AMERICAN VANDAL

AMERICAN VANDAL

Mark Twain Abroad

ROY MORRIS, JR.

THE BELKNAP PRESS OF
HARVARD UNIVERSITY PRESS
Cambridge, Massachusetts
London, England
2015

Library of Congress Cataloging-in-Publication Data

Morris, Roy, Jr.

American vandal : Mark Twain abroad / Roy Morris, Jr.

pages cm

Includes bibliographical references and index.

ISBN 978-0-674-41669-7 (alk. paper)

1. Twain, Mark, 1835-1910—Travel.   I. Title.

PS1334.M67 2015

818'.409—dc23   2014033055

FOR STEVE ELLIS

Thanks for the ride

CONTENTS

A NOTE ON NAMES

The man who signed himself "Mark Twain" on the covers of his books was born, of course, Samuel Langhorne Clemens. Everyone knows that. But since a good deal of his traveling was done under the aegis and persona of his trade name, and since this is a book about those travels, it seems a needless affectation to split the single person into two parts. I have chosen simply to call him "Mark Twain," as indeed he chose to call himself.

INTRODUCTION

For a man who enjoyed being called—not without reason—*the* American, Mark Twain spent a surprising amount of time living and traveling abroad. Beginning with his five-month-long visit to Hawaii (not yet a U.S. territory) in 1866, Twain passed the better part of a dozen years outside the boundaries of the continental United States. He made twenty-nine separate transatlantic crossings; circumnavigated the globe via the Atlantic, Pacific, and Indian Oceans; cruised the Mediterranean, Caribbean, Black, Caspian, and Aegean Seas; crisscrossed India from Bombay to Darjeeling; hiked the Alps and the Tyrolean Black Forest; floated down the Neckar and Rhone Rivers on a raft; and lived and worked for extensive periods of time in London, Paris, Berlin, and Vienna, as well as various smaller European cities and resorts. It was all part of his lifelong need to see and experience new things, a need that in itself was deeply and characteristically American. "I am wild with impatience to move—move—*Move!*" Twain wrote to his mother in 1867. "My mind gives me peace only in excitement and restless moving from place to place. I wish I never had to stop *anywhere*." He seldom did.[1]

On the fame-making cruise to the Mediterranean and the Holy Land that provided Twain with his first great book-length success, *The Innocents Abroad,* in 1869, he introduced readers to the American Vandal, a broadly drawn burlesque figure representing the best (and worst) of the national character. The American Vandal, male or female, was a brazen, unapologetic visitor to foreign lands, generally unimpressed with the local ambience—to say nothing of the local inhabitants—but ever ready to appropriate any religious or historical trinket he or she could carry off. Literally nothing was sacred to the Vandal. In an illustration from the book that later was used on the front of its advertising prospectus, Twain cheerfully posed as the Vandal himself, toting a tomahawk, a bow and arrow, and a monogrammed "M.T./U.S." carpetbag. It was a role he would continue to play, when the mood struck him, for the rest of his life, long after the new had worn off and he had become, as most people do, a sadder and a wiser man.

Twain would write a trio of books about his world travels—*The Innocents Abroad, A Tramp Abroad,* and *Following the Equator*—that correspond neatly to the beginning, middle, and end of his writing career. Besides tracking the progress of the author's personal life, the books reflect the evolving perspectives of American travelers, starting with Twain himself. From the comparatively youthful neophyte in *The Innocents Abroad* encountering the wonders of Europe and the Holy Land for the first time, Twain grew into the more confident and self-sufficient middle-aged "tramp" who measured a country's charms chiefly by his reactions to them, and finally into a world-famous international celebrity who dined with the German Kaiser, swapped jokes with the Austrian emperor, traded quips with the king of England, and negotiated with the president of Transvaal for the release of war prisoners.

Like his own country at the turn of the twentieth century, Twain found himself a major player on the world stage. Arthur L. Scott tracks that remarkable evolution: "This raw Westerner was shaped into a New Englander. During the 1880's he became an ardent nationalist, and finally he grew into a cosmopolite, an internationalist—sage but not serene."[2]

Twain's emergence, personally and artistically, underscored the rise of the American middle class in the latter half of the nineteenth century, a social class whose signature virtues of industry, honesty, and sheer hard work he embodied throughout his life, even after he married into great (if ultimately fleeting) wealth. Unlike the other towering American novelist of the age, Henry James, Twain did not come from the moneyed Eastern elite. He did not grow up in a roomy New York City brownstone, attend Harvard Law School, or spend large stretches of his youth traveling and studying abroad. He did not speak fluent French, revere the English aristocracy, or aspire to a Europeanized existence and sensibility. And again unlike James, who became an English citizen late in life, Twain did not seem embarrassed by his own national identity. He did not desire, as did James, to keep readers guessing whether he was "an American writing about England or an Englishman writing about America." Everyone knew Mark Twain was an American. Consequently, when Twain first went overseas, he brought America with him, much as James's title character, the symbolically named Christopher Newman, does in *The American:* "You are the great Western Barbarian, stepping forth in his innocence and might, gazing a while at this poor corrupt old world and then swooping down on it." James did not mean it as a compliment.[3]

But if James was a defender of the Old World and its courtly traditional values, Twain was an avatar of the New, training a fresh set of eyes on the glories and ruins of the past. As Shelley Fisher Fishkin has noted, Twain's travel writings gave other Americans of the time the confidence needed "to stand before the cultural icons of the Old World unembarrassed, unashamed of America's lack of palaces and shrines, proud of its brash practicality and bold inventiveness, unafraid to reject European models of 'civilization' as tainted or corrupt." Brash, bold, and unafraid himself, Twain encouraged other Americans to follow his example and travel freely, believing that "contact with men of various nations and many creeds teaches him that there are other people in the world beside his own little clique, and other opinions as worthy of attention and respect as his own." For his part, said Twain, "I am glad the American Vandal goes abroad. It does him good. It makes a better man of him. It rubs out a multitude of his old unworthy biases and prejudices." So it was for Twain himself.[4]

Twain was already an experienced traveler long before he first set foot outside the continental United States—indeed, before he was even Mark Twain. Leaving his hometown of Hannibal, Missouri, at the age of seventeen, the youthful Sam Clemens crisscrossed the country for the next six years, working as an itinerant printer in St. Louis, New York, Philadelphia, Keokuk, and Cincinnati before landing his dream job as a riverboat pilot on the Mississippi River, a job that afforded him entry into the exclusive ranks of "the only unfettered and entirely independent human being[s] that lived on the earth." He fully intended to remain a riverboat pilot for the rest of his life "and die at the wheel when my mission was ended."[5]

The advent of the Civil War effectively destroyed those plans and ultimately left Twain stranded back in Hannibal, where he briefly joined a local Confederate militia unit to avoid having to serve as a pilot on Union Army troopships. The few weeks he spent thrashing about the rain-drenched Missouri woods—the sum total of Twain's military career—were a boyish lark, at least in his later retelling of it. He and the other would-be warriors in the Marion Rangers spent the majority of their time looking for food and shelter, arguing about grand matters of strategy, and dodging imaginary hordes of enemies, including a then little-known Union colonel named Ulysses S. Grant. Finally, "incapacitated by fatigue through persistent retreating," Twain deserted the Marion Rangers. Like his most famous literary character, he lit out for the territory.[6]

With his brother, Orion, who had just been appointed secretary to the governor of Nevada Territory, Twain embarked on an epic three-week-long stagecoach ride across Nebraska, Colorado, Utah, and the Great American Desert. The brothers arrived in Carson City, Nevada, the territorial capital, in mid-August 1861. The real action was taking place twelve miles to the north, at Virginia City, where the richest silver strike in American history, the fabled Comstock Lode, had been discovered two years earlier by a couple of hardscrabble desert rats. In three decades' time, the lode would yield upwards of four hundred million dollars in gold and silver, and dozens of dirt-poor prospectors would become overnight millionaires. Twain, hoping to join their ranks, spent a few desultory months digging, blasting, picking, and scratching through the stony Nevada soil before discovering his true fortune above ground as a cub reporter on the *Virginia City Territorial Enterprise*. It was there that he adopted his short, punchy nom de plume, taken from his days as a riverboat pilot, and began filling long columns of newsprint with vigorous accounts, sometimes true, of the madcap comings and goings of the various prospectors, outlaws, settlers, and loafers in the West's most raucous boomtown.

Eventually Twain abandoned Virginia City for San Francisco, where he pursued his lifelong ambition of becoming a dandy. A few blissful months of "butterfly idleness" ended abruptly when his former partners sold off his nest egg of Nevada mining stock without bothering to tell him about it. Very much against his will, he reentered the workforce as a general assignment reporter for the *San Francisco Morning Call*, but the newspaper's eighteen-hour workdays quickly proved to be soul-killing drudgery for someone as professedly lazy as Twain. After four months of enforced servitude, he turned in his resignation. His managing editor was not greatly dismayed.[7]

The unexpected success of his 1865 tall tale "Jim Smiley and His Jumping Frog," now better known as "The Celebrated Jumping Frog of Calaveras County," gave Twain his first national exposure, and he subsequently spent five months of "luxurious vagrancy" in Hawaii in the spring and summer of 1866, reporting on the islands for his new employer, the *Sacramento Union*. While in Hawaii he hiked across the floor of an active volcano, surfed the waves off Waikiki Beach, looked into the local leper colony, toured the death site of Captain Cook, climbed mountains, rode horses, smoked cigars, sampled poi, interviewed survivors of a deadly shipwreck, and unsuccessfully courted a bevy of land-rich sugar plantation heiresses. It was a crowded visit.[8]

Upon returning to the States, Twain mounted a well-received lecture tour of California and Nevada, delivering a drolly exaggerated account of his adventures among "Our Fellow Savages in the Sandwich Islands." The tour added to his growing fame as a writer and humorist, and another newspaper, the *San Francisco Alta California*, offered him a plum assignment as its roving travel correspondent, "not stinted as

to time, place or direction." The editors sketched out an ambitious itinerary: France, Italy, the Mediterranean, India,
China, and Japan. "We feel confident his letters to the *Alta* will
give him a world-wide reputation," they predicted. They were
proved right, if not perhaps in the way they expected. Twain
would quickly outgrow the newspaper business.[9]

For the next forty years, alone or with his family, Mark
Twain traveled the world as "a self-appointed Ambassador at
Large of the U.S. of America," functioning as both tour guide
and tourist. Modern readers are often surprised to learn that
the author of perhaps the greatest novel in American literature was much better known in his own time as a travel writer.
Certainly it did not surprise Twain, who fell back on his travel
writing whenever—and it was often—he found himself financially embarrassed. Wherever he went, he felt at home. "I can
stand any society," he declared. "All that I care to know is that
a man is a human being—that is enough for me; he can't be
any worse."[10]

Whether surfing the waves at Waikiki, trekking the Holy
Land in the footsteps of Christ, braving icy ravines in the Swiss
Alps, strolling the leafy boulevards of pre–World War I Berlin,
riding an elephant through the streets of New Delhi, or clat-
tering by train across the South African veldt, Twain displayed
at all times an avid curiosity for his physical surroundings and
the baffling, sometimes exasperating people who lived there.
He was truly a citizen of the world, and one of the great travelers of the nineteenth—or indeed any—century. "The world
is a book and those who do not travel read only a chapter," said
St. Augustine, and Mark Twain in his time read many chapters. He even wrote a few himself.

CHAPTER ONE

INNOCENTS ABROAD

hen thirty-one-year-old journalist Mark Twain made his way gingerly down the ice-encrusted gangplank of the steamship *America* in New York harbor on January 12, 1867, after an arduous twelve-day voyage from San Francisco, it marked the first time he had set foot in the great city in nearly fourteen years. Then a "pure and sinless sprout" fresh from his brother's newspaper in Hannibal, Missouri, he had spent a scuffling six months in New York working as a printer at the John A. Gray Company on Cliff Street, earning a penurious twenty-three cents per "em" of type. Now, after six eventful years in the West, including stints as a miner, prospector, stockbroker, duelist, dandy, newspaper reporter, and traveling lecturer, he was back. Having grown accustomed to life in arid Nevada, balmy California, and temperate Hawaii, he found New York's frigid winter weather a shock to his system, the thermometer hovering "180 degrees below zero, I should judge." An old newspaper acquaintance from San Francisco encountered Twain on the street one afternoon, "shivering and chattering his teeth at the 'damnation cold weather,' and complaining of the 'infernal long distances'" between saloons.[1]

Checking into the Metropolitan Hotel at Broadway and Prince, just below Greenwich Village, Twain spent much of his time attempting to patch together a book of his old western newspaper clippings and sending back dispatches to the *Alta California* on a variety of titillating topics, from Broadway plays and women's fashions to the distinguished membership of the Century Club—average hat size, eleven—and the scantily dressed wonders of the New York stage. At the recommendation of Moses S. Beach, owner and editor of the *New York Sun* and a member of renowned minister Henry Ward Beecher's flock at Brooklyn's Plymouth Congregational Church, Twain attended Sunday services at the church on February 3. As usual, the church was packed. Jammed into the last seat in the upstairs gallery—"about large enough to accommodate a spittoon"—Twain watched with detached professional admiration as Beecher cast a well-practiced spell over his listeners. The famous preacher, he observed, "went marching up and down his stage, sawing his arms in the air, hurling sarcasms this way and that, discharging rockets of poetry, and exploding mines of eloquence, halting now and then to stamp his foot three times in succession to emphasize a point." It was not Twain's style—he went in more for laconic understatement and well-timed pauses—but it was undeniably entertaining. Twain fought back an urge to stand up and applaud.[2]

A few days later, Twain learned of plans for a five-month-long pleasure cruise to Europe, the Holy Land, and "intermediate points of interest," to be led by Beecher himself. The cruise aboard the 1,428-ton side-wheeler *Quaker City*, a converted Union navy supply ship, was open to the public, subject to the approval of a "pitiless" one-man screening committee, tour organizer and ship's captain Charles C. Duncan. In the company of his friend Edward H. House, drama critic for the *New York Tribune*, Twain paid a visit to Duncan's office at 117 Wall Street. Duly fortified with a few drinks beforehand, the two reporters wafted into his office, Duncan remembered a decade later, on "the fumes of bad whiskey." House introduced his rumpled companion as "the Reverend Mark Twain, a clergyman of some distinction, lately arrived from California." Twain, playing along, inquired whether his fellow man of the cloth, the Reverend Beecher, might consent to share the pulpit with him on the voyage over. Duncan assured him that Beecher would be delighted to make room, ecumenically speaking, for a brother minister. Professing himself satisfied with the arrangements, Twain put down a $120 deposit for a berth on the ship, enjoying the novelty, he said, of being for once a member of the elect. It was not a category in which he usually found himself.[3]

The *Quaker City* voyage, the first prepackaged luxury cruise in American history, promised to be a star-studded affair. Besides Beecher, who was said to be going to the Holy Land to gather details for a new biography of Jesus Christ, other rumored passengers included former Union generals William Tecumseh Sherman and Nathaniel Banks, Broadway actress Maggie Mitchell, and sixteen-year-old Robert Henry Hendershot, the self-proclaimed "Brave Drummer Boy of the Rappahannock." As it stood, Duncan's tour roster was greatly exaggerated. Hoping to recoup his fortunes after losing all his money to a thieving business partner during the Civil War, Duncan tacitly encouraged Beecher's followers to believe their champion would be leading the trip. In fact, Beecher had no intention of going to Europe or the Holy Land, nor did the Civil War figures, either commanding generals or not-so-humble drummer boy. Sherman was preparing to head west to persecute Indians, a task for which he was eminently better qualified, and the precocious Hendershot was making plans to elope with a slightly older Poughkeepsie College classmate. Even the usually accommodating Banks, who as one of Stonewall Jackson's ill-fated opponents in the Shenandoah Valley had left behind so many abandoned supplies that hungry Confederates dubbed him "Commissary" Banks, presumably had something better to do. He was serving in Congress.[4]

After putting down his deposit, Twain cabled his editors back in San Francisco: "Send me $1,200 at once. I want to go abroad." Remarkably, they agreed. In return for the advance, Twain contracted to send the newspaper fifty travel letters at twenty dollars apiece. The swift withdrawal of forty previously booked Plymouth Church passengers, who declined to sally forth without their leader, left the *Quaker City* operating at roughly 75 percent capacity. Duncan, in something of a panic, advertised in the *New York Evening Post* for additional passengers who possessed the requisite "good moral character, good health, and a fair share of good humor." Twain met at least two of the captain's three published criteria, and in the end no paying applicants were refused passage. The final tally, surprisingly inexact for a professional cruise ship—albeit one on its maiden voyage—was somewhere between sixty-five and eighty passengers, including several newly acquired fundamentalists from upstate New York, Pennsylvania, Ohio, Missouri, and various other midwestern states.[5]

Nervous and impatient in the best of times, Twain seethed at the dwindling passenger list and frequent changes in departure date. "Curse the endless delays!" he groused to his mother. "They always kill me—they make me neglect every duty & then I have a conscience that tears me like a wild beast. I wish I never had to stop *anywhere* a month. I do more mean things, the moment I get a chance to fold my hands & sit down than ever I can get forgiveness for." In this he was telling the truth, as he occasionally did. One night he was thrown into jail for brawling on a public street, a crime he professed himself innocent of committing. "Anybody can get into the Station House here without committing an offense of any kind," he reported unapologetically in the *Alta California*. "And so he can anywhere that policemen are allowed to cumber the earth." According to Twain, he offered the New York policemen a perfectly reasonable bribe to let him go, "but there were too many witnesses present, and they actually refused." Hauled off to jail, he spent a diverting hour or two "looking through the bars at the dilapidated old hags, and battered and ragged bummers, sorrowing and swearing in the stone-paved halls." It was probably not as much fun as Twain claimed it was—most jail stays aren't—but he was released back into the general population the next day.[6]

Two days prior to departure, Beach held a get-acquainted dinner for his fellow passengers at his mansion in Richmond Heights. Twain was in good spirits that night, pronouncing his prospective shipmates "a crowd of tip-top people" and predicting that they would have "a jolly, sociable, homelike trip." He made a labored joke about going out with the tide, presumably one of the "ebullitions of wit" with which he was reported to have "enlivened the crowd." The next night he and a few of his newfound companions christened their impending voyage with a nine-hour orgy of eating and drinking. Among those joining Twain in the revels was his preassigned roommate for the voyage, Dan Slote, a thirty-nine-year-old New York banker. The balding, rotund, easy-going Slote was, Twain reported happily, "splendid, immoral, tobacco-smoking, wine-drinking [and] godless"—in short, much like Twain himself. Slote came prepared with a great supply of shirts, a written history of the Holy Land, a cribbage board, and three thousand cigars. "I will not have to carry any baggage at all," bragged Twain.[7]

On June 8, the *Quaker City* eased away from the East River pier and headed out to sea—but not for long. A mid-Atlantic storm roiled the waters so badly that Duncan was forced to lie at anchor off Gravesend Bay for the next two days, in plain view of the Plymouth Congregational Church. That Sunday, the Reverend Twain noted vaguely, one of the three actual shipboard ministers "preached from II Cor 7 & 8th about something." Finally, at 12:30 p.m. on June 10, the *Quaker City* steamed into the open seas. The passengers launched into a Pentecostal hymn, "Homeward Bound," accompanied lustily on the organ by Captain Duncan's eleven-year-old son Harry. "I say goodbye & God bless you all," Twain wrote to his mother, "& welcome the wind that wafts a weary soul to the sunny lands of the Mediterranean!" No mention was made of the Holy Land.[8]

In heading abroad, Twain was joining an avalanche of American travelers in the years immediately following the Civil War. It was a crush that had been gaining momentum for decades, interrupted only by the vicissitudes of war. Journalist Henry Tuckerman, writing in the May 1844 issue of *United States Magazine and Democratic Review*, noted approvingly that "our times might not inaptly be designated as the age of traveling." The development of steam-powered ships greatly increased the numbers of Americans traveling abroad. That number had risen tenfold, from 1,927 per year in 1820 to 19,387 in 1860 for departures from the four major Atlantic ports of Boston, New York, Philadelphia, and Baltimore. "Steam is annihilating space," Tuckerman observed. "The ocean, once a formidable barrier, not to be traversed without long preparation and from urgent necessity, now seems to inspire no more consideration than a goodly lake, admirably adapted to a summer excursion." A trip that previously had taken upward of three weeks now could be accomplished in nine or ten days.[9]

As a former riverboat pilot himself, Twain knew all about the advantages of steam power—and the disadvantages as well. His younger brother, Henry, had been killed in a boiler explosion on the Mississippi River nine years earlier, and Twain himself had narrowly avoided injury on several occasions. Such technological advances as the iron hull, screw propeller, and compound engine made foreign travel more accessible for American travelers, which in turn altered the fundamental nature of such travel. Before the advent of steam-powered ships, transatlantic voyages were slow and expensive, limited for the most part to the wealthiest Americans, mainly roistering young college men and museum-haunting artists, who had the time and wherewithal needed to undertake the grand tour of European capitals. Larger ships and cheaper travel had a democratizing effect on American travel, creating an eager new pool of self-improving middle-class tourists who longed to see the outside world and its wonders, even as they carried with them the virtues and values of their homeland.

Henry James, no democrat himself, would come to lament the unwelcome onslaught of his fellow countrymen on European shores. "A very large proportion of the Americans who annually scatter themselves over Europe are by no means flattering to the national vanity," he would write in his 1878 essay "Americans Abroad." "Their merits, whatever they are, are not of a sort that strikes the eye—still less the ear," James fussed. "They are ill-made, ill-mannered, ill-dressed." Ralph Waldo Emerson, a lifelong friend of James's father, Henry James Sr., was even more critical of what he termed "the superstition of Travelling." "I have no churlish objection to the circumnavigation of the globe for the purposes of art, of study, and benevolence," Emerson allowed in his essay "Self-Reliance." But purely recreational travel, he warned, was nothing more than "a fool's paradise. He who travels to be amused, or to get somewhat which he does not carry, travels away from himself, and grows old even in youth among old thing. . . . He carries ruins to ruins."[10]

Despite Emerson's Olympian warnings, Americans after the Civil War took to the open roads and waters in massive numbers. In May 1868, *Putnam's* magazine noted the "traveling mania which has gradually increased until half of the earth's inhabitants, or at least of its civilized portion, are on the move." The explosion of travel created an unslakable hunger for travel books. A staggering two thousand such books were published in the United States before 1900, counting only those books related to overseas travel. Virtually all American newspapers and periodicals of the time featured regular travel sections, catering not only to prospective travelers but to stay-at-home readers who wanted to experience exotic locales vicariously from the comfort of their parlors. "Their experience of Europe came strictly at home, where they read widely pop-

ular travel literature or viewed stereocards and chromolitho-
graphs of famous art works and well-known European vistas
and monuments," notes scholar Richard S. Lowry. And, as Jeffrey Alan Melton has observed, travel books were the "virtual
reality for the nineteenth century."[11]

For those equipped mentally, emotionally, and financially
to make the trip, Europe remained the strongest lure, since
most Americans at that time were still of European heritage.
One of the first prominent American writers to make the
transatlantic journey was Washington Irving, whose 1820 account, *Sketch-Book of Geoffrey Crayon, Gent*, set the template
for future travel writers. In it, Irving announced his desire "to
wander over the scenes of renowned achievement—to tread,
as it were, in the footsteps of antiquity—to loiter about the ruined castle—to meditate on the falling tower—to scamper, in
short, from the common-place realities of the present, and lose
myself among the shadowy grandeurs of the past." Irving's success inspired fellow authors James Fenimore Cooper, Herman
Melville, and Nathaniel Hawthorne to undertake travel books
of their own, although in Melville's case it was the South Seas,
not Europe, that served as the subject of his first book, *Typee*,
published in 1852.[12]

By far the most popular American traveler writer was
Pennsylvania-born poet and journalist Bayard Taylor. Beginning with his best-selling 1846 work, *Views A-Foot*, Taylor virtually invented the craft of personalized travel writing. His account of a two-year walking tour of Europe established a
working model for future writers, and subsequent books on
his travels to the Sudan, India, China, Japan, the Arctic Circle,
and the American West were equally well received. Taylor
based his books on letters he wrote during his journeys for
Horace Greeley's *New York Tribune*, which helped to give his

accounts a sense of immediacy and spontaneity. Readers felt as though they were walking alongside Taylor on his jaunts; his air of exuberant enjoyment and sheer American can-do spirit made it easy for his audience to relate to him. "He was a valiant and adaptable traveler," notes Larzer Ziff, "quick to learn languages, uncomplaining in pain, willing to go it alone, able to cover long distances on foot, keen to don the local garb, adept at passing as a native—and he traveled to extraordinary places." Taylor was the first American writer to travel purely for the purpose of writing about his travels, and he made good money doing so—an example that would not be lost on Twain.[13]

Another popular travel writer, British-born Frederick Marryat, whose works Twain had read as a boy in Hannibal, toured the United States in the late 1830s. In his whimsical essay "How to Write a Book of Travels," Marryat gave future writers a sardonic but largely accurate checklist for travel writing: "Traveling—remarks on country passed through— anecdote—arrival at a town—churches—population—historical remarks—egotism—remarks on women (never mind the men)—another anecdote—reflections—an adventure—and on to bed." Throughout his own travel-writing career, Twain would follow Marryat's prescriptions carefully, if not always religiously.[14]

The *Quaker City* voyage would provide Twain with the perfect opportunity to test the limits of conventional travel writing. His account would be less a strict chronological record of the trip than his retrieved memories of it, filtered through the thought processes of a talented fiction writer who, to that point in his life, had not yet written a novel or, indeed, a book of any kind. In doing so, as Jeffrey Steinbrink notes,

Twain would align himself with the great tsunami of postwar American tourists, "less genteel, less familiar with the process of living within long-standing traditions, less often classically educated, less often the master of a language other than his own." Like them, he "tended to place his confidence in himself, in his country, and in the sufficiency of the present rather than the sanctity of the past; he was curious, active, and acquisitive; he was simultaneously skeptical and deferential, and quite unabashedly—and identifiably—American."[15]

In approaching the trip as "a picnic on a gigantic scale," Twain would be going against the strictures of both Bayard Taylor and Wilbur Fisk, the latter of whom had solemnly vowed in his 1838 account, *Travels in Europe,* to shine a light on "any important truths, any facts connected with politics or morals, education or religion, [which] can be wrought into the incidents of a journal so as to make them readable or acceptable." Twain had no such concerns. As he later would say in his famous introductory notice to readers of *Huckleberry Finn:* "Persons attempting to find a motive in this narrative will be prosecuted; persons attempting to find a moral in it will be banished; persons attempting to find a plot in it will be shot." His preface to *The Innocents Abroad* would emphasize that point: "This book is a record of a pleasure trip," he would write. "Yet not withstanding it is only a record of a picnic, it has a purpose, which is, to suggest to the reader how *he* would be likely to see Europe and the East if he looked at them with his own eyes instead of the eyes of those who traveled in those countries before him. . . . I offer no apologies for any departures from the usual style of travel-writing that may be charged against me—for I think I have seen with impartial eyes, and I am sure I have written at least honestly, whether

wisely or not." *Impartial* and *honestly* may have been
stretching the point, considering the creative liberties Twain
would take with his book, but he definitely saw things with
his own set of eyes, and he wrote about what he saw in a wised-
up, drolly unimpressed voice—the voice of the free-ranging
American Vandal.[16]

In the absence of Beecher, Sherman, and other previously
announced celebrities, Twain found himself by default
the most prominent traveler remaining aboard ship. He was
not exactly famous—certainly not to the degree he would
become—but many of his fellow passengers had read his
Jumping Frog story and knew something of his reputation as
a western journalist and wit. In recognition of his comparatively elevated status, Duncan gave Twain the choice upper-
deck corner cabin, Number 10, which had formerly been reserved for the erstwhile conqueror of Atlanta. With the help
of two free cases of Veuve Clicquot and Lac d'Or champagne
delivered to him as a parting gift by a New York importing
house, Twain set about preparing his cabin as a secular
oasis, a worldly respite from the psalm-singing, shuffleboard-
playing activities favored by his more sedate shipmates. "I
and my room-mate have set apart every Saturday as a solemn
fast day, wherein we will entertain no light matters of frivo-
lous conversation, but only get drunk," he told his abstemious
mother, but added quickly, "That is a joke." Joking or not,
Twain soon convened the first of a regular series of meetings
of the "Quaker City Night Hawks," an ad hoc group of like-
minded passengers who quickly set about decimating Twain's

two cases of champagne and Slote's three thousand cigars. Along with Twain and Slote, the other Night Hawks included Dr. Abraham Reeves Jackson, the ship's surgeon; John Van Nostrand, of Greenville, New Jersey; Frederick Greer, of Boston; Daniel Leary, of New York City; and Julius Moulton, of St. Louis.[17]

On the fringes of the group was seventeen-year-old Charles Jervis "Charley" Langdon of Elmira, New York, the son of a fabulously wealthy coal magnate, who was destined to play a larger role in Twain's future than anyone else on board their ship. Initially, Twain judged the timid young man "fearfully green & fearfully slow"; he had even forgotten to bring his passport with him. Charley was similarly unimpressed with Twain, reporting home that "we have some hard cases with us. [Mark Twain] is one of the hardest." When Charley dared to advise Twain on his poker-playing—one of the last things on earth the author needed advice about—the less-than-pleased advisee leveled him with a stern gaze. "Young man," said Twain, "there's a prayer-meeting forward in the dining saloon and they need you there." Charley left.[18]

Twain did not spend all his time drinking and playing cards in his smoke-filled cabin. During the day he mingled freely with his fellow travelers, the vast majority of whom were a good deal older, richer, and more religious. Except for native New Yorkers, the largest single contingent of passengers came from the First Presbyterian Church of Cleveland, Ohio. The unquestioned, if unofficial, leader of the Cleveland bloc was Mary Mason Fairbanks, the thirty-nine-year-old wife of *Cleveland Herald* owner and publisher Abel Fairbanks. Mrs. Fairbanks, a former schoolteacher who spoke fluent French, was one of several *Quaker City* passengers who had contracted to

write regular accounts of the voyage for their hometown newspapers. ("Everyone taking notes," Twain observed sourly.
"Cabin looks like a reporters' congress.") Despite being only
eight years older than Twain, she took a maternal interest
in the rough-edged journalist, who obligingly dubbed her
"Mother" and declared her "the most refined, intelligent, and
cultivated lady in the ship, and altogether the kindest and
best." They would remain good friends for the next three
decades.[19]

In all, there were seventeen women among the ship's passengers—only four were single—and several took note immediately of the wisecracking bad boy of the cruise. Among the
single women was Julia Newell of Janesville, Wisconsin.
Newell, too, was planning to write articles about the voyage
for a newspaper, in her case the *Janesville Gazette*. She had
taken the trouble to read Twain's Jumping Frog story before
they set sail; she found parts of it profane. As for its author,
she thought Twain "rather a handsome fellow," but too inclined
to be funny at the expense of others. And though Janesville
was not that far from Hannibal on the map, she considered
Twain's languorous Missouri drawl "abominable." In any event,
Newell's attentions soon shifted, and she became romantically
involved with another of the Night Hawks, Abraham Jackson.
The other unmarried women on the trip were Kate Brown of
Circleville, Ohio; Carrie Chadeyne of Jersey City, New Jersey;
and Emeline Beach, Moses Beach's pretty, seventeen-year-old
daughter. Twain took little notice of Brown, who was traveling
with her father, and he found the flirtatious Chadeyne a little
"questionable." But he liked Emma Beach and spent a fair
amount of time playing chess with her on deck and allowing
her to chide him good-naturedly about his faults. As with
Mary Fairbanks, he would keep in touch with Emma for the

rest of his life, later naming her one of the eight people on the voyage whom he would always consider a friend.[20]

Without a doubt, the most colorful character on board the *Quaker City* was the grandly named Bloodgood Haviland Cutter, a diminutive (he weighed less than one hundred pounds) millionaire farmer from Long Island who, at the somewhat advanced age of fifty, had discovered his true calling as a lyric poet. The "Poet Lariat," as Twain styled him, was given to versifying at the drop of a hat and bestowing his work, generally unrequested, on "any man who came along whether he has anything against him or not." Cutter had petitioned Duncan for free room and board in return for his services as the ship's resident poet. Duncan turned him down, but Cutter generously dispensed his talents for free. Emily Severance, another of Twain's shipboard friends, judged Cutter to be "a peculiar man. He may be intelligent in some ways, but is scarcely a poet." Twain wouldn't go that far. To him Cutter was "a shameless old idiot" whose debut performance, "Recollections of the Pleasant Time on Deck Last Night," consisted of seventy-five stanzas of torturous rhymed couplets. Other poetic effusions included "Apostrophe to the Rooster in the Waist of the Ship," "Ode to the Ocean in a Storm," and an untitled quatrain to a flying fish that read, in full: "My friends, to gratify your wish, / I hang up here a flying fish; / Last night 'twas said he flew on board, / And was not to the sea restored." It was actually one of Cutter's better works.[21]

Other shipmates were even less amusing. Mrs. J. O. Green of Washington, D.C., a thirtyish matron, was traveling with

her small black-and-tan terrier, Little Boy. Twain, who never
particularly liked dogs as a species—he much preferred cats—
described Mrs. Green's pet as "a mongrel with long sharp ears
that stick up like a donkey's." The dog, observed Twain, "jumps
into her lap & repeats it over & over again, & his damned spirit
will not down till she takes him to her bosom, wraps her shawl
about him & talks affectionate baby talk to him." Even the
long-suffering Mary Fairbanks, to whose cabin Mrs. Green initially was assigned as a roommate, quickly got enough of the
canine baby talk and invited Mrs. Green and her dog to move
to a vacant cabin. Emily Severance pronounced the woman
"not exactly sane."[22]

Another eccentric passenger was Dr. William Gibson of
Jamestown, Pennsylvania, a physician-turned-railroad-
builder who had written to the U.S. Department of Agriculture before the trip and offered to collect specimens for the
Smithsonian Institution. The noncommittal, politely worded
official reply emboldened Gibson to style himself "Commissioner of the United States of America to Europe, Asia, and
Africa." The honorific, said Twain, was all well and good, but
"to my thinking, when the United States considered it necessary to send a dignitary of that tonnage across the ocean, it
would be in better taste, and safer, to take him apart and cart
him over in sections, in several ships." Twain would later get
a measure of revenge by mischievously arranging for Gibson
to be surrounded by a pestering group of Arab beggars while
he attempted to pose for a commemorative photograph at the
Egyptian pyramids.[23]

A second Pennsylvanian, Harrisburg jurist Jacob S. Haldeman, presented an altogether humbler, more tragic de-
meanor. Haldeman, a former Republican state legislator, had
served during the Civil War as Abraham Lincoln's minister

to Sweden. An ongoing battle with alcoholism had led to his rather less exalted position with the Pennsylvania State Agricultural Society. Haldeman was traveling abroad in search of a cure. To steady his nerves, he was taking large substitute doses of morphine, which rendered him increasingly unsteady on his legs. Despite his generally tipsy physical state and extravagant traveling costume (red flannel shirt printed with hunting scenes, florid neckties, and knee-high patent-leather boots), the judge was elected president of the Quaker City Club, which met to share information about upcoming destinations on the trip's itinerary. The thought, perhaps, was to keep him out of trouble.

At the captain's insistence, a nightly prayer meeting was held between the hours of eight and nine in the upper-deck saloon—Twain dubbed it the "Synagogue"—and attendance, though not compulsory, was strongly encouraged. The captain's log details a typical meeting: "Singing—prayer by Col. Denny of Virginia—another hymn—prayer by Mr. Severance of Ohio—again a hymn—Scripture read—after which addresses and prayers by Messrs. Quereau, Church, Beckwith & Bullard—closing prayer by the Captain. Doxology—Praise God from whom all blessings flow & benediction by Mr. Bullard." Twain, in his self-ordained role as "chief hypocrite," took a turn presiding over one prayer meeting, but he fell back on his brief parliamentary experience as a recording secretary for the Nevada state legislature to question the validity of the meetings. "We held one hundred and sixty-five prayer meetings in the Quaker City," he noted, "and one hundred and eighteen of them were scandalous and illegal, because four out of the five real Christians on board were too sea sick to be present at them, and so there wasn't a quorum. I know. I kept a record."[24]

Besides the prayer meetings, there were birthday parties, magic lantern shows, lectures, charades, horse billiards (described by Twain as "a mixture of hop-scotch and shuffleboard played with a crutch"), a debating club, and evening dances that took on the character of a cross-country steeplechase. "When the ship rolled to starboard the whole platoon of dancers came charging down to the starboard with it, and brought up in a mass at the rail," wrote Twain, "and when it rolled to port, they went floundering down to port with the same unanimity of sentiment. . . .The Virginia reel, as performed on board the *Quaker City*, had more genuine reel about it than any reel I ever saw before."[25]

After ten days at sea—the longest single maritime stretch of the voyage—the *Quaker City* hove into view of Flores, in the Azores, at 3 a.m. on June 21. Twain, awakened by excited shipmates pounding on his door, ventured the observation that he "did not take any interest in islands at three o'clock in the morning." The pounding continued until he agreed to join the other rain-drenched passengers on deck. The view was less than awe-inspiring. To Twain, Flores "seemed only a mountain of mud standing up out of the dull mists of the sea." Steering around the island in an ongoing gale, Duncan made for the neighboring island of Fayal, whose green farmland, divided by stone walls and alternating black-lava hills, put Twain in mind of a giant checkerboard. The island's residents, he judged, were an unimpressive lot, "all ragged and barefoot, uncombed and unclean, and by instinct, education, and profession beggars." One toothless old woman proved so persistent in following Twain around that he was

forced to fend her off with a white lie: "Madame, these attentions cannot but be flattering to me, but it must not be—alas,
it cannot be—I am another's." The island women all wore
Portuguese-inspired hoods, called *capotes*, that reminded
Twain of the prompter's box at a play.[26]

After two humdrum days in the harbor at Fayal, enlivened
only by a hired donkey ride that carried away one of the passengers and unsaddled him in the doorway of a parlor, the ship
continued east through stormy seas toward the Strait of Gibraltar. Most of the passengers were confined to their cabins
with seasickness, and even Twain, ordinarily a good sailor, admitted that he didn't feel "very bright" himself. He treated his
symptoms by staying up all night drinking bourbon and
playing dominoes with the ship's purser, Robert Vail. At dawn
the two beheld the abrupt sight of "the granite-ribbed domes"
of Spain on their left and "the tall yellow-splotched hills" of
Africa on their right. Soon the Rock of Gibraltar came into
view, "a lonely and enormous mass of rock, standing seemingly
in the centre of the wide strait and apparently washed on all
sides by the sea." It was none too soon; the coal-burning
Quaker City, running low on fuel, had to put on a full rigging
of sails to safely clear the strait and make landfall.[27]

Gibraltar proved scarcely more interesting than Fayal.
Mary Fairbanks bought a few lemons the size of oranges at
an open-air market, then took off to San Roque with Emily
Severance and her husband, Solon, to see a bullfight. Moses
and Emma Beach, Charley Langdon, and a few others took
the ferry to Cadiz, where they planned to proceed across Spain
by railroad to Madrid, Paris, and Switzerland before rejoining
the ship at Livorno, Italy. Twain, bereft of his closest companions, organized a side trip to Tangier, Morocco, "a filthy, dirty
town" peopled by a polyglot collection of Arabs, Bedouins,

Jews, Riffians, Dervishes, and "original, genuine negroes as black as Moses." Accompanying Twain was the usual gang of Night Hawks—Slote, Jackson, Van Nostrand, and Moulton—along with Major John Barry of St. Louis, five bottles of whiskey, and seventy-five cigars.[28]

It was a memorable thirty-six hours. Tangier was an outlaws' town, notorious for smuggling, spying, armed robbery, and kidnapping, and like many such wide-open towns, it was an irresistible magnet for writers, artists, and counterculturalists of all stripes. Delacroix and Matisse, among others, frequented the city to sketch and paint. Twain felt somewhat less at home. "This is the infernalest hive of infernally costumed barbarians I have ever yet come across," he wrote his family. He and his traveling companions paid a courtesy call on the American consul-general of Tangier, Jesse McNath. The lonesome McNath was glad for the company and offered his services as volunteer guide. It was well that he did. Major Barry had already committed a near-fatal faux pas by blundering into a Muslim mosque; he was chased down the street by a stone-throwing mob of infuriated worshipers and barely escaped with his infidel life.[29]

With McNath as their guide, the party spent the next day and half seeing the sights. These included the Cave of Hercules, various Roman ruins, and the teeming bazaar, at which Twain bought half a pint of Moroccan coins for one shilling, "though I care nothing for wealth." Fascinated as always by jails, Twain toured Tangier's house of detention, where he observed Moorish prisoners making baskets and mats and heard a gruesome account of a recent triple execution in which, he said, authorities had taken three murderers out beyond the city walls and used them literally for target practice. "Moorish guns are not good, and neither are Moorish marksmen," wrote Twain. "In this instance, they set up the poor criminals at long range, like so many targets, and practiced on them—kept them hopping about and dodging bullets for half an hour before they managed to drive the centre."[30]

Reboarding the *Quaker City* at Gibraltar, Twain and his companions entertained the other passengers with hair-raising accounts of their onshore adventures, decked out in full Moroccan drag—white pajama pants, long white blouses, head scarves, and bright yellow leather slippers like something out of *The Arabian Nights*. The next day was spent commemorating, at wearisome length, the Fourth of July, while the ship steamed northeastward through the Mediterranean toward Marseilles. At daybreak the ship's two swivel cannons boomed a patriotic salute, and American flags were flown aloft or draped over the sides. The entire company gathered under the aft-deck awning, said Twain, to listen as "the flute, the asthmatic melodeon, and the consumptive clarinet crippled The Star-Spangled Banner." A reading of the Declaration of Independence came next, followed by "that same old speech about our national greatness which we so religiously believe and so fervently applaud." Only Duncan's closing address passed muster with Twain, making up in brevity what it lacked in eloquence: "Ladies and gentlemen: May we all live to a green old age and be prosperous and happy. Steward, bring up another basket of champagne." Cutter concluded the festivities with another of his inimitable poems: "No matter where we are on earth, / We'll celebrate our nation's birth; / If we cannot do it on the land / Then on deck 'neath our flag we'll stand."[31]

The *Quaker City* made landfall at Marseilles at 8 o'clock that same night. Lampooning the flowery language of guide books, Twain would later recount the ship's arrival in port,

where they "saw the dying sunlight gild its clustering spires
and ramparts, and flood its leagues of environing verdure
with a golden radiance that touched with an added charm
the white villas that flecked the landscape far and near.
(Copyright secured according to law)." After a quick visit to
the Chateau d'If in Marseilles harbor, where Alexandre Du-
mas's Count of Monte Cristo and the Man in the Iron Mask
had been held in captivity, Twain, Slote, and Jackson traveled north by train to Paris on July 6 to see the great Exhibition of 1867. They alighted at the Gare de Lyon and took a
room at the Grand Hotel du Louvre, across a wide boulevard
from the great museum. With the help of *Gaglignani's New
Paris Guide for 1867*, the party spent the next three days
touring the city's famous sights: the Tuileries, Notre Dame
Cathedral, the Pantheon, the Jardin des Plantes, the Tomb of
Napoleon, the Bois du Boulogne, Pere Lachaise Cemetery, and
various churches, museums, libraries, and galleries. Twain
found Parisians as a whole "so moustached, so frisky, so af-
fable, so fearfully and wonderfully Frenchy!" Given his later
low opinion of their homeland, it was scant praise.[32]

The Paris Exhibition, which attracted an estimated 100,000
Americans that summer, merited only two hours of Twain's
time. He was less interested in the seven concentric, doughnut-
shaped galleries devoted to the world's manufacturing glories—
the prize U.S. exhibit was a mobile military hospital—than in
what was taking place outside. Like its first iteration a dozen
years earlier, the Exhibition was the brainchild of French
Emperor Napoleon III, who made up in ceremonial pomp
what he lacked of his immortal cousin's battlefield prowess.
Despite still being in official mourning over the fate of his
recently executed fellow royal, Archduke Maximilian, by
Mexican nationalists, the emperor led a grand military re-

view down the Champs Elysees. Climbing onto a barrel near the Arc de Triomphe de l'Étoile, Twain enjoyed a front-row seat for the ruler's royal progress with his distinguished guest of honor, Sultan Abdul-Aziz of Turkey. Twain was fascinated by the contrast between the two rulers and their cultures: "Napoleon III, the representative of the highest modern civilization, progress, and refinement; Abdul-Aziz, the representative of a people by nature and training filthy, brutish, ignorant, unprogressive, superstitious—and a government whose Three Graces are Tyranny, Rapacity, Blood." The emperor, Twain told *Alta California* readers, was "the greatest man in the world today. There is no element of true greatness which Napoleon does not possess." Three years later, Otto von Bismarck and the Prussian army would forcibly refute that opinion, overwhelming Napoleon III's forces at Sedan and compelling the emperor to surrender his sword, his crown, and most of his greatness.[33]

The remainder of Twain's Paris visit involved less majestic sights. In the company of a charlatan guide with the improbable name A. Billfinger, the first in a series of irritating guides that Twain and his companions would endure on the trip, the party toured the Paris morgue, "that horrible receptacle of the dead who die mysteriously and leave the manner of their taking off a dismal secret." They looked into a room filled with "the clothing of dead men; coarse blouses, water-soaked; the delicate garments of women and children; patrician vestments, hacked and stabbed and stained with red; a hat that was crushed and bloody." Most terrible of all was the body of a drowned man, "naked, swollen, purple; clasping

the fragment of a broken bush with a grip which death had
so petrified that human strength could not unloose it—mute
witness of the last despairing effort to save the life that was
doomed beyond all help."[34]

A visit to a Paris dancehall to see the notorious cancan girls
was considerably more diverting. "The music struck up, and
then—I placed my hands before my face for very shame," Twain
would recall. "But I looked through my fingers. They were
dancing the renowned 'Can-can.' A handsome girl in the set
before me tripped forward lightly to meet the opposite gentleman—tripped back again, grasped her dresses vigorously
on both sides with her hands, raised them pretty high, danced
with an extraordinary jig that had more activity and exposure
than any jig I ever saw before, and then, drawing her clothes
still higher, she advanced gaily to the centre and launched a
vicious kick full at her *vis-à-vis* that must infallibly have removed his nose if he had been seven feet high. It was a mercy
he was only six. That is the *can-can*."[35]

Twain, Slote, and Jackson took the train back to Marseilles
on July 13. Landing the next day at Genoa, the *Quaker City*'s
passengers disembarked, minus Mary Fairbanks, the Beaches,
the Severances, Charley Langdon, and others who were still
traveling across Europe by train. After three days in Genoa,
whose women Twain judged the prettiest on the continent—
"I fell in love with a hundred and eighty women myself, on
Sunday evening, and yet I am not of a susceptible nature"—
he and his companions began a hectic twelve-day race across
northern Italy, visiting four major cities and numerous villages. It was the sort of headlong pace that American tourists were known for, and it swept past in a blur of incense-
reeking cathedrals filled with "fat and serene" priests and
bogus religious relics. In Genoa they were shown a chest pur-

porting to contain the ashes of Saint John the Baptist, the second such reliquary they had seen, said Twain, and "we could not bring ourselves to think St. John had two sets of ashes." They were also shown a portrait of the Madonna, supposedly painted from life by the Apostle Luke. "We could not help admiring the Apostle's modesty in never once mentioning in his writings that he could paint," Twain allowed. He kept a running tally of the number of relics they were shown: a piece of the True Cross in every church they went into, a keg's worth of nails from said cross, three separate crowns of thorns, and enough bones of the martyred Saint Denis "for them to duplicate him, if necessary."[36]

In Milan it was more of the same. Cathedral priests showed them two of St. Paul's fingers, one of St. Peter's, bones from Judas Iscariot (suitably black) and various other disciples, a handkerchief imprinted with the face of Jesus, a fragment of the Savior's purple robe, more crowns of thorns, and another of St. Luke's patented Madonna portraits. Twain found Leonardo da Vinci's celebrated painting of the Last Supper severely lacking in both setting and preservation. The painting, much faded, was located on a wall of the nuns' dining room at the church of Santa Maria delle Gracie, "an ancient tumble-down ruin of a church." Twain watched a dozen artists copying Da Vinci's masterpiece. "I could not help noticing how superior the copies were to the original, that is, to my inexperienced eye," he wrote. He was driven to distraction by the "ejaculations of rapture" coming from his fellow tourists about the painting's grace, colors, touch, and expression. Twain, for his part, could only see a battered, scarred, stained, and badly discolored work. Napoleon's horses, he said, had "kicked the legs off most of the disciples when they (the horses, not the disciples,) were stabled there more than half a century ago." As for the disciples themselves, "Simon looks seedy; John looks sick, and half of the other blurred and damaged apostles have a general expression of discouragement about them."[37]

On several occasions during their journey across Italy, Twain and his fellow passengers were forced to endure a claustrophobic and utterly ineffective fumigation process that was designed to combat an ongoing cholera epidemic. As a child of the American frontier, Twain was no stranger to the deadly and particularly nasty disease, which kills by inducing fatal dehydration in its victims due to catastrophic vomiting and diarrhea. He had, in fact, been born in upstate Missouri, not St. Louis, as originally intended, because a cholera scare had induced his parents to relocate in the scruffy inland hamlet of Florida rather than the more cosmopolitan destination on the banks of the river. During the 1840s, when Twain was a boy, another cholera epidemic struck the Mississippi River valley. For every person killed by cholera, he said, three more died of fright.

Twain may have been blasé about the threat of cholera, but Europeans were not. Four separate pandemics had struck the continent since 1817, killing millions of people, including King Charles X of France, Prussian military theorist Karl von Clausewitz, and Russian composer Peter Tchaikovsky. In the United States, former President James K. Polk was also a victim. Determined to limit the spread of the waterborne disease, Italian authorities herded travelers from affected areas into closed rooms, where they were forced to stand for half an hour amid swirling smoke from burning pots of chloride of lime and sulfur. Twain called the experience "the Black Hole of Calcutta on a small scale" and groused about the "combination of miraculous stinks and stenches such as only Italian ingenuity could contrive." Travelers might survive cholera easily enough, he said, "but whether they can undergo Italian purification and live is another matter." His unfinished novel, *3,000 Years among the Microbes*, is narrated by a cholera microbe.[38]

Bypassing such literary landmarks as Padua and Verona, Twain and his companions pulled into Venice at eight o'clock on the evening of July 24. The slowly sinking aqueous city so beloved by Henry James and Ernest Hemingway did not much captivate Twain, who found it a ruined and desolate shell of its former self. "Her glory is departed, and with her crumbling grandeur of wharves and palaces about her she sits among her stagnant lagoons, forlorn and beggared, forgotten of the world," he wrote. As for the city's fabled gondolas, the author judged the conveyance to be "an inky, rusty old canoe with a sable hearse-body clapped onto the middle of it," powered by "a mangy, barefooted guttersnipe with a portion of his raiment on exhibition which should have been sacred from public scrutiny." The city reminded him most strongly of "an overflowed Arkansas town, the streets full of mud and rubbish."[39]

From Venice the party rushed through Florence to Pisa, whose leaning tower Twain declared "the strangest structure the world has any knowledge of." On July 29, they reboarded the *Quaker City* in the harbor at Livorno, having spent ten days tearing across northern Italy, enduring several forced fumigations and viewing "thirteen thousand St. Jeromes, and twenty-two thousand St. Marks, and sixteen thousand St. Matthews, and sixty thousand St. Sebastians, and four millions of assorted monks, undesignated." In self-defense, Twain's traveling party adopted a stock response to all the blathering guides, hired or self-appointed, who afflicted them with rote descriptions and trite apostrophes to local glories. "After they have exhausted their enthusiasm pointing out to us and praising the beauties of some ancient bronze image or broken-legged statue," he wrote, "we look at it stupidly and in silence for five, ten, fifteen minutes—as long as we can hold out, in fact—and then ask: 'Is—is he dead?' That conquers the serenest of them."[40]

Hoping to avoid more fumigations, Twain and Slote took a French steamer to Civitavecchia, which Twain deemed "the finest nest of dirt, vermin and ignorance we have found yet, except that African perdition they call Tangier, which is just like it." From there they caught a train to Rome, beating the other *Quaker City* passengers by twelve hours. Judging by Twain's patent disinterest in the Eternal City, they might as well have taken their time. "What is there in Rome for me to see that others have not seen before me?" he wondered. "What is there for me to touch that others have not touched? What is there for me to feel, to learn, to hear, to know, that shall thrill me before it passes to others? What can I discover?—Nothing. Nothing whatsoever." Confronting sights already long familiar to American travelers by 1867, Twain struggled to find something new to say about Rome. A visit to the Coliseum put him in mind of the early Christian martyrs, and he pretended to discover an old playbill for a typical day's performance that promised such delights as "grand broadsword combat," "grand moral battle-ax engagement," "general slaughter!" and a sword fight between the Roman champion Marcus Marcellus Valerian (real name Smith) fighting left-handed, against "six Sophomores and a Freshman from the Gladiatorial College!" Twain also claimed to have discovered—another lucky chance—a stained but legible copy of the *Roman Daily Battle-Ax*, with running drama criticism of the same day's events. In it, one gladiator was deemed "not thoroughly up in the backhanded stroke, but it was very gratifying to his numerous friends to know that, in time, practice would have overcome this defect. However, he was killed." A special matinee performance was scheduled for the children, with several Christian martyrs to be eaten by tigers.[41]

After five days in Rome, Twain and the others made the eight-hour train ride south to Naples, where they were to re-board the *Quaker City*. Unfortunately, the ship was under quarantine for another three days, with neither the remaining passengers nor crew allowed to leave. This inconvenient condition moved Bloodgood Cutter, again, to verse:

> *Why don't your doctor come on board*
> *And see what in our ship is stored;*
> *Although our ship is nice and clean*
> *On her at all he is not seen.*

> *But no, he came near in his boat,*
> *Under his umbrella there doth float;*
> *Says a few words then goes away,*
> *Leaving us confined in Naples Bay.*[42]

The ship's photographer, William E. James, entertained hopes that Italian authorities, upon hearing the first part of Cutter's twelve-stanza poem, would immediately release the ship from quarantine to avoid having to hear the rest of it, "but, as in many other things concerned with this excursion, we were

doomed to disappointment." Twain and the other nonquar-
antined passengers amused themselves, if not their captive
shipmates, by rowing past the ship and inviting them to come
ashore. He spent a busy several days seeing the sights of Naples, from the supposed "miraculous liquefaction of the blood
of St. Januarius" to "a made-up Madonna—a stuffed and
painted image, like a milliner's dummy—whose hair miracu-
lously grew and restored itself every twelve months."[43]

Twain took a dim view of the Neapolitans, "a people who
want two cents every time they bow to you." The local merchants, he said, "cheat everybody they can, and they always
are expecting to get cheated themselves. They always ask four
times as much money as they intend to take, but if you give
them what they first demand, they feel ashamed of themselves
for aiming so low, and immediately ask for more. . . . One
cannot buy and pay for two cents' worth of clams without
trouble and a quarrel." The normally mild-mannered Emily
Severance shared Twain's disapproval. "We all have the
feeling," Mrs. Severance wrote in her journal, "that the Neapolitans themselves are the lowest dregs of humanity we have
yet seen. I would not trust them with the smallest sum."[44]

The difficulties in negotiating with the natives did not prevent Twain from organizing a donkey ride up Mount Vesuvius.
Peering over the lip of the volcano, he beheld "yellow banks
of sulphur and with lava and pumice-stone of many colors. No
fire was visible any where, but gusts of sulphurous steam issued silently and invisibly from a thousand little cracks and
fissures in the crater, and were wafted to our noses with every
breeze." Some in the party—Twain was probably one—thrust
long slips of paper into the holes to set them on fire and light
their cigars. Others cooked eggs over boiling fissures in the
rocks. As a natural wonder, Twain judged "the Vesuvius of

today a very poor affair compared to the mighty volcano of Kilauea," which he had visited during his stay in Hawaii nine months earlier.[45]

More impressive were the ruins of Pompeii, a forty-five-minute carriage ride away. Wandering through "this old silent city of the dead," Twain tried to conjure the people's lives before "that awful November night [November 9, 79 AD] of eighteen centuries ago" when as many as thirty thousand residents died in a blazing, asphyxiating cloud of superheated ash. In this endeavor he had expert help. Thanks to the pioneering archaeological advances of Naples-born Giuseppe Fiorelli, who had taken over as director of excavations at Pompeii four years earlier, visitors to the site could see recently molded plaster casts of the victims. The Fiorelli Process pumped wet plaster into holes left in the hardened ash by the decomposed bodies of the dead, revealing the minutest details of the victims' clothing, hair styles, and even facial expressions at the time of death. Morbidly fascinated, Twain took in a bakery where workers had found fossilized loaves of bread the doomed baker had not had time to remove, and saw the remains of a man, a woman, and two young girls. "The woman had her hands spread wide apart, as if in mortal terror," he reported, "and I imagined I could still trace upon her shapeless face something of the expression of wild despair that distorted it when the heavens rained fire in these streets, so many ages ago. The girls and the man lay with their faces upon their arms, as if they had tried to shield them from the enveloping cinders."[46]

When the quarantine was lifted, the *Quaker City* prepared to leave Naples and its unsavory residents. Passengers hurried back on board with boatloads of last-minute purchases—linen suits for the men, rolls of silk and velvet for the women, jewelry, wine, statues, and shawls. The American Vandals were in full cry. Reverend G. W. Quereau of Aurora, Illinois, having discovered a taste for paintings, unscrolled numerous copies of the Old Masters and laid them out on deck for his fellow shipmates to admire. One enterprising old Neapolitan rowed out to the ship and commenced an impromptu bagpipe concert, simultaneously manipulating two wooden dancing dolls. Two young Italian maidens, strumming guitars, sang and waved as the Americans tossed money to them.

At 6 a.m. on August 8, Captain Duncan pointed the *Quaker City* out to sea, only to quickly cut the engines after it was discovered that Judge Haldeman, the recovering alcoholic, had apparently fallen off the wagon and gone missing. A search party was organized, and eventually the judge was rowed back to the ship, frantically waving his arms in fear of being left behind. Two hours later, the ship steamed out of Naples harbor. Twain, like the others, was glad to leave Italy behind. "As far as I can see," he informed readers of the *Alta California*, "Italy, for fifteen hundred years, has turned all her energies, all her finances, and all her industry to the building up of a vast array of wonderful monuments of human folly, and starving half her citizens to accomplish it. She is today one vast museum of magnificence and misery."[47]

If Naples was frustrating for the travelers, the next port of call, Athens, was infuriating. With cholera still raging at near-epidemic levels in Italy, Greek officials were understandably leery about welcoming in a new boatload of tourists from the infected country. Ten years earlier, thoughtless British sailors had broken quarantine and sneaked ashore at

Piraeus, instigating an outbreak that ultimately claimed ten thousand lives. Seeking to prevent a repeat performance, harbor officers rowed out to the *Quaker City* and placed the passengers and crew under quarantine for the next eleven days. Frustrated passengers crowded the rails, looking wistfully at the square-topped hill, the Acropolis, crowned by the storied Parthenon. Huddled among the various lower hills were clumps of tents sheltering thousands of refugees from Greece's ongoing war with Turkey who were probably carrying more potential cholera microbes than the frequently quarantined and regularly fumigated pilgrims aboard the *Quaker City*. In any event, the quarantine was not strictly enforced: supply boats ferried fresh fruits and ices out to the ship, and Moses Beach unpacked his small sailboat and took groups of shipmates larking around the harbor and over to the swimming beach to cool off.[48]

Like Ben Jonson's Shakespeare, Twain had "small Latin and less Greek," but he shared with the other passengers an idealized vision of Athens as the cradle of Western civilization. He wanted to see for himself the streets down which Plato, Aristotle, Sophocles, Aeschylus, and Euripides had walked, upon which Pericles had proclaimed the birth of democracy. His first impressions were not favorable. "I suppose that ancient Greece and modern Greece compared, furnish the most extravagant contrast to be found in history," Twain observed. "The fleets that were the wonder of the world when the Parthenon was new, are a beggarly handful of fishing-smacks now, and the manly people that performed such miracles of valor at Marathon are only a tribe of unconsidered slaves today. The classic Illyssus has gone dry, and so have all the sources of Grecian wealth and progress." As for the surrounding countryside, it was little more than "a bleak, unsmiling desert, without agriculture, manufactures or commerce." He wondered how the government managed to support itself.[49]

A helpful harbor official told the passengers that he had no way of checking to see if anyone rowed to shore under cover of darkness, provided they returned to the ship before daylight. Taking the hint, Twain, Abraham Jackson, Colonel W. S. Denny of Winchester, Virginia, and Dr. George B. Birch from the author's hometown of Hannibal donned the red fezzes they had purchased in Tangier to blend into the crowd and sneaked ashore by clouded moonlight. The quartet, stumbling through the dark, was trailed by a squadron of barking dogs—so many that the passengers remaining aboard ship later claimed that they could follow the party's progress by the sound of the barks. Stealing grapes along the way, the men climbed uphill through barren countryside "a little rougher piece of country than exists anywhere else outside of the State of Nevada." Bribing the guards at the Parthenon, the party toured the rubble-strewn ruins. After a breathless view of Athens by moonlight, Twain and the others headed back to the ship, followed by an armed escort of vineyard owners who understandably objected to the Americans' casual thievery, along with "our usual escort of fifteen hundred Piraean dogs howling at our heels." Dodging the harbor patrol, they made it back to the ship at daybreak, having "seen all there was to see in the old city."[50]

Deciding to leave Athens rather than wait out the quarantine, Duncan piloted the *Quaker City* through heavy seas toward Constantinople. Much to their relief, the ship was given a clean bill of health by Turkish inspectors. "The 'barbarous' Turks proved better Christians than their more pretentiously wise neighbors, the Greeks," noted Moses Beach, "and the door of entrance to the Turkish capital was thrown wide open." It did not stay open long. At war with the Greeks over Crete, a regular occurrence, the Turks displayed a persistent bias against the supposedly pro-Greek Americans. The *Quaker City* pilgrims, in turn, found their first views of the Middle East equally negative. "The narrow dirty crowded and stinking streets, shockingly paved were utterly disgusting," Duncan observed. And Emily Severance, the mildest of women, was moved to complain: "We have spoken of the filth of the Italian cities, but they were clean compared with this place. The very first thing to attract our attention was the dogs. They are to be seen everywhere—surly, dirty and ill-formed. . . . The night is made hideous with their noise." Twain said the dogs had been "misrepresented."[51]

He had less patience for the celebrated Mosque of St. Sophia, which Twain termed "the rustiest old barn in heathendom. Everywhere was dirt, and dust, and dinginess, and gloom." Turkish women were "rather pretty," he said, but went about the city shrouded head to toe in chaste Muslim fashion. Meanwhile, the men "dressed in all the outrageous, outlandish, idolatrous, extravagant, thunder-and-lightning costumes that ever a tailor with delirium tremens and seven devils could conceive of." The city as a whole was "the very heart and home of cripples and human monsters," Twain reported, with such horrific sights as a man with a foot composed of a single gigantic toe, a three-legged woman, a man with an eye in his cheek, another man with no eyes at all, and a third "with a prodigious head, an uncommonly long body, legs eight inches long and feet like snow-shoes."[52]

Twain adjudged the Turks to be "fantastic pagans," overrun with beggars, freaks, and dancing dervishes. There were plenty of mosques, churches, and graveyards, "but morals and whiskey are scarce. The Koran does not permit

Mohammedans to drink. Their natural instincts do not permit them to be moral." Inside the Mosque of St. Sophia, he watched the daily Islamic services with undisguised distaste: "Squatting and sitting in groups were ragged Turks reading books, hearing sermons, or receiving lessons like children, and in fifty places were more of the same sort bowing and straightening up, bowing and getting down to kiss the earth, muttering prayers the while, and keeping up their gymnastics till they ought to have been tired, if they were not." Moses Beach estimated that "a score of the best missionaries who ever existed" could spend a lifetime evangelizing the Turks of Constantinople to no apparent effect.[53]

So unsatisfying was their stay in Constantinople that Twain drafted a resolution formally petitioning Duncan to change the cruise's itinerary and bypass the famous Crimean War battlefield at Sevastopol in order to spend more time in Palestine. Noting that "there is nothing to see at Sebastopol but a bare & uninteresting battle-field where military fortifications have been but no longer exist," Twain the Confederate army deserter declared that "several among us having stood in the midst of scenes of this character of infinitely greater importance in our own country in the smoke and carnage of battle." In the end, the petition was never delivered, and the *Quaker City* sailed north through the Bosporus and into the Black Sea, docking at Sevastopol on August 21.[54]

At Sevastopol the pilgrims were welcomed with surprising hospitality by the Russians, perhaps because they weren't English. The city, said Twain, "is probably the worst battered town in Russia or anywhere else. Ruined Pompeii is in good

condition compared to Sevastopol." Two days had been set
aside to tour the battle sites, but two hours was all anyone
needed. Twain, never much fascinated by actual warfare,
spent a desultory few hours picking through the ruined houses
and bare hillsides. He gave a cursory, inaccurate survey of the
fighting around Sevastopol—the French assault on Mal-
akhov Hill took one day, not three as he claimed, and the
Russians never retook it—before heading back to the ship.
There he found the Vandals again hard at work, having carried off heaping handfuls of relics from the battlefield. "They
have brought cannon balls, broken ramrods, fragments of
shell—iron enough to freight a sloop," Twain reported. "Some
have even brought bones . . . and were grieved to hear the
surgeon pronounce them only bones of mules and oxen."
One traveler "turned his state-room into a museum of worth-
less trumpery," labeling one of his finds, a jawbone with a
couple of loose teeth in it, "Fragment of a Russian General."
When Twain pointed out that the jawbone in question actually came from a horse, rank unspecified, the man said his
aunt back home would never know the difference.[55]

The *Quaker City* steamed northwest across the Black Sea
to Odessa. Twain had a momentary scare when, having forgotten his passport, he was forced to use Dan Slote's to enter
the country (Slote had remained behind in Constantinople).
Somehow he managed to pass for the pudgier, balding Slote,
all Americans presumably looking alike to Russians, and was
granted free range of the city. There wasn't much to see, with
one notable exception—male and female residents, young and
old, bathed nude together in full view of the ship. "I have often
thought that our style of bathing was rather subdued than
otherwise, and lacked many elements of cheerfulness," Twain
reported. "You cannot say that of the Russian style. I never

was so outraged in my life. At least a hundred times, in the
seven hours I stayed there, I would just have got up and gone
away from there disgusted, if I had had any place to go to."[56]

While the ship was recoaling at Odessa, the passengers
were invited to pay a courtesy call on the Russian czar, Alexander II, who had succeeded his father, Nicholas I, as ruler
of all the Russias in 1855. Alexander was summering nearby
at Luvidia, his vacation dacha in Yalta, unscathed and presumably untroubled by a recent assassination attempt in Paris.
Wildly excited by the invitation, the passengers spent several
hours practicing their curtsies and bows, while Twain headed
a five-man committee drafting a formal address to the czar.
The resulting address was so obsequious that one almost sus-
pects Twain was burlesquing the form: "We are a handful of
private citizens of America, traveling simply for recreation—
and unostentatiously, as becomes our unofficial state—and
therefore, we have no excuse to tender for representing ourselves before your Majesty, save the desire of offering our
grateful acknowledgments to the lord of a realm, which
through good and through evil report, has been the steadfast
friend of the land we love so well." Alexander had recently
proved his friendship by selling Alaska to the United States
for seven million dollars, or two cents an acre.[57]

The next morning, Twain and sixty other passengers made
the pilgrimage to Yalta, where the American consul, Frederick
Smith, arranged them in a semicircle in the palace garden. The
czar graciously did not keep them waiting, but appeared forth-
with, accompanied by the czarina and their youngest son and
daughter. In a spirit of noblesse oblige, the royal family wore
no jewels or uniforms, while the visitors, conversely, were
decked out in morning suits and ball gowns "Good morning,"
said the czar in passable English. "I am glad to see you—I am

gratified—I am delighted—I am happy to receive you!" Consul Smith made the introductions, the Americans bowing and scraping like so many Ukrainian serfs, and then read Twain's speech. The czar smiled, muttered, "Very good, very good, I am very, very grateful," and handed the manuscript to a nearby aide, "to be filed away among the archives of Russia—in the stove, perhaps," Twain conjectured. The author paid particular attention to the czar's fourteen-year-old daughter, Marie. "She was only a girl, and she looked like a thousand others I have seen," he noted, "but never a girl provoked such a novel and peculiar interest in me before"—the nude female bathers at Odessa notwithstanding. The guests were invited into the summer palace for a quick tour; then the ruler gave a final friendly wave and left. The audience had lasted fifteen minutes.[58]

As a consolation prize, the visitors were invited to share a light breakfast at the nearby home of Grand Duke Michael, the czar's younger brother. In full Cossack regalia, Michael made a stronger impression than the dressed-down czar. "He is a rare brick, the princeliest figure in Russia," noted Twain. "He is even taller than the Czar, as straight as an Indian, and bears himself like one of those gorgeous knights we read about in romances of the Crusades. He looks like a great-hearted fellow who would pitch an enemy into the river in a moment, and then jump in and risk his life fishing him out again." Michael proved a gracious host, exchanging small talk with his visitors over crackers, tea, and cold cuts. Mary Fairbanks, for one, was carried away. "I can assure you," she wrote, "it made my heart throb with delight to hear those fine looking Russians say in their broken French or English, 'We love your country.'" Not everyone was so enchanted with the czar, at any rate. Fourteen years later, while Twain was putting the finishing touches on his novel *The Prince and the Pauper*, Alexander was blown to bits by bomb-throwing anarchists in St. Petersburg.[59]

The *Quaker City* returned to Constantinople to take on more coal. It was a maddening process, exacerbated by a work slowdown by the Turks, who apparently were annoyed at the Americans for paying court to their traditional enemy the czar. Sultan Abdul-Aziz, last seen riding alongside Napoleon III in Paris, was miffed that they did not call on him as well. With nothing better to do, the passengers went into the city to buy more things—embroidered slippers, hookah pipes, Turkish towels, turbans, even personalized gravestones with their names carved on them in Arabic. Back on board ship, they endured extensive ribbing from the ship's crew, who satirized their slavish visit to the czar by holding their own royal reception, with the galley cook standing in for the Russian sovereign, cavorting about in a soiled tablecloth with a tin pot on his head, holding a scepter that looked suspiciously like a belaying pin. Other sailors took the roles of pilgrims, male and female, sashaying about in tarpaulin dresses, hoop skirts, and frock coats, bowing and scraping before their ruler with "a system of complicated and extraordinary smiling which few monarchs could look upon and live." A deckhand produced a piece of paper and began reading solemnly: "We are a handful of private citizens from America, traveling simply for recreation." The opening lines would be repeated by crewmen for the rest of the voyage. Said Twain, "I never was so tired of any one phrase."[60]

After five more days in port at Constantinople, the *Quaker City* steamed south along the Turkish coast to Smyrna, first stop on the long-anticipated Holy Land portion of the tour. The ancient port, one of the Seven Churches of the Apocalypse mentioned in Revelation, reminded Twain of the *Arabian Nights*, with its covered bazaars, honeycombed streets, spice-laden camel trains, clarion-calling muezzins, and pretty, smiling Armenian girls. "They average a shade better than American girls," he observed, "which are treasonable words I pray may be forgiven me." His fellow passengers were more interested in seeing the nearby biblical ruins of Ephesus than underage Armenians, and Twain joined a party of day-trippers led by Duncan. The outing began with a three-hour ride on an English-run railroad, followed by a bone-jarring hour mounted aboard donkeys to the ruins. In the furnace-hot sun-light the travelers struggled to control their donkeys. Periodi-cally, one of the riders would pitch headfirst onto the ground. For fear of falling off, the women had to ride immodestly astride their mounts rather than sidesaddle.[61]

At Ephesus, where the Apostle Paul had written 1 Corin-thians, the pilgrims walked worshipfully in his footsteps. They posed for photographs in the well-preserved amphitheater, read Bible passages aloud to one another, shared sacramental cups of wine, and then fell, like good Vandals, to the task at hand, carrying off every semiportable memento they could find. Bloodgood Cutter distinguished himself by carrying away an entire portion of columned wall. Twain implied that he, too, had joined in the looting, bragging later: "I never resist a temp-tation to plunder a stranger's premises." But the real treasure, from his point of view, came after he returned to the ship, when Charley Langdon showed him an ivory miniature of his sister Olivia. In Twain's famous retelling of his Saul of Tarsus moment, he fell in love immediately with the delicate twenty-two-year-old girl in the cameo and vowed to marry her one day. Charley was less than enthusiastic, turning down Twain's request to hand over the miniature for future viewings. For the time being, at any rate, Olivia was safely out of reach with their parents in Elmira, New York, but a chord had been struck in Twain's memory, and he never forgot a face—certainly not hers.[62]

Now began the most exhausting, exhilarating part of the journey. For most *Quaker City* passengers, the visit to the Holy Land was the ultimate tour destination. "We sailed from Smyrna, in the wildest spirit of expectancy," reported Twain, "for the chief feature, the grand goal of the expedition, was near at hand—we were approaching the Holy Land!" Since signing onto the tour back in the spring, Twain and his fellow passengers had been primarily tourists. Now they would be—some of them at least—pilgrims, in the purest sense of the term, walking with bowed heads and clasped hands the same ground that Jesus and the Apostles had walked two millennia before. Twain, who had used the term "pilgrim" more or less interchangeably during the preceding months of the trip to describe himself and the other *Quaker City* voyagers, now began using it specifically to denote the more pietistic members of the party. For himself and other less religiously observant travelers, he employed a different word—sinners.[63]

Hugging the eastern Mediterranean coast, the ship docked at Beirut, Lebanon, on September 10. There was an immediate complication. Duncan had arranged in advance for round-trip overland passage for the pilgrims from Beirut to Damascus, Syria, a distance of seventy miles, on the French-run Continental Stage Coach and its private road, but the line could only carry twelve passengers per day—a third of those wishing to see Damascus. The other two dozen would have to find alternative means of transportation and then link up with the *Quaker City* at Jaffa. Twain was in the second group, along with the other able-bodied men. His traveling party included Dan Slote, Jack Van Nostrand, Julius Moulton, George Birch, William Denny, J. W. Davis, and William Church. They would strike east through Lebanon's Beqaa Valley, then head south through Damascus and down into Palestine. It was a risky journey, said Twain, "for any but strong, healthy men, accustomed somewhat to fatigue and rough life in the open air." It was debatable how rough and ready the eight men really were. Twain's own years in the American West had been spent, for the most part, in Virginia City saloons, San Francisco hotels, and Hawaiian tourist resorts. He was not exactly Buffalo Bill.[64]

Under the experienced eyes of a Muslim guide and translator named Abraham, the party set out with an entourage that included nineteen servants, twenty-six pack mules, tents, food, and supplies. The first night out Twain and the others were served a full-course dinner on fine linen tablecloths with silver candlesticks, while the servants set up gaily colored tents complete with iron bedsteads, soft pillows and mattresses, and snow-white sheets. "And they call *this* camping out," Twain smirked. The countryside reminded him of Nevada and Arizona, while the Bedouins who peopled the region put him in mind of the Digger Indians out West, which given his habitual disregard of Native Americans was not a compliment. Mounted on a tailless horse named Jericho that spent most of its time shying at shadows, kicking at flies, and biting at Twain's legs—"I do not care particularly about that, only I do not like to see a horse too sociable"—the author rode through barren, rocky countryside in scorching heat. The trip was briefly enlivened by his first glimpse of a camel, with Twain giving a vivid description of the animal: "When he is down on all his knees, flat on his breast to receive his load, he looks something like a goose swimming; and when he is upright he looks like an ostrich with an extra set of legs. They have immense, flat, forked cushions of feet, that make a track in the dust like a pie with a slice out of it."[65]

At a nameless Lebanese village they viewed the tomb of Noah. "Noah built the ark," Twain observed helpfully. He computed the tomb to be 210 feet long and four feet high. "He must have cast a shadow like a lightning-rod." At Baalbek, the well-preserved ruins of the fabled Greco-Roman city of Heliopolis, the party spent a desultory few hours going through the Temple of the Sun, the Temple of Jupiter, and other lesser temples. Twain marveled at the giant rocks used in the construction, but he railed against the countless "John Smiths, George Wilkinsons, and all the other pitiful nobodies" who had graffitied their names on the walls. "It is a pity some great ruin does not fall in and flatten out some of these reptiles," he raged, "and scare their kind out of ever giving their names to fame upon any walls or monuments again, forever."[66]

Twain's mood was not improved by their arrival at Damascus, which he found "the most fanatical Mohammedan purgatory out of Arabia." In a passage with all-too-modern resonance, Twain described the persistent anti-Western feeling inside the city, where "they so hate the very sight of a foreign Christian that they want no intercourse whatever with him." Even the beggars and merchants left them alone. Recalling a massacre of Christians inside the city six years earlier, Twain broke character as the amiable travel writer to snarl: "I never disliked a Chinaman as I do these degraded Turks and Arabs, and when Russia is ready to war with them again, I hope England and France will not find it good breeding or good judgment to interfere." Earlier he had expressed the similar wish that Russia would "annihilate Turkey a little—not much, but enough to make it difficult to find the place again without a divining-rod or a diving-bell."[67]

The next day Twain fell ill with a mild form of cholera possibly caused by dunking his head in a water tank at his hotel. It was a welcome break from Syrian travel, he joked; having cholera was the high point of his visit to Damascus. Weakened by illness, Twain spent a miserable next few days riding south through Palestine, while "the sun-flames shot down like the shafts of fire that stream out before a blow-pipe." With the feverish Twain taking minimal interest, they passed Juneh, the traditional site of St. Paul's conversion; the tomb of Nimrod at Kefr Hauwar; the Bainias Fountain, one of the principal sources of the Jordan River; and various Arab desert villages before coming to the fabled Sea of Galilee. It, too, failed to impress Twain, who judged it "a solemn, sailless, tintless lake, reposing within its rim of yellow hills and low, steep banks, and looking just as expressionless and unpoetical . . . as any bath-tub on earth." The entire setting, he said, was one of "exquisitely dismal solitude." One night Arab bandits pelted their camp with stones in an unsuccessful attempt to stampede the horses. Had they succeeded, Twain and the others might well have died from thirst and exposure. As it was, the only casualty of the trip occurred when a camel sneaked up on one of the pilgrims and bit him on the shoulder.[68]

A six-hour ride brought them to Jesus's boyhood home at Nazareth. Twain had difficulty picturing the Messiah spending the first thirty years of his life in such an unimpressive village. "One finds oneself saying, all the time, 'The boy Jesus has stood in this doorway—has played in that street—has touched these stones with his hands—has rambled over these chalky hills,'" he noted. "Whoever shall write the Boyhood of Jesus ingeniously, will make a book which will possess a vivid interest for young and old alike." It would not be Twain. Although he prudently kept his more irreligious musings to himself, reserving them for the back of his notebook, he remained at heart a committed agnostic. Not even his long, devoted marriage to a conventionally devout young woman would change Twain's fundamental religious skepticism, if not outright disbelief.[69]

Dutifully Twain toured the grotto of the Annunciation where the Holy Infant had lived with Joseph and Mary, the workshop where Joseph and Jesus had worked, the synagogue where the young Jesus had taught, and the huge stone slab upon which Jesus and his disciples had sat after their return from the Sea of Galilee. At the Fountain of the Virgin, where Mary supposedly went to draw water twenty times a day, Twain again found himself looking appraisingly at the local girls. "The Nazarene girls are homely," he wrote. "Some of them have large, lustrous eyes, but none of them have pretty faces. . . . We can all believe that the Virgin Mary was beautiful; it is not natural to think otherwise; but does it follow that it is our duty to find beauty in these present women of Nazareth?" All in all, Nazareth was a depressing letdown: "Dirt and rags and squalor; vermin, hunger and wretchedness; savage costumes, savage weapons and looks of hate." Mary Fairbanks, whose traveling party had left Nazareth two days earlier, concurred. The entire town, she said, was "a filthy, unattractive spot."[70]

At midday on September 23, Twain and his party rode into Jerusalem. Somewhere along the way he had parted company with his troublesome horse Jericho—no word on the horse's ultimate fate—and acquired a less vicious but also less able-bodied mount, a half-blind, toothless, broken-nosed swayback that he named Baalbec "because he is such a magnificent ruin." The other pilgrims were arriving, too, having survived their own misadventures with fractious horses, thieving Arabs, scorching weather, and ill health. Julia Newell had been thrown from her horse at Haifa, Abraham Jackson (now her fiancé) was suffering from heat stroke, and Kate Brown and William James had been struck by rocks thrown by unwelcoming locals at Samaria, leading Twain to remark that if the city was actually the home of the Good Samaritan, he must have been "the only one that ever lived there."[71]

Surprisingly, their first glimpse of Jerusalem did not induce an emotional response from the travelers. The city, situated on a plateau in the Judean Mountains, was holy to Jews, Christians, and Muslims alike; conflicting claims had caused the city to be besieged seventy-five times since its founding in the dusty murk of the fourth millennium. Since then, Jerusalem had changed hands forty-four times, ruled variously by Jews, Egyptians, Assyrians, Babylonians, Persians, Macedonians, Romans, Selucids, Muslims, Christians, Tartars, Mamluks, and Mongols. Except for a brief nine-year interregnum by Egypt in the 1830s, the Ottoman Turks had controlled the city since the sixteenth century, bringing with them such modern innovations as paved roads and a postal system. Within the Old City, four quarters traditionally held sway: Christian, Jewish, Muslim, and Armenian. Outside the city walls, a new Russian compound had sprung up in 1860 to accommodate the six thousand Russian pilgrims arriving yearly. Churches, synagogues, and mosques jostled uneasily for space on the scattered hillsides. The sky itself seemed cordoned off.[72]

Twain and his party checked into Mediterranean Hotel, Jerusalem's finest, and the next day he toured the city's sacred sites. He found the city surprisingly small: "A fast walker could go outside the walls of Jerusalem and walk entirely around the city in an hour." All shades of nationality and languages were represented there, but the Muslim majority dominated: "Rags, wretchedness, poverty and dirt, those signs and symbols that indicate the presence of Moslem rule more surely than the crescent-flag itself, abound," Twain noted. The city was swarming with lepers, cripples, the blind, and the mad. The sheer numbers of "maimed, malformed, and diseased humanity" made the author think that the angel of Lord was about to descend. "Jerusalem is mournful, and dreary, and lifeless," he wrote. "I would not desire to live here."[73]

During the course of one crowded day, Twain visited the Dome of the Rock, the Church of the Holy Sepulchre, the Pool of Bethesda, Pontius Pilate's house, and the Via Dolorosa. In a tart observation jotted down in his notebook, he remarked on the broken stone pillar where Christ was said to have dropped his cross. "We might have thought this story the idle invention of priests and guides, but the broken column was still there to show for itself," Twain wrote. "One cannot go behind the evidence." Except for the hill at Calvary, which he accepted as an actual site, he considered the other sacred spots merely "imaginary holy places created by monks." Emily Severance was likewise unmoved by the Church of the Holy Sepulchre. "I do not confess to feelings of solemnity during our visit," she noted. "Priests chanting mass over the Stone of Unction and clouds of incense do not make holy those places I am sure would never have been hallowed."[74]

Many of the pilgrims shared Twain's disappointed disgust with travel writer William Prime's *Tent Life in the Holy Land,* which had been their touchstone on the voyage over. Mary Fairbanks said Prime's book was "a charming book to read in your library, but when with your finger upon a certain line of glowing description you look around in vain for the original of the picture, a feeling of resentment comes over you as when you have been deceived." To Twain's way of thinking, Prime's guidebook was "a bitter disappointment. The fairy land was modified too much. It was a howling wilderness instead of a garden." Twain found Prime hopelessly lachrymose in his re-actions to the holy sights. Of Prime's entrance into Jerusalem, Twain noted: "He wept, and his party all wept, and the drag-oman wept, and so did the muleteers, and even a Latin priest, and a Jew that came straggling along. He never bored but he struck water." As for himself, Twain conceded that he had shed tears of his own at the Grave of Adam, but only because he was moved "to discover the grave of a blood relation" so far from home."[75]

Jesus's birthplace at Bethlehem was also a disappointment. Mary Fairbanks and Emily Severance did not even bother to go there. Twain did, but spent little time or reflection on his visit. Bethlehem, he said, was filled with the usual "troops of beggars and relic-peddlers." At the Church of the Nativity, he saw the very manger, so it was claimed, where the Holy In-fant had been born. It was marked by a silver star on the floor, "tricked out in the usual tasteless style observable in all the holy places of Palestine." The ordinarily loquacious Twain was struck mute by the scenes, although not from religious awe. "I have no 'meditations' suggested by this spot where the very first 'Merry Christmas!' was uttered in all the world, and from whence the friend of my childhood, Santa Claus, departed on his first journey," he joked. "I touch, with reverent finger, the actual spot where the infant Jesus lay, but I think—nothing." The entire last part of the trip, as scholar Harold T. McCarthy points out, proved to be "a serious exhausting affair driving Twain to a savage assessment of the Pilgrims that was, in part, a reaction to the bitter recognition that his own concept of Christianity had been a wishful dream."[76]

After gathering up a cache of souvenirs for his family—a Bible encased in olive wood for his mother, an olive-wood card case and beads for his sister Pamela, a branch torn from King Godfrey's tree and bottles of holy water from Bethesda, the River Jordan, and the Dead Sea for his brother Orion—Twain left Bethlehem and its "clap-trap side-shows and unseemly impostures." One last day of sightseeing in Jerusalem brought him to the Hill of Evil Counsel where Judas Iscariot had hanged himself. Twain wondered why Judas couldn't have hanged himself a little closer to town. On September 30, Twain rode into the port city of Jaffa and reboarded the *Quaker City* to begin the long westward journey home. A note he jotted down during a brief visit to the Dead Sea summed up his thoughts on the Holy Land: "No Second Advent," he wrote. "Christ been here once, will never come again." Once again, he kept the impious thought to himself.[77]

Two more stops in the Middle East remained, at Alexandria and Cairo, Egypt. The two-day voyage from Jaffa to Alexandria was rough and crowded; besides the full contingent of *Quaker City* pilgrims, Duncan had taken on board another forty-one refugees from a failed religious commune at Jaffa led by a former actor and excommunicated Mormon elder named George Jones Adams. Under Adams's charismatic spell, some one hundred sixty colonists from the state of Maine had forsaken all their earthly belongings and sailed to Palestine to found the New Jerusalem. The commune quickly failed, Adams took to drink, and most of his followers returned home. The rest hunkered down, waiting for divine intervention, which came at last in the form of a fifteen hundred dollar advance from Moses Beach to pay their passage back to America and a spot on the storm-tossed deck of the *Quaker City* for the connecting voyage to Alexandria. Someone else later claimed to have been the colonists' anonymous benefactor instead of the modest Beach. "Such is life," Twain philosophized.[78]

From Alexandria, Twain and a group of pilgrims made a daylong train ride along the Nile River to Cairo to see the great pyramids and the Sphinx at Giza. Twain and others climbed the Pyramid of Cheops, assisted by native guides who tugged and pushed them toward the summit, all the time "threatening to throw us down the precipice, which was persuasive and convincing." At the summit, Twain looked out over a great sea of sand on one side and a broad green floodplain on the other. At the bottom another "howling swarm of beggars" descended on the company before being driven off by a bribed bodyguard swinging a long wooden staff. "Millions for defense," said Twain, "but not a cent for bucksheesh."[79]

The highlight of the Egyptian visit was the visit to the Sphinx. "The great face was so sad, so earnest, so longing, so patient," Twain wrote. "There was a dignity not of earth in its mien, and in its countenance a benignity such as never any thing human wore. It was stone, but it seemed sentient. . . . It was gazing over the ocean of Time—over lines of century-waves which, further and further receding, closed nearer and nearer together, and blended at last into one unbroken tide, away toward the horizon of remote antiquity." The vista was somewhat marred by the jarring sight of William Gibson, the self-styled "Commissioner of the United States of America to Europe, Asia, and Africa," attempting to chip off part of the Sphinx's jaw for the Smithsonian Institution. He failed.[80]

Four months after leaving the harbor in New York City, the *Quaker City* departed Alexandria on October 7 and commenced her return voyage. It was a long six weeks. Again the specter of cholera arose, and several planned stops were canceled due to quarantine. Malta, Sardinia, Algiers, and Malaga all declared themselves off-limits to the ship, even though no one on board was actually sick. "I begin to see understand why Ulysses' voyage was so prolonged," Mary Fairbanks wrote. Nine days out they anchored at Gibraltar to take on coal, and Twain, Jack Van Nostrand, Julia Newell, and Abraham Jackson jumped ship for a weeklong horseback ride across southern Spain. Back on board, the pilgrims battled seasickness, homesickness, and epidemic boredom. Twain noted a typical day's delights: "Morning, dominoes. Afternoon, dominoes. Evening, promenading the deck. Afterwards, charades. Monotony till midnight—Whereupon, dominoes."[81]

A five-day layover in English-speaking Bermuda afforded Twain his first view of what later would become one of his favorite vacation spots. The "happy little paradise" allowed the pilgrims to catch their breath before churning through a vicious mid-Atlantic storm for the final four days of their voyage. Judge Haldeman became the trip's only civilian casualty when he caught his foot in a carelessly opened door frame and broke

his ankle. (A crewman had jumped overboard at Constantinople and presumably drowned.) Finally, on November 19, the
same day that Charles Dickens landed in Boston to commence
his second reading tour of the United States, the *Quaker City*
sailed into New York harbor. Everyone, said Twain, was under
strict orders to wear Christian garb for their arrival, although
there was "a latent disposition in some quarters to come out
as Turks." During the course of five months and one week,
Twain and his companions had traveled more than twenty
thousand miles, docked in fifteen ports, and visited twelve
major cities and countless flyspeck villages in eight sovereign
countries and three islands. In true Vandal fashion they had
brought back great steamer trunks full of souvenirs—legally
purchased or illegally appropriated—and memories enough
to last a lifetime. Thanks to Mark Twain, they would last far
longer than that.[82]

CHAPTER TWO

TRAMPS ABROAD

Within weeks of the *Quaker City*'s return, Twain received an offer from publisher Elisha Bliss of the Hartford, Connecticut-based American Publishing Company to write a "humorously inclined" book about the cruise. Twain was usually so inclined, and he went to Hartford to meet with Bliss. He was determined, he told his mother, that "I wasn't going to touch a book unless there was *money* in it, & a good deal of it." He had already taken a staff position in Washington, D.C., with Nevada senator William M. Stewart, an old friend from his prospecting days out West, but he unhesitatingly agreed to write a six hundred-page book for Bliss. He drove a prescient bargain, turning down a flat ten thousand dollar offer and holding out instead for a 5 percent royalty on each book sold, one percent higher than customary. The company sold its books door-to-door on a subscription basis to largely middle-class, middlebrow families—the ideal target audience for a popularly written travel book by an experienced journalist such as Twain. Despite what some reviewers—and many ministers—would say about the book, particularly its less than reverential views of the Holy Land, the combination of author and subject matter proved to be a match made in heaven, or at least its outlying environs. Priced between $3.50 and $7, depending on the subscriber's choice of binding, the book would make its author both rich and famous.[1]

Writing as many as sixteen hours at a stretch in his smoke-filled Washington rooming house—he soon quit his job with Stewart—Twain dove headlong into completing the book, which he provisionally titled *The New Pilgrim's Progress*. With the aid of a scrapbook kept by his sister Pamela of his various travel letters, along with information supplied by his former tour companions Mary Fairbanks and Emma Beach, he quickly completed the first ten chapters, bringing him up to the point of their arrival at Marseilles. A crisis suddenly arose when Twain learned that his former employer, the *San Francisco Daily Alta California*, was withholding permission for him to use his previously published letters to the newspaper. He borrowed one thousand dollars from Bliss and immediately sailed for San Francisco, where he took a room in his favorite hotel, the Occidental, and somehow managed to convince *Alta*'s editors to let him use the letters free of charge and unencumbered.

Twain's initial choice of a title, *The New Pilgrim's Progress*, was revealing on several levels. The original *Pilgrim's Progress*, of course, is one of the most popular and enduring works of religious literature in the English language, known to generations of readers from the moment it was published in 1678 by Baptist minister and Church of England dissenter John Bunyan. Twain, the son of a devoutly religious mother, was familiar with the book from childhood, and during his lifetime he would own several copies himself, including a facsimile of Bunyan's original. He assumed a similar level of familiarity with the book among his readers. In the end, to avoid undue confusion with the original, Twain decided to call his book something else. It was a wise decision. As described by Bunyan, the allegorical journey of Christian from the City of Destruction to the City of God, with a lengthy detour through the Slough of Despond, reenacts the soul-trying journey of the true believer on the twisting road to salvation. The comparatively luxurious journey undertaken by Twain and his fellow *Quaker City* pilgrims to Europe and the Holy Land was another matter altogether. They too traveled to foreign lands and visited holy sites, the fundamental test of any true pilgrim, but their trials were the normal hardships of travelers everywhere—not fundamental issues of faith, doubt, and salvation. Twain's personal attitude toward Bunyan's book may be inferred from the perplexed reaction of another comparative innocent, Huckleberry Finn, who encounters the book in the Grangerford family library during his flight down the Mississippi. *The Pilgrim's Progress*, says Huck, is a book "about a man that left his family but didn't say why." After reading more of the book Huck concludes, fairly enough, that "its statements was interesting, but tough." He puts it back on the shelf.[2]

Twain's own approach to writing, his endlessly amused engagement with larger-than-life characters both real and imagined, was closer to Geoffrey Chaucer than John Bunyan. He would make that affinity clear in his novel *A Connecticut Yankee in King Arthur's Court*, in which he devotes an entire chapter to a pilgrimage peopled by the same sort of prototypical English personalities who populate Chaucer's *Canterbury Tales*—knights, friars, peasants, damsels—en route to the Valley of Holiness to drink at the Holy Fountain. Later in his career, Twain would consider writing a comic operetta based on Chaucer's work and featuring Chaucer himself in a lead role, a potentially promising idea that ultimately he abandoned. Another rejected brainstorm involved a sort of multimedia *Pilgrim's Progress*, with models dressed as Bunyan's characters posing at suitably illustrative sites: a mountain gorge for the Valley of the Shadow of Death, the city of Paris standing in for Vanity Fair, and so on. The resulting "stereoptical panorama" would then be displayed on screens in local theaters to afford audiences a presumably uplifting and entertaining experience. Again, Twain thought better of the idea.[3]

By June 1868, Twain had finished the manuscript. Several frustrating delays pushed back publication of the book, now titled *The Innocents Abroad* (Twain insisted on retaining *The New Pilgrim's Progress* as a subtitle), for a nearly a year. In the interim, the author undertook a forty-one-city lecture tour of the East and the Midwest that amounted to an extended promotional campaign for his book. The subject of the lecture was "The American Vandal Abroad." As characterized by Twain, the American Vandal was a proud member of "the roving, independent, free-and-easy character of that class of traveling Americans who were not elaborately educated, cultivated, and refined, and gilded and filigreed with the ineffable graces of the first society." He opened the tour in Mary Fairbanks's hometown of Cleveland, and despite Twain's jab at the Vandals' social and educational deficiencies, she generously praised her old shipmate for the "beauty and poetry" of his lecture, which she said proved that "a man may be humorist without being a clown." Most critics agreed. Although not perhaps as funny as Twain's debut lecture, "Our Fellow Savages of the Sandwich Islands," the new talk functioned perfectly as an introduction to *The Innocents Abroad*, and its conclusion invited other Americans to experience, at least vicariously, the broadening aspects of foreign travel. "I am glad the American Vandal goes abroad," concluded Twain. "It does him good. . . . It liberalizes the Vandal to travel." He spoke from personal experience.[4]

The book finally appeared in July 1869. The green leather cover was embossed in gold with the title, subtitle, and various images of the Sphinx, a pyramid, a man riding a camel, an elephant, the Parthenon, the dome of St. Peter's, Mount Vesuvius in eruption, a Muslim mosque, and assorted minarets. The author's name was barely visible on the face of the pyramid. The text comprised nearly 192,000 words, broken into sixty-one chapters and enlivened by 234 illustrations, many of them by the publishing company's talented staff artist True Williams. With the help of Twain's just-concluded lecture series and a flurry of favorable reviews in the influential eastern press, most particularly from William Dean Howells in the style-setting *Atlantic Monthly*, *The Innocents Abroad* sold nearly 83,000 copies in its first eighteen months and continued to sell at the rate of more than 1,000 copies a month well into the next decade, making it the best-selling American book since *Uncle Tom's Cabin*. Only Elizabeth Stuart Phelps's oleaginous novel *The Gates Ajar*, which appeared one year after *The Innocents Abroad*, would rival the sales of *The Innocents Abroad*. It dealt with the consolatory virtues of religion in the wake of the ruinous Civil War, a war that Twain had largely avoided by lighting out for the territory. Unchastened by his noncombatant status, Twain later would mercilessly lampoon Phelps's vision of a homey Americanized afterlife—dead pets allowed—in his satirical novella *Captain Stormfield's Visit to Heaven*.

In retrospect, the runaway success of *The Innocents Abroad* is understandable. To begin with, it is very funny, with Twain using all the tricks he had learned as "the Wild Humorist of the Pacific Slope" to move the action along at a breakneck pace. Small-town readers—added to the subscription ranks by publisher Elisha Bliss's bustling army of sales agents— could experience in the comfort of their own homes a sense of what it was like to tear across Europe and the Holy Land in the amusing company of Mark Twain and his fellow travelers. Then, too, there was the sense, intuited immediately by his old friend and fellow writer Bret Harte, that the trip amounted to "a huge practical joke, of which not the least amusing feature was the fact that 'Mark Twain' had embarked on it." Everyone likes to feel that they are in on the joke, and Twain craftily salted the book with enough winks, nods, eye rolls, and elbow pokes to clue in the most superficial reader. As Bruce Michelson notes, *The Innocents Abroad* functions as "a pleasure tour through modes of narration. It ranges through sentimentality, and parody, patriotism and anti-Americanism, whimsy and plodding factuality; the persistent, overriding assertion of the prose being that 'I Mark Twain am out to have myself a good time.' And we are meant to enjoy his narrator's pleasure trip, his tour through the world of literary voices." How he told a story was always more important to Twain than the story itself, a trick that he learned from his yarn-spinning mother.[5]

The years immediately following Twain's life-changing cruise on the *Quaker City* were ones of great personal and professional change, highlighted by his marriage in February 1870 to the lovely and fragile sister of his old cruise companion Charley Langdon. The unlikely matrimonial pairing of Samuel Langhorne Clemens of Hannibal, Missouri, and Olivia Louise Langdon of Elmira, New York, would endure for the next thirty-four years, literally in sickness and in health, and would bear witness to Mark Twain's greatest joys and deepest heartaches. Livy, as she was called by her family and friends, would strive constantly to "sivilize" her cigar-smoking, Scotch-drinking husband. He, in turn, would show her the great wide world, even when the only part of it she really wanted to see was the sunlit view outside her kitchen window in garden-lovely Hartford.

The wooing of Olivia Langdon, like many of the turning points in the first half of Mark Twain's life, seems almost preordained. Had her brother not been sent on the *Quaker City* cruise by their concerned parents, apparently to keep him out of Elmira's saloons, and had Twain not gone on the same cruise, a spur-of-the-moment decision that depended on swift outside funding from his San Francisco newspaper, the author would never have seen Livy's photograph in Charley Langdon's locket in the harbor at Smyrna. And had Twain not successfully courted and married Livy (and unexpectedly inherited a quarter of a million dollars two years later after her generous, good-natured father, Jervis Langdon, died abruptly of stomach cancer), the course of his life might well have mirrored that of his recently deceased friend and fellow humorist Artemus Ward—a wearying round of one-man shows played out in smoky lecture halls, seedy hotel rooms, late-night bars, and clamorous railroad stations. Certainly, he would not have settled into comfortable upper-middle-class luxury in sedate Hartford with Olivia Langdon, "the most perfect gem of womankind that ever I saw in my life." But against all odds, he did.[6]

Twain spent the first two years of his married life working as editor of the *Buffalo Express*, a daily newspaper in which he had earlier bought a one-third interest with the help of a

$12,500 loan from his father-in-law. Much of the time, how-
ever, he was occupied with his own extra-journalistic career:
traveling, lecturing, and writing his next book, *Roughing It,*
a genial hybrid of travel book, memoir, tall tales, and fictional
recreations of his years out West, beginning with his epic
stagecoach ride to Nevada with his brother, Orion, in 1861.
As with *The Innocents Abroad,* the American Publishing Company sold *Roughing It* by subscription. It too did well, selling
some 73,000 copies in the first two years before tapering off
slightly by the end of the decade. Although *Roughing It* has
proven to be one of Twain's most popular works, it was not,
strictly speaking, a travel book along the lines of *The Innocents
Abroad.* Many of the events it documented had taken place
more than a decade earlier, and Twain based his account more
on memory, his own and Orion's, than on published letters or
contemporaneous notes. Many sections were closer to fiction
than to fact: the imaginary traveling companion Bemis, with
his "pepper-box" pistol and slapstick penchant for lassoing
wild buffaloes up a tree; the deadly gunslinger Jack Slade, who
offers Twain the last cup of coffee at a stage depot—"I politely
declined. I was afraid he had not killed anybody that morning
and might be needing diversion"; the burning down of a mountainside near Lake Tahoe by Twain and a fellow "lumber tycoon"; various gunfights, blizzards, windstorms, tarantulas,
prospectors, gamblers, and Indians. It was a boy's-eye-view
of the Wild West, recollected in tranquillity by a thirty-seven-
year-old husband and father of two writing in the newfound
comfort of his mansion in Buffalo, New York. As Huck Finn
might have said, *Roughing It* was mostly true, but with some
"stretchers" thrown in.[7]

Indirectly, the publication of *Roughing It* took Twain back
overseas, this time to England, where London publisher

George A. Routledge was to bring out an English edition of the book in return for a modest one-time fee of two hundred pounds to the author. This time, at least, Twain was being paid something for his work, a marked improvement over his previous experience with English publishers. The problem for Twain and other American writers was the lack of an international copyright law. Twain's fellow novelist John W. De Forest, who coined the term "the great American novel," had warned in 1868 that such a work would not be forthcoming until American publishers stopped pirating English novels and publishing them for free, which had a suppressing effect on new American novels and encouraged English publishers to pirate American books in return. One particularly shameless English pirate was John Camden Hotten. The thirty-nine-year-old Hotten had made his reputation—and a tidy pile of money—as the English publisher of leading American humorists, including James Russell Lowell, Artemus Ward, Oliver Wendell Holmes—and Mark Twain. Hotten was able to publish at no inconvenient cost to himself the works of any American writers he chose, including the great but not notably humorous poet Walt Whitman. He had chosen to break up *The Innocents Abroad* into two separate volumes—*The Innocents Abroad: The Voyage Out*, and *The New Pilgrim's Progress: The Voyage Home*. Hotten had also worked up two collections of Twain's shorter works, to which he gave the lurid titles *Eye-Openers* and *Screamers*. Unknown to all but those in the Victorian underground, Hotten had a lucrative sidelight as London's leading publisher of pornography. Among the titles in his private catalogue were *The Romance of Chastisement; Aphrodisiacs and Anti-Aphrodisiacs; Flagellation and the Flagellants: A History of the Rod in all Countries, from the Earliest Period to the Present Time* (with "numerous illustrations"); and the rather more pithily titled *Lady Bum-tickler's Revels.*[8]

Twain's alliance with Routledge was an attempt to forestall more piracy by Hotten. To make his case in person, the author sailed to England from New York City in August 1872. He was leaving Livy behind with a new baby and an even newer grief. On March 19, she had given birth to their first daughter, Olivia Susan Clemens, called Susy, who was destined to be both the brightest light and the darkest shadow in the family in years to come. Susy's birth was soon eclipsed by the death of her brother, Langdon, who died on June 2 from diphtheria at the age of eighteen months. Livy was still fighting a crushing depression—"My pathway was to be from this time forth lined with graves," she told her sister, Susan—but Twain stoically carried on with his work, even as he privately blamed himself for contributing to his son's death by neglecting to cover him with a blanket during a freezing carriage ride. The author had a career to conduct, and that meant going to London to oversee the foreign publication of *Roughing It* and perhaps research a new travel book on England. Off the coast of Ireland, Twain sent Livy a consolatory letter encouraging her to imagine him "standing high on the stern of the ship, looking westward, with my hands to my mouth, trumpet fashion, yelling across the tossing waste of waves, 'I LOVE YOU, LIVY DARLING!'" Perhaps it helped.[9]

The need for his trip was immediately made evident to Twain on the train ride east from Liverpool to London. Sitting across from him, a fellow traveler was reading a pirated copy of *The Innocents Abroad*. Even worse, from the writer's point of the view, the man wasn't cracking so much as the shadow of a smile. "It was a sad beginning, and affected me dismally," Twain recalled. "It gave me a longing for friendly companionship and sympathy." The longing was still there the next morning, and Twain hurried over to the offices of Routledge and Sons in Charing Cross, where he found a warm welcome and a heaping luncheon table. The Routledges, father and sons, possessed apparently insatiable appetites, and Twain spent most of the day eating. That night Edmund Routledge, one of the sons, took him to dinner at the Savage Club, where he was introduced to fellow humorist Tom Hood, celebrated actor Henry Irving, and Anglo-American explorer Henry Morton Stanley, who had just returned from tracking down Dr. David Livingstone in darkest Africa. Twain, as usual, made an immediate impression on his hosts, joking that it was really he, not Stanley, who had located the missing missionary. In time, Twain would be elected to lifetime membership in the club, an honor that would prove useful in his subsequent world travels about the fraying edges of the British Empire.[10]

A few nights later Twain was taken to dinner at another of Routledge's clubs, Whitefriars, in Mitre Square (later to be the scene of some of Jack the Ripper's more gruesome depredations). The guest of honor that night was not Twain but fellow American writer Ambrose Bierce, who had relocated to London a few months earlier to try his hand at Fleet Street journalism after half a dozen years as a much-feared newspaper columnist in San Francisco. Bierce and Twain had only intersected briefly in California, and for unknown reasons possibly having to do with their divergent Civil War careers, they did not much like each other. Bierce, as a volunteer lieutenant in the Ninth Indiana Infantry, had seen more combat than any other American writer, Northern or Southern, in the war. Twain, of course, had skedaddled at the first sign of trouble. Now Bierce was well on his way to a legendary career as a notorious gadfly and curmudgeon, the future author of *The Devil's Dictionary,* "An Occurrence at Owl Creek Bridge," *The Parenticide Club,* and other black-humored works of the darkest sort. In time Twain would come to echo some of Bierce's depthless bitterness, but in Twain's case it would be the product of personal tragedies and financial setbacks. Bierce's misanthropy was more innate and more generalized, a strictly philosophical program, he said, of "calm disapproval of human institutions in general . . . human suffering and human injustice in all their forms to be contemplated with a merely curious interest, as one looks into an anthill."[11]

That night Bierce was in one of his rare good moods, and he welcomed Twain to London with a humorous anecdote about their first meeting in San Francisco five years earlier. Twain, much more practiced at public speaking than Bierce, contrived to undercut his countryman's speech with some judicious deadpanning, looking off distractedly into the middle distance and affecting an air of long-suffering boredom. The British audience, taking its cue from Twain, maintained a deathly silence throughout Bierce's soon faltering speech. When it was over, the speaker sank back into his seat, white-faced and embarrassed, while Twain resumed his conversation with others at his table as though nothing noteworthy had occurred. In Twain's defense, he may have been settling a score dating back to Bierce's gratuitous remark about Twain's marriage in 1870. "Mark Twain has got married," Bierce noted in the *San Francisco News Letter.* "It was not committed while laboring under temporary insanity; his insanity is not of that type, nor does he ever labor—it was the cool, methodical, cumulative culmination of human nature, working in the breast of an orphan hankering for some one with a fortune to love— some one with a bank account to caress." Whatever the case, Twain got in the last word—or a silence that spoke more loudly than words. After that night, Bierce never again spoke in public.[12]

Another old acquaintance from Twain's San Francisco days also turned up at the dinner. Indiana native Joaquin Miller, born Cincinnatus Heine, had reinvented himself out West in the best frontier fashion as "the Poet of the Sierras" and "the Byron of the Rockies." With his shoulder-length hair, white buckskins suits, knee-length cowboy boots and spurs, Miller was a dead ringer for Buffalo Bill Cody, and he entertained English crowds with his outlandish personality and ringing, declamatory verse. Arriving fashionably late at Whitefriars, Miller jingled over to a fishbowl, pulled out a goldfish, swallowed it whole, and boomed, "A wonderful appetizer!" Twain and Bierce, who were used to Miller's attention-seeking antics, ignored the stagecraft, and Miller left the gathering in a huff.[13]

The warmth of his English reception took Twain by surprise. Everyone wanted to see him, he bragged to Livy, and he found himself welcomed into the best private houses and clubs. "As Americans have *no* rank, it is proper to place us either *above* or *below* the nobles," he told her. "Courtesy rather forbids the latter, & so we get the good seats." He spent so much time dining out that he got little writing done. "Confound this town," he complained to his left-behind wife. "Time slips relentlessly away & I accomplish next to nothing. Too much

company—too much dining—too much sociability." True to
his word, Twain spent the next eight weeks eating, drinking,
and traveling about the lovely late-summer countryside. He
journeyed through Warwickshire and Stratford with American publisher James Osgood, hopped down to the Channel-
side town of Brighton with Tom Hood, went to Oxford for a
day, took part in a stag hunt on the five hundred-year-old
estate of a squire with the rather Dickensian name of Broom,
and attended the Lord Mayor of London's formal installation
at the ancient and venerable Guildhall in the City, where he
was introduced to the crowd and received "such a storm of
applause as you never heard. I was never taken so aback in
my life. I did not know I was a lion."[14]

Twain received so many invitations to speak—from the best
gentlemen, as he was quick to point out to Livy—that he was
forced to publish an open letter in the *London Times* pleading
the press of family concerns and promising to come back to
England the following year to lecture on "such scientific topics
I know least about." He returned to America in late November,
having formed a lifelong affection for the British people and
their country, whose rural landscape, he said, was "too absolutely beautiful to be left outdoors—[it] ought to be under a
glass case." As always, he filled his notebook with impressions
of the sights he encountered along the way, but no travel book
would come from his first English visit. "England seemed prosaic to him after the Tsar, the Coliseum, Pompeii, Jerusalem,
and the Pyramids," notes Arthur L. Scott, "but what really
killed the book was British kindness. . . . He could not write
a funny book about these gracious people, so he wrote no book
at all." Some of Twain's notes would later find their way into
two of his own favorite novels, *The Prince and the Pauper* and
A Connecticut Yankee in King Arthur's Court.[15]

Much to his disappointment, Twain got no satisfaction from John Camden Hotten, who had the law (or lack thereof) on his side. Besides publishing Twain's works without paying him, Hotten had the effrontery to pad his Twain collections with new bits of nonsense that he, Hotten, wrote himself. All Twain could do was complain, in a public letter to the *London Spectator*, about the man he called John Camden Hottentot. "My books are bad enough just as they are written," wrote Twain. "What must they be after Mr. John Camden Hotten has composed half-a-dozen chapters & added the same to them?" Twain confessed to having half a mind "to take a broom-straw & go & knock that man's brains out. Not in anger but only to see, that is all. Mere idle curiosity." Hotten kept his brains— for a while longer, anyway. He would die of apoplexy nine months later, and his rhyming epitaph, suitable for Boot Hill cemetery in Virginia City, Nevada, was a group effort by Ambrose Bierce and other victims of the publisher's creatively maintained ledger books: "Hotten/Rotten/Forgotten."[16]

Keeping his promise, Twain returned to England the next spring with Livy and thirteen-month-old Susy in tow. He had a new book to discuss with his English publishers. Over the previous six months, he and his Hartford neighbor, newspaper editor Charles Dudley Warner, had collaborated on a political novel, Twain's first outright foray into fiction, with the instantly iconic title, *The Gilded Age*. The title was better than the book itself, which combined autobiographical elements of Twain's life, particularly the Clemens family's long and troubled stewardship of 70,000 acres of land in Fentress County, Tennessee, with unequal parts of political chicanery, romance, comedy, melodrama, and farce. Despite its title, the book had little to do with the country's ongoing economic warfare or crushing monopolies; they were still a few years down the road. Ulysses S. Grant was just commencing his second term in the White House, and the president and his henchmen had not yet had sufficient time to complete the most corrupt administration in American history. That would come later.

The traveling party took rooms in the Edwards Royal Cambridge Hotel overlooking Hanover Square. "My wife likes Edwards's Hotel," Twain told a friend, "& so would I if I were dead; I would not desire a more tranquil and satisfactory tomb." Soon they relocated to the more lavish Langham Hotel on Regent Street in Oxford Circus, where Twain had stayed the year before. As it was, they were rarely in their rooms. Leaving Susy with her English nurse, the perfectly named nanny Nellie Birmingham, Twain took Livy on a sweeping tour of the countryside, including a visit to William Shakespeare's tomb at Stratford-on-Avon, the aquarium at Brighton, and Sir Walter Scott's home in Abbotsford on the Tweed River south of Edinburgh. Side trips to Belfast, Dublin, and Liverpool followed, then the couple made a brief cross-Channel junket to Paris. Back in London, a steady stream of illustrious visitors came to their door. Although still only the author of one travel book and a yet to be published co-written novel, Twain found himself consorting with some of Europe's the leading literary lights: Robert Browning, Lewis Carroll, Herbert Spencer, Ivan Turgenev, Benjamin Disraeli, Anthony Trollope, Wilkie Collins, and Thomas Hughes. After England's reigning poet laureate, Lord Tennyson, expressed the desire to hear him speak, Twain sent him a fawning personal note and complimentary tickets, but scheduling conflicts prevented Tennyson from attending.[17]

All the attention proved too much for Livy, who fell ill during their visit to Scotland and scarcely had time to recover in London. "I am blue and cross and homesick," she wrote to her mother. "I can't bear the thought of postponing going home." She was also pregnant again, although she may not have known it yet. While they were en route from Paris in mid-September, the stock market crashed in America, initiating a six-month-long panic and a five-year-long depression that led to the demise of eighteen thousand private businesses, cost the nation five hundred million dollars, and put three million Americans out of work. The primary cause of the Panic of 1873 was the failure of the giant New York banking concern, Jay Cooke and Company, whose chief operating officer Twain knew personally and in whose bank he had deposited some of Livy's inheritance. To make matters worse, the couple had been spending lavishly during their months abroad, and Twain estimated that he had spent another ten thousand dollars on household furnishings for their new home in Hartford. The ongoing crisis hit them hard, emotionally as well as financially. "The financial panic in America has absorbed about all my attention & anxiety," Twain told Livy's Scottish physician, Dr. John Brown, forgetting for a moment Livy's ongoing health issues.[18]

To recoup his losses, Twain decided to accept a standing offer from London impresario George Dolby, Charles Dickens's business manager, to give a series of public lectures. He dusted off his old talk, "Our Fellow Savages of the Sandwich Islands," and made six well-attended appearances in London and Liverpool in mid-October before boarding the S.S. *Batavia* to

escort Livy, Susy, and their traveling companions back
home to Hartford. In what Twain biographer Ron Powers
has aptly termed "one of the longer courtesy detours in
19th-century travel," Twain accompanied the ladies to their
doorstep, checked on the progress of their new home, which
was still under construction, and hopped another transatlantic steamer back to London five days later. For company
he replaced Livy with transplanted California writer Charles
Warren Stoddard, who was going to England to work as a
correspondent for the *San Francisco Chronicle*. Stoddard
agreed to serve as Twain's private secretary, which amounted
mainly to fetching the ingredients for his new employer's favorite cocktail—Scotch, Angostura bitters, lemons, ice, and
sugar—attending his lectures, and sitting up with him afterwards while Twain unwound. By the end of the season, Stoddard said without exaggeration, "I could have written his
biography."[19]

Twain's lecture series went over well. Between December
1, 1873, and January 10, 1874, he made twenty-seven appearances, evenings and matinees, alternating his familiar talk on
his Hawaiian escapades with a new lecture, "Roughing It on
the Silver Frontier," which dealt with his picaresque adventures in the American West. English reviewers praised Twain's
"insouciance and aplomb," his "personal comeliness," his
"grandeur of character," and his "native sweetness of disposition." One night, during the heaviest fog that London had seen
in twenty years, Twain brought down the house at the Queen's
Concert Rooms in Hanover Square by joking mildly: "Ladies
and gentlemen, I hear you, & so I know that you are here—&
I am here, too, notwithstanding I am not visible." Despite his
continued warm reception, Twain found himself missing Livy
and their life in Hartford. "If I'm not homesick to see you," he

wrote, "no other lover ever *was* homesick to see his sweet-heart." He advised Livy to have his favorite cocktail ready for him when he got home. "Nothing but *Angostura* bitters will do." Presumably, she did.[20]

After departing Liverpool on the S.S. *Parthia* on January 13, 1874, Twain would not return to England for more than five years, and then for only one month. In the meantime, he oversaw the completion of the family's new home at 351 Farmington Avenue in tranquil West Hartford. The first years in Hartford were exceedingly happy ones. Livy gave birth to their second daughter, Clara, on June 23, 1874. The "Great American Giantess," as her father called her, weighed eight pounds at birth, nearly twice as much as either of the two previous children, and Twain displayed her picture wonderingly to everyone he came across. Livy recovered quickly and took the lead in furnishing their home, often described as "Steamboat Gothic" for its passing resemblance to a Mississippi riverboat with its wooden railings, steeply gabled roof and balconies, and long, covered front porch. The house, designed by local architect Edward Potter, contained three stories, nineteen rooms, and seven bathrooms (complete with flushing toilets). The first floor included the dining room, drawing room, library, and kitchen. The family quarters were located on the second floor, and the third floor was largely given over to a billiards room, where Twain worked and wrote when he was not busy stuffing kittens into the side pockets of the pool table for amusement—his, not the kittens'—and smoking many of the eighteen cheap cigars he allowed himself each day.[21]

During their first years in Hartford, Twain produced two major works centered on his boyhood memories of Hannibal and the great turbulent river that ran past its shore. (Much of the actual writing was done during summer-long visits to sister-in-law Susan Crane's farm in Elmira.) He began writing his first solo novel, *The Adventures of Tom Sawyer*, in the summer of 1874 and finished it in the summer of 1875. The timing was appropriate. *Tom Sawyer* seems to take place in perpetual summer. In its fictional guise of St. Petersburg, Twain's old hometown glows in retrospective sunlight, the realm of joyous boyhood, pranks and adventures, camping and fishing, skylarking and picnicking and puppy love. In time, the novel would sell more copies than any of Twain's other books and spawn two sequels, neither of which would recapture the ineffable magic of the first book. You can't remain a boy forever.

Before *Tom Sawyer* was published in December 1876, Twain produced his second remembrance—this one unfictionalized— about his early life on the Mississippi. Published serially in seven issues of his friend William Dean Howells's prestigious *Atlantic Monthly* in 1875, "Old Times on the Mississippi" presented a fondly romanticized account of Twain's four-year career as a riverboat cub, when he became one of "the only unfettered and entirely independent being[s] that lived on the earth." Under the no-nonsense eyes of riverboat captain Horace Bixby, he gradually learned how to be a pilot, to read what he called "the face of the water." There was a lot to learn. The 1,200-mile stretch between New Orleans and St. Louis was one of the most treacherous river passages in the world, each mile menaced by ever-shifting currents, rapids and sandbars, floating islands, loose debris, hidden rocks, sunken ships, and the ever-present dangers of collision, fires, and boiler explosions such as the one that would claim the life of Twain's brother Henry in 1858. After a fairly unpromising beginning—"Well, taking you by and large, you do seem to be more different kinds of an ass than any creature I ever saw before," Bixby exploded—Twain became fully licensed on April 8, 1859, an achievement that he always considered the single proudest moment of his life, his marriage to Livy and the births of their children notwithstanding.[22]

As a respite from the continual nailing, sawing, and hammering at the new house, Twain spent a good deal of time at the nearby home of his new friend Joseph Twichell, minister of Hartford's Asylum Hill Congregational Church. Twain had met Twichell at a church social in 1868 and liked him at once, notwithstanding the fact that Twichell's communicants included so many wealthy bankers, businessmen, and stockbrokers that Twain dubbed it "the Church of the Holy Speculators." A tall, handsome man with a drooping walrus mustache like Twain's, Twichell was a new kind of minister, a proponent of "muscular Christianity" who focused more on good deeds and community outreach than on narrow theological questions and pulpit-pounding sermons. A graduate of Yale, Twichell had served for three years during the Civil War as the chaplain of the famous Seventy-first New York Zouaves, a hard-fighting, hard-drinking regiment that took part in some of the war's bloodiest battles. Following the war, Twichell graduated from Andover Theological Seminary and was called to the ministry in Hartford. He helped officiate at Twain's wedding in 1870, cementing his friendship with the author. The friends regularly took ten-mile walks around Hartford on Sunday afternoons, and in the winter of 1874 they set off on a one hundred-mile hike to Boston, managing to cover about a third of the distance before freezing weather forced them to turn back and catch a train. The truncated jaunt was good training for a more ambitious hike they would undertake together a few years later.[23]

During the centennial summer of 1876, Twain briefly involved himself in national politics. Increasingly, the former Confederate guerrilla (retired) had been edging over to the Republican Party, toasting and entertaining President Grant and Generals William Tecumseh Sherman and Phil Sheridan at various banquet halls across the Northeast. The carnival of crime coming out of Washington had led to a groundswell of popular support for New York's reformist governor Samuel Tilden, the Democratic Party's presidential nominee, but Twain threw his support behind the Republican standard-bearer, Ohio governor Rutherford B. Hayes. At the urging of Howells, who was Hayes's cousin by marriage and was writing a campaign biography of the great man, Twain agreed to appear at a Republican campaign rally in Hartford on September 30. His political speech, unlike his theatrical lectures, was short on humor and long on denunciations. It apparently did not occur to Twain, although it did to his listeners, that the federal government had been in the hands of the Republican Party for the past sixteen years, and that most of the "idiots," "ignoramuses," and "flatheads" serving in government had been appointed to their posts by Republican presidents. Said the GOP-leaning *Boston Transcript*, "Somebody should have led him from the platform by the ear."[24]

Twain survived his lead-footed intrusion into electoral politics, but he got into even more trouble the next year at a venue that should have been more comfortable and familiar: the after-dinner banquet stage. Once again, Howells was the unwitting instigator. The occasion was the seventieth-birthday celebration for Quaker poet and abolitionist John Greenleaf Whittier, which took place on the night of December 17, 1877, in the dining room of Boston's tony Brunswick Hotel. The dinner was the brainchild of *Atlantic Monthly* publisher Henry O. Houghton, whose magazine had published most of the assembled writers in the room, including Twain, Howells, Whittier, Henry Wadsworth Longfellow, Oliver Wendell Holmes— virtually the entire school of "Fireside Poets," as they were known at the time. Twain had planned his after-dinner speech for days, going to the trouble of rereading many of the often yawn-inducing works of his fellow guests. With practiced informality, he rose to speak. And then, as Howells would remember: "The amazing mistake, the bewildering blunder, the cruel catastrophe was upon us."[25]

Years earlier, Twain said, he had been traveling in the West (many of his best stories began that way) when he came upon an isolated cabin in the Sierra Nevada foothills. He knocked on the door. "A jaded melancholy man of fifty, barefooted, opened the door to me," said Twain. "When he heard my nom de guerre he looked more dejected than before." Twain, the prospector told him wearily, was "the fourth littery man that has been here in twenty-four hours—I'm going to move." Who were the others? Twain asked innocently. "Mr. Longfellow, Mr. Emerson, and Mr. Oliver Wendell Holmes—consound the lot!" said the miner. Twain, taken aback, asked the prospector to describe his visitors. Longfellow, said the man, had the cropped hair and pulverized nose of a professional prize fighter, Emerson was "a seedy little bit of a chap," and Holmes was "as fat as a balloon; he weighed as much as three hundred, and

had double chins all the way down to his stomach." The trio
had proceeded to spend the long night drinking, cursing, gam-
bling, and generally helling about. Their reluctant host could
only watch helplessly as they trashed his cabin, drank up his
liquor, ate up his beans and bacon, stole his only pair of boots,
and declaimed incoherent, sententious nonsense about "stately
mansions" and "footprints on the sands of time." "Why, my
dear sir, these were not the gracious singers to whom we and
the world pay loving reverence and homage," Twain protested.
"These were impostors." "Ah! impostors, were they?" the miner
responded, adding the story's carefully timed snapper: "Are
you?"[26]

In the subsequent recollections of both Twain and Howells,
the speech was an unmitigated disaster. In their retelling,
which was far funnier than the speech itself, Twain stumbled
and stuttered through "a silence weighing many tons to the
square inch," his joke "laying dead on his hands," while the
scandalized guests looked on in horror. Twain's "hideous mistake," shuddered Howells, was nothing less than "an effect of
demoniacal possession." Howells couldn't bear to watch. As
for Twain, he became uncomfortably aware early in his speech
that "a sort of black frost" had formed on the faces of his listeners, but he seemed powerless to stop himself. The Whittier Birthday Speech has passed into literary legend, with its
enduring image of the famous monologist, bathed in flop
sweat, scandalizing a roomful of self-satisfied stuffed shirts.
Contrary to Twain's and Howells's accounts, however, no one
that night took particular offense at the speech. Local newspapers reported the next day that Twain had set the crowd into
roars of laughter and "produced the most violent bursts of hi-
larity." The *Boston Globe*, the newspaper of record for the self-
proclaimed American Athens, reported that "Mr. Longfellow

laughed and shook, and Mr. Whittier seemed to enjoy it keenly." Only the increasingly senile Emerson "seemed a little puzzled about it," as indeed he was about everything then. Twain's memory notwithstanding, he did not stumble immediately from the dining room in a daze, but remained seated for the remaining two hours of the program, placidly smoking his corncob pipe and nodding agreeably at the other speakers' remarks.[27]

Whatever his actual reception that night, Twain continued to brood about his performance for weeks to come. "I haven't done a stroke of work since the Atlantic dinner; have only moped around," he told Howells, adding that he felt like "a great & sublime fool." The disappointing sales figures for *Tom Sawyer*, combined with his continued worries over Livy's investments in such uneasy financial times, induced Twain to turn again to travel writing as a convenient source of cash. "I have about made up my mind to take my tribe & fly to some little corner of Europe & budge no more until I have completed one of the half dozen books that lie begun," he informed his mother. "We propose to sail the 10th April." He missed his projections by one day. On April 11, 1878, the traveling party, which included Twain, Livy, their two girls, Livy's friend Clara Spaulding, and German-speaking nursemaid Rosina Hay, sailed from New York for Hamburg, Germany, aboard the S.S. *Holsatia*.[28]

It was a rough crossing. Livy called it a "horror," and even her usually seasick-proof husband termed it "two almost devilish weeks at sea." The only bright spot was his shipboard acquaintance with noted travel writer Bayard Taylor, who was

going to Germany to assume his post as American minister
to that country in the Hayes administration. After resting a
week in Hamburg, which Livy considered "the finest city I was
ever in," the party continued by train to Heidelberg. Twain discovered a lifelong liking for Germany and its people. In a letter
to Howells he gushed, "What a paradise this land is! What
clean clothes, what good faces, what tranquil contentment,
what prosperity, what genuine freedom, what superb government!" And in a notebook jotting that future generations of
Americans and Europeans would have good cause to quibble
with, the author observed, "The chief German characteristic
seems to be kindness, good will to men." He had already commenced his comical and largely unsuccessful efforts to learn
the language. "Drat this German tongue," he complained in a
letter to Howells. "Never knew before what Eternity was made
for. It is to give some of us a chance to learn German." Some
German words, he said, were so long that they had their own
perspective, like the receding lines of a railroad track. For his
part, he "would rather decline 2 drinks than one German verb,"
and only God could read a German newspaper. Six-year-old
Susy, with her inherited knack for aphorisms, complained,
"Mamma, I wish Rosa was made in English."[29]

Settling into the Hotel Schloss on a mountainside overlooking Heidelberg, Twain spent an increasingly restless seven
weeks in the bosom of his family. He took a room nearby where
he could work in peace, away from the various annoying
sounds—cuckoo clocks, yodelers, noisy pets, crying children,
clanging church bells—that interrupted his thoughts. Any day
now, he kept assuring Howells by letter, he would be ready to
write. In fact, he was already bored with the well-ordered
scenery and well-regulated citizenry of central Germany. He
needed a diversion. Livy, who had studied music as a girl,

dragged him off to Mannheim for an operatic performance of *King Lear.* "It was a mistake," wrote Twain. "We sat in our seats three whole hours and never understood anything but the thunder and lightning; and even that was reversed to suit German ideas, for the thunder came first and the lightning followed after." A performance of Wagner's *Lohengrin* was even worse, from Twain's perspective. "The banging and slamming and booming and crashing were something beyond belief," he wrote. "The racking and pitiless pain of it remains stored up in my memory alongside the memory of the time I had my teeth fixed. . . . At times the pain was so exquisite that I could hardly keep the tears back. At those times, as the howlings and wailings and shriekings of the singers, and the ragings and roarings and explosions of the vast orchestra rose higher and higher, and wilder and wilder, and fiercer and fiercer, I could have cried if I had been alone." Not one in fifty Americans liked opera, said Twain, and the funerals of those who did "do not occur often enough."[30]

In late July the family departed Heidelberg for the hot-springs spa at Baden-Baden. The weather was bad, cold rain alternating with intervals of "hellish heat," and the town itself was inane, "filled with sham, and petty fraud, and snobbery." Thousands of yelping dogs and cats preyed on Twain's ever-fragile nerves, and the busy crowds of equally noisy American and English tourists didn't help matters. "See Naples & then die," he advised the visitors, "but endeavor to die *before* you see Baden-Baden." As for the famous spa, "In it one may have any sort of bath that has ever been invented, and with all the additions of herbs and drugs that his ailment may need or that the physician of the establishment may consider a useful thing to put into the water." Twain said he had suffered from rheumatism for years, but after boiling in the

bathwater at Baden-Baden, "I fully believe I left my rheumatism in Baden-Baden. Baden-Baden is welcome to it. It was
little, but it was all I had to give. I would have preferred to
leave something that was catching, but it was not in my
power."[31]

After the opera and the spa—he was not sure which was
worse—Twain settled down to the trip's real business: traveling around and writing about it. Livy and the girls could
hardly be expected to accompany him (and would not have
been suitable comic foils if they had), so Twain sent back to
America for his favorite walking companion, Joseph Twichell,
offering to pay his way over and back in return for the company. A delighted Twichell accepted immediately. "To walk
with you, and talk with you, and sleep with you, and say my
prayers with you, and see things with you, for six weeks together, why, it's my dream of luxury." He arrived in Baden-
Baden on August 1 and immediately joined Twain for a
walking tour through the Black Forest. "The true charm of
pedestrianism does not lie in the walking, or in the scenery,
but in the talking," Twain observed. "It is no matter whether
one talks wisdom or nonsense. The bulk of the enjoyment
lies in the wagging of the gladsome jaw and the flapping of
the sympathetic ear."[32]

Initially, Twain had intended to write about his European
adventures as he went along, jotting down his impressions in
his ever-present notebook, but this soon proved impractical.
"It is no sort of use to try to write while one is traveling," he
told publisher Frank Bliss. "I am interrupted constantly—and
most of the time I am too tired to write, anyway." Instead, with

Twichell on hand to serve as his sidekick, he devised a new plan, an extended burlesque of Bayard Taylor–inspired travel books. The title of the envisioned book, *A Tramp Abroad*, would consciously pun on the concept of both hikers and hiking, "a lazy, delightful, irresponsible high-holiday time on the road." A running joke in the book, he confided to Howells, would be the avidity with which the hikers jumped on and off trains, carriages, wagon carts, and boats. "I allow it to appear,—casually & without stress,—that I am over here to make the tour of Europe on foot. I am in pedestrian costume . . . but mount the first conveyance that offers, making but slight explanation or excuse."[33]

Leaving the family behind in Baden-Baden, Twain and Twichell set off on a walking tour of Bavaria. The two wore identical hiking uniforms: "Broad slouch hats, to keep the sun off; gray knapsacks; blue army shirts; blue overalls; leathern gaiters buttoned tight from knee down to ankle; high-quarter coarse shoes snugly laced. Each man had an opera glass, a canteen, and a guide-book case slung over his shoulder, and carried an alpenstock in one hand and a sun umbrella in the other. Around our hats were wound many folds of soft white muslin, with the ends hanging and flapping down our backs,—an idea brought from the Orient and used by tourists all over Europe." The first leg of their journey took them into the enchanted depths of the Black Forest. "No single ray is able to pierce its way in," noted Twain, "but the diffused light takes color from moss and foliage, and pervades the place like a faint, green-tinted mist, the theatrical fires of fairyland. The suggestion of mystery and the supernatural which haunts the forest at all times, is intensified by the unearthly glow." The younger, more vigorous Twichell set a brisk pace between long asides on grammar, camp dentistry during the Civil War, and the daily habits of the worker ant, an insect Twain considered "strangely overrated." After a mere two days tramping by foot, the pair caught a train north to Heidelberg and Wimpfen, and then hitched a ride on a peasant's cart to Heilbronn, seven miles east on the Neckar River. Along the way, Twain ventured a confidence in their native language. "Speak in German, Mark," advised Twitchell. "These Germans may understand English."[34]

At the bridge pier in Heilbronn, Twain hailed the owner of the largest raft, an over-aged, overweight Huck Finn sporting a straw hat, rolled-up trousers, and bare feet. Chartering his raft, Twain and Twichell set off downriver. "Germany, in the summer, is the perfection of the beautiful," Twain recalled, "but nobody has understood, and realized, and enjoyed the utmost possibilities of this soft and peaceful beauty unless he has voyaged down the Neckar in a raft." Sitting on the edge of the raft with their own pants rolled up and their legs dangling in the river, the pair watched the matchless scenery float by. Twain, as was his wont, soon spied a naked woman—or rather, a twelve-year-old girl—bathing in the water. "She was a pretty creature, and she and her willow bough made a very pretty picture," he observed, "one which could not offend the modesty of the most fastidious spectator." What the Christian minister Twichell had to say about the sight of an underaged, naked girl went unrecorded.[35]

The river was busy with other vessels—steamboats, keelboats, tugboats—which Twain observed with his experienced eye before falling again into reveries about damsels imprisoned in gloomy castles, crusaders returning from the Holy Land, knights, dragons, enchanted caves, and the mythical Rhine maidens known as the Lorelei. Even American Indians—always a bugaboo for Twain—turned up in his thoughts as an effective way to hold down unwanted European emigration. "The fact that a band of 6,000 Indians are now murdering our frontiersmen at their impudent leisure, and that we are only able to send 1,200 soldiers against them, is utilized here to discourage emigration to America," he noted. "The common people think the Indians are in New Jersey." Twain's dreams were disturbed by a series of real explosions: Italian workmen were dynamiting the hillside for a new railway line. "We ran that whole battery of nine blasts in a row," he wrote, "and it was certainly one of the most exciting and uncomfortable weeks I ever spent, either aship or ashore." He was seized by the thought that he would die an absurd death resulting in an equally absurd obituary: "Shot with a rock, on a raft." They survived the blasting, a nighttime storm, and a raft wreck, "and I have never regretted it."[36]

Returning by rail to Heidelberg, Twain and Twichell continued south to Lucerne, Switzerland, for the next leg of their journey. Livy and the girls had arrived before them, and Twain enjoyed a brief family reunion while he toured the almost overly picturesque Lucerne. "Lucerne is a charming place," he noted. "It begins at the water's edge, with a fringe of hotels, and scrambles up and spreads itself over two or three sharp hills in a crowded, disorderly, but picturesque way, offering to the eye a heaped-up confusion of red roofs, quaint gables, dormer windows, toothpick steeples, with here and there a bit of ancient embattled wall lending itself over the ridges, worm-fashion, and here and there an old square tower of heavy masonry." The town was filled with tourists, half of them English, and a number of fellow Americans, including an attractive young woman who recognized Twain, forcing him to pretend that he recognized her as well.[37]

Going to the nearby village of Weggis, Twain and Twichell set out to climb six thousand-foot-high Rigi-Kulm in the Swiss Alps. The climb, which took less than a day in real time, stretches over the course of two chapters in *A Tramp Abroad*, with the author comically inflating their actual experience into an epic adventure. Ignoring a recently constructed railway from the village to the mountain summit, the two men set out to make their ascent. They have their hearts set on seeing an alpine sunrise, Twain reports, and they hire a boy to carry their packs and overcoats for them—"That left us free for business"—but stop so often to rest and smoke that the youth asks them dryly if they had hired him by the job or by the year. "We told him he could move along if he was in a hurry," writes Twain. "He said he wasn't in such a very particular hurry, but he wanted to get to the top while he was young. We told him to clear out." The youth says he will go on ahead and find them a hotel, "but if they were all full he would ask them to build another one and hurry up and get the paint and plaster dry against we arrived."[38]

Checking into a hotel halfway up the mountainside—Twain thinks they are already at the summit—the pair make plans to wake for sunrise, but "sleep like policemen" and miss the dawn by five or six hours. Setting off at the crack of noon, they climb steadily, interrupted regularly by Swiss yodelers. They pay one man a franc to yodel again, the next half a franc to perform the same office, then gradually work their way through a virtual battalion of yodelers who they eventually pay a franc apiece not to yodel any more. At Kaltbad Station they find another hotel, go to bed early to see the sunrise, and wake at three the next afternoon. In search of another hotel that reputedly woke its guests with an alpine horn so loud "that would raise the dead," they get lost in the fog and rain and huddle together cursing, afraid of plunging off the side of the mountain in the dark. When they finally turn around, they see the Rigi-Kulm Hotel right behind them. They try again the next day, but once more manage to oversleep. Finally, awaking in time, they make the wrong-headed decision to watch the sunrise from their room, only to discover that they again are facing the wrong way. "There is a hitch about this sunrise somewhere," observes Twain. "It doesn't seem to go. What do you reckon is the matter with it?" When Twichell points out the error, Twain explodes. "It was exactly like you to light a pipe and sit down to wait for the sun to rise in the west." "I find out all the mistakes," says his companion. "You make them all, too," Twain replies.[39]

Gemmi Pass, near Kandersteg, is their next target. Twain directs his friend to climb the three hundred-foot-high ladders built into the precipice: "I ordered [Twichell] to make the ascent, so I could put the thrill and horror of it in my book." Twichell subcontracts the climb to another hiker. "It makes me shudder yet when I think of what I felt when I was clinging there between heaven and earth in the person of that proxy," writes Twain. "At times the world swam around me, and I could hardly keep from letting go, so dizzying was the appalling danger. Many a person would have given up and descended, but I stuck to my task, and would not yield until I had accomplished it. . . . I shall break my neck yet with such fool-hardy performance, for warnings never seem to have any lasting effect upon me."[40]

In writing his semifictional account of the climb through Gemmi Pass, Twain appropriated, and quoted liberally, from the experiences of two earlier alpine adventure writers, Thomas Hinchcliff (*Summer Months among the Alps*, 1857) and Edward Whymper (*Scrambles amongst the Alps*, 1871). Inspired by their examples, he declares boldly in chapter 37 of *A Tramp Abroad*: "I will ascend the Riffelberg." This leads to the comic climax of the book, in which Twain inflates the actual four-hour climb into a weeklong endurance contest requiring, by careful count, 154 luggage-carriers, 44 mules, 17 guides, 15 barkeepers, 143 pairs of crutches, 27 kegs of paregoric, 12 waiters, 4 surgeons, 3 chaplains, 4 pastry cooks, a butler, and a barber. Supplies included 22 barrels of whiskey, 16 cases of hams, and 2,000 cigars.[41]

The expedition starts out, single-file, linked by one 3,122-foot-long rope. Twain and Twichell take up the most dangerous position, in the extreme rear. The guides fear that they have become lost; Twichell produces his Baedeker to prove that it is the mountain that is lost. A rumor sweeps camp that a barkeeper had fallen over the cliff, but happily it is only a chaplain. "I had laid in an extra force of chaplains, purposely to be prepared for emergencies like this," says Twain, "but by some unaccountable oversight had come away rather short-handed in the matter of barkeepers." After unbearable hardships, they arrive at the summit, the Riffelberg Hotel, where they are greeted by seventy-five hardy travelers who had preceded them, "mainly ladies and little children." No matter, as Huck Finn might have said. "The ascent had been made, and the names and dates now stand recorded on a stone monument to prove it to all future tourists," Twain records modestly. "Let the tourist rope himself up and go there; for I have shown that with nerve, caution, and judgment, the thing can be done."[42]

One last adventure awaits the pair, the ascent of Mount Blanc, the highest peak in Europe. At the exchange office in Chamonix, which coordinated all the mountain-climbing and guide-assigning for the peak, Twain observes a German tourist receiving his official diploma signifying he had successfully completed the harrowing climb. "I tried to buy a diploma for an invalid friend at home who had never traveled, and whose desire all his life has been to ascent Mount Blanc," Twain recalls, "but the Guide-in-Chief rather insolently refused to sell me one." He attempts to buy the German's just-awarded certificate, but "he wanted his diploma for himself—did I suppose he was going to risk his neck for that thing and then give it to a sick stranger?"[43]

In the end, Twain settles again for mountain-climbing by proxy, this time by telescope. "I wanted to stand with a party on the summit of Mont Blanc, merely to be able to say I had done it, and I believe the telescope could set me within seven feet of the uppermost man." He asks the telescope operator if there is any danger. "He said no,—not by telescope; said he had taken a great many parties to the summit, and never lost a man." For the price of three francs, Twain bends to the task. "The old dare-devil spirit was upon me, and I said that as I had committed myself I would not back down; I would ascend Mont Blanc if it cost me my life." He watches a party of twelve make the ascent. "Presently we all stood together on the summit! What a view was spread out below!" Twain returns to the exchange office for his climbing diploma, "but the Chief Guide put us off, with one pretext or another, during all the time we staid in Chamonix." The chief expresses the wish that the town had a lunatic asylum, which cheers Twain a bit. He advises others who might want to follow his example for climbing Mount Blanc to "choose a calm clear day; and do not pay the telescope man in advance."[44]

The mountain-climbing adventures, real and imagined, concluded Twichell's visit to Europe. He left for America on

September 9, having more than fulfilled his role as Twain's designated traveling companion. "Dear Old Joe," Twain wrote him the next day. "It is actually all over! I couldn't seem to accept the dismal truth that you were actually gone, and the pleasant tramping and talking at an end. Ah my boy! it has been such a rich holiday for me, and I feel under such deep and honest obligations to you for coming." Now, reunited with Livy and the girls, he spent the autumn months reluctantly squiring them through Italy, never one of his favorite countries. "Italy, the home of art & swindling; home of religion & moral rottenness," he confided to his journal. Turin and Milan were fine, but all the great paintings gave him a bellyache. "The eternal repetition of Virgin & Child affects me at least as much as an eternity of Washington Crossing the Delaware by an infinitude of Artists would," he complained. Venice bored him as usual, and Rome was about as interesting as East Hartford. Livy and Clara Spaulding, Twain wrote, were "having a royal time worshiping the Old Masters, and I as good a time gritting my ineffectual teeth over them."[45]

The family wintered in Munich while Twain struggled to complete his travel book. He worried in a letter to Twichell that he had lost his faculty for writing travel sketches and that the new book "is either going to be compared with the Innocents Abroad, or contrasted with it, to my disadvantage." He hoped at least that the book would be "no dead corpse of a thing." He was even less hopeful to Howells, raging that "I hate travel, & I hate hotels, & I hate the opera, & I hate the Old Masters—in truth I don't ever seem to be in a good enough humor with anything to satirize it. I want to make a book which people will read, & I shall make it profitable reading in spots—in spots merely because there's not much material for a larger amount." It was concise and cogent self-criticism of a book that he was already tired of writing.[46]

In March 1879 the family relocated to Paris for another four months, taking rooms on the right bank in the Hotel de Normandie adjacent to the Rue de Rivoli and the Tuileries Gardens. After his unsuccessful wrestling match with the German language, Twain flatly refused to join Livy and the girls in attempting to learn French. "You won't ever catch me fooling around with any more foreign languages," he wrote to Mary Fairbanks, "particularly as I don't intend to wander off to any more foreign lands till after I'm dead." Not that he had much opportunity to speak to the locals anyway. "I have been sick—sick—and sick again—with rheumatism and dysentery," he complained to Frank Bliss. "I have spent four-fifths of my six week's residence in Paris in bed. This is an awful set-back." Eventually he rallied enough to exchange courtesy calls and books with Russian novelist Ivan Turgenev, whom he had met in London six years earlier. "Brought me one of his books," Twain noted, without saying which. "Gave him Tom Sawyer." One hopes it was a fair exchange.[47]

The unusually wet and chilly spring weather added to Twain's miseries. "I wish this eternal winter would come to an end," he groused. "Have had rain almost without intermission for 2 months & one week." The book was not going well either. "I've been having a dismal time for months over this confounded book," he told Mary Fairbanks. Still, he promised Frank Bliss, he would finish soon. "There is nearly matter enough," he wrote, "but I shall probably *strike out* as well as *add*," a promise he didn't keep. He yearned for the simple basics of American life: "hot biscuits, *real* coffee with *real* cream—and *real* potatoes. Fried chicken, corn bread, *real* butter, *real* beefsteak, *good* roast beef with *taste* to it." In

search of some good, old-fashioned home cooking, he attended
meetings of the Anglo-American Stomach Club, but there was
more talking involved than eating. "We are mighty hungry," he
reported to Twichell. "We want to get home & get something
to eat."[48]

The longer he stayed in France, the less Twain found to like.
He only admired three things about the country, he said: the
French Revolution, Napoleon, and Joan of Arc. Otherwise, the
national motto stood for "Liberty (to rob, burn and butcher)—
Equality (in bestiality)—Fraternity (of Devils)." "France has
neither winter nor summer nor morals," wrote Twain. "Apart
from these drawbacks it is a fine country." Even the Paris cab-
bies came in for aspersions: "The French cabman never treats
you to a civility—never leaves his seat to assist a lady—receives
his fare without even a grunt, whether it be too much or too
little." Worst of all, there were no French translations of his
works, so even in the cosmopolitan capital of Paris the average
man on the street had little idea, or interest, in who Mark
Twain was—a disinterest that was returned in spades. The two
great branches of French thought, he judged, were "science and
adultery."[49]

In mid-July the family escaped Paris for London, but the
weather continued to be unseasonably bad. "Rainy and cold,"
Twain noted after they had reoccupied their rooms in the
Brunswick House on Hanover Square. "Have had a rousing
big cannel-coal fire blazing away in the grate all day. A remarkable summer, truly." Despite the inclemency, Twain crowded
his return visit with dinners and social calls. One night he
dined with two other London-based American celebrities,
James McNeill Whistler and Henry James. He did not record
his conversation with the other great writer of his generation,
about whom he had once complained to William Dean How-

ells that he "would rather be damned to John Bunyan's heaven" than be forced to read *The Bostonians*. Livy, on the other hand, reported that she had met James and "enjoyed him very much. I had a little chat with him before dinner, and he was exceedingly pleasant and easy to talk with. I had expected just the reverse, thinking one would feel looked over by him and criticized." Another dinner party included Lewis Carroll, whom Twain judged to be "the stillest and shyest full-grown man I have ever met except Uncle Remus [Joel Chandler Harris]." Perhaps there was something about writing children's fables that made men shy, although it didn't seem to faze Twain. On his way to Liverpool to catch the steamer home, Twain took a side trip to Windermere, in the Lake Country, to dine with Charles Darwin. Again, he did not record his impressions of the great man (or vice versa), although he learned later from Charles Eliot Norton of Harvard that Darwin "always read himself to sleep with my books"—not necessarily the highest praise for a writer.[50]

The traveling party left out of Liverpool on the S.S. *Gallia* on August 23 and docked in New York on September 2, having been away from the United States for a little more than sixteen months. With them they brought back twelve jam-packed steamer trunks and twenty-two freight packages, much of the contents intended to furnish the Hartford house. A reporter for the *New York Sun* observed that Twain had changed so much during his months in Europe that only his drawl remained familiar. "He looked older than when he went to Germany," said the reporter, "and his hair has turned quite gray." Demonstrating that no two reporters ever see things

the same way, another writer in the *New York Times* insisted
that Twain still seemed ageless, "the nearest surviving kin
of the jumping frog," and that his hair was "no whiter than
when he last sailed to Europe."[51]

Back in Hartford, Twain completed the manuscript for
A Tramp Abroad in January 1880, and it was published two
months later by American Publishing Company. By the end
of the year it had sold 62,000 copies, a respectable figure but
hardly in line with his sales for *The Innocents Abroad*. Reviews, by Twain's standards, were also subpar. Howells loy-
ally if anonymously praised the "paradoxical charm of Mr. Clemens's best humor," which he said sprang from "a personal
hatred for humbug or pretension." But even Howells had to
admit that some of the pseudo-events in the book, such as the
torturous climb up the Riffelberg, "went on a little too long."
The appendices—there were six—were "all admirable." An un-
signed article in the *Saturday Review*, attributed afterward
to Sir Leslie Stephen, the father of Virginia Woolf, found the
book dull in places and impossible to read straight through,
but conceded that "there are also plenty of passages, stories,
bits of observation, scraps of character and conversation, and
so forth, which are delightfully bright and clever. And a practiced reader can always skip the dull parts." That seems, on
balance, a fair assessment. Twain biographer Ron Powers hits
the mark—he frequently does—by calling the book "mainly
set-piece horsing around . . . a crazy quilt of dropped-in anecdotes, some of them uproarious." Twain himself told an in-
terviewer that *A Tramp Abroad* was "a book written by one
loafer for a brother loafer to read."[52]

In retrospect, for both author and reader, *A Tramp Abroad*
proved to be much harder work than that. Inevitably, Twain's
second major foreign trip was considerably less exhilarating

than his first. The scruffy young Western reporter of the *Quaker City* tour had morphed into a well-tailored, respectable middle-aged Easterner, a married father of two who now confronted European culture on his own relatively sophisticated terms. This confrontation was less a collision of strangers than a meeting of equals, an encounter that mirrored the experience of other American travelers at the tag end of the first great wave of foreign tourism. They, like Twain, had seen it all before—no one can see things twice for the first time. "Broader experience made him more cautious in his comments," Arthur L. Scott observes. "He did his best to recapture the cavalier Western viewpoint of *The Innocents Abroad*, but the novelty of Europe had worn thin for him, and his youthful spontaneity was gone. The gigantic cultural breach between Mark Twain and Europe was gradually closing, bringing him ever closer to the Old World in sympathies." Still, as Jeffrey Alan Melton notes, *A Tramp Abroad* in its own rambling way is an accurate reflection of the evolving perspectives of American tourists on foreign shores. "If in *The Innocents Abroad* Twain struggles to hold on to his picture of the imaginary touristic Old World, *A Tramp Abroad* shows that such struggles are the work of an innocent; the high-tide tourist has apprehended that all is irrelevant," writes Melton. "For the leisure tourist, the primary goal is not to see the world but to be the center of it." By the late 1870s, Mark Twain was used to being the center of the world—if not indeed the universe.[53]

CHAPTER THREE

INNOCENTS ADRIFT

E xcept for one notable trip down the Mississippi River to revisit his halcyon steamboating days, Twain did most of his traveling over the next twelve years in the third-floor study of the family home in Hartford or at his sister-in-law's farm outside Elmira. During this time, probably the happiest period of his life, he wrote four of his best-loved books: *The Prince and the Pauper, Life on the Mississippi, Adventures of Huckleberry Finn,* and *A Connecticut Yankee in King Arthur's Court.* Two were based on his travels up and down the Mississippi; the other two depended, in part, on personal impressions he had formed while visiting England during the previous decade.

Befitting their locales, the American books feature homespun, rough-edged characters, including the author himself in his hardscrabble youth, whereas the English volumes concern monarchs, noblemen, lords, and ladies—the medieval trumpery of rank and privilege. The democratic-minded Twain (lowercase "d"; he generally voted Republican) ironically reversed the notions of royalty by giving the low-born English pauper and the small-town Missouri river urchin an innate nobility of spirit. Conversely, the knights of King Arthur's court and the aristocrats advising young Prince Edward are shown to be guided by base instincts and selfish motives. It takes the poor but honest peasant boy and the hardheaded Yankee shop mechanic to demonstrate the basic virtues of honesty, individuality, and self-reliance to those in power, which was very much how Twain saw his own role in life, long after he had left behind his humble roots and entered the genteel moneyed class he affected to disdain.

The two Mississippi books, of course, drew on Twain's own personal history, deepening and extending his experience on the river to drive home characteristically American themes of freedom, mobility, and self-creation. Fictitious Huck Finn and real-life Sam Clemens both made their escape down the great national waterway, leaving behind their provincially learned narrow-mindedness and drawing a new, empowered identity from their river journeys. *Life on the Mississippi* reprised material from Twain's earlier magazine series, "Old Times on the Mississippi," which had appeared eight years earlier. To the fourteen chapters detailing his education as a cub pilot on the river, Twain added thirty-nine new chapters and four appendices recounting his month-long return to the river in 1882, including a lengthy section recording his first return to his hometown of Hannibal in nearly thirty years.

Among his most vivid recollections of Hannibal, Twain records the time he gave some matches to a nameless drunken tramp who then accidentally burned himself to death in the town jail. Someone remembers the victim as "Jimmy Finn, the town drunkard," but Twain recalls the incident differently. The real Jimmy Finn, he says, "died a natural death in a tan vat, of a combination of delirium tremens and spontaneous combustion." The true victim was nameless, but the name Finn lives on (as do the delirium tremens) in Twain's greatest novel, *Adventures of Huckleberry Finn*, which he published ten months after *Life on the Mississippi*. Little remains to be said about Huckleberry Finn, the novel or character, except to underline biographer Ron Powers's assertion that Huck Finn is "the Vandal of American literature." Although scarcely an innocent and certainly no pilgrim, Huck *is* a tourist in a way, dropping in on various riverfront towns along the way and even meeting up with a very curious pair of "royals"—the inimitable King and the Duke. Reflexively honest in his way, Huck vandalizes nothing and takes only what he needs to survive on the river with his newfound friend Jim. Tom Sawyer, much closer in spirit to his creator, would have been right at home on the *Quaker City* cruise.[1]

The English books, which Twain himself always rated higher than *Huckleberry Finn* on his list of achievements, were a radical departure from the Mississippi books. To begin with, each was set in the far-distant past. *The Prince and the Pauper* takes place in the year 1547, when King Henry VIII died and was succeeded by his nine-year-old son, Edward VI. The book's well-known plot involves the young prince inadvertently switching places with a poor commoner, Tom Canty, who is born on the same day as the prince and bears a miraculous physical resemblance to him. Through a series of unlikely misunderstandings, the two boys, promoted in age to around fourteen to make their adventures more believable, undergo contrasting rites of passage, literally living for a time in each other's shoes. The prince, in particular, has his eyes opened by the sorry plight of London's poor and ultimately ascends the throne as an altogether kinder and more humane ruler, "a singularly merciful one for those harsh times." Fittingly, for what is primarily a children's book, Twain dedicated it to "those good-mannered and agreeable children, Susie and Clara Clemens."[2]

The somewhat less agreeable title character—not necessarily the hero—of *A Connecticut Yankee in King Arthur's Court* hails from Twain's adopted home. Hank Morgan, a Hartford native, is a factory superintendent and amateur inventor, good at making things or figuring out how they work. Magically transported back to the sixth century AD, he finds himself at large in the fabulous realms of Camelot, which is quite pointedly different from the romanticized vision of Sir Walter Scott, whose high-blown medievalism Twain always blamed for encouraging Southerners to start the Civil War. Morgan, a prototypical American with the can-do spirit of the Gilded Age, sets out to transfer his democratic values to the oppressed and oppressive world of medieval Europe. He first introduces the woefully ignorant Arthurian courtiers to the simple pleasures of soap, matches, paper, ink, and glass; then he moves on to such modern inventions as bicycles, telephones, factories, coal mines, dynamos, steamships, locomotives, and the great American game of baseball. Ultimately, he brings the people dynamite, torpedoes, and Gatling guns—a decidedly mixed blessing with which, in an ironic echo of the American Civil War, they slay countless thousands of their fellow citizens. Not surprising, given its antimonarchical tone, English reviewers were unamused by the book. It didn't help that the portly Queen Victoria was portrayed in one of the book's illustrations as a literal hog. American readers, by and large, were indifferent to Her Majesty's stature, but they were less than enchanted by the science fiction elements of the plot. The book sold only middling well.

Settling into his suburban Connecticut home, Twain had no more plans to travel abroad. He was content, he told William

Dean Howells, to stay at home with his all-female family. Besides Livy, Susy, and Clara, a third daughter, Jean, was born in 1880. "I have seen all the foreign countries I want to except heaven and hell," Twain joked to Howells, "and I have only a vague curiosity as concerns one of those." Unfortunately for the author and his dependents, he would prove to have a good deal more curiosity about, if no more direct personal knowledge of, complex financial matters, most notably a get-rich-quick scheme that proved to be neither quick nor enriching: the Paige compositor. Always fascinated with gadgets, Twain devoted an inordinate amount of time and money over the next decade to the research and development of a mechanical typesetting machine, which he was convinced would revolutionize the world of publishing. The machine he had in mind was the brainchild of inventor James W. Paige, another transplanted Hartfordian from upstate New York whom Twain met through a mutual acquaintance the same year that Jean was born.[3]

Paige, who formally—and accurately—listed his profession as "patentee," was one of a virtual army of inventors seeking to perfect a new typesetting device in the early 1880s. Inventors had been working on prototype machines for many years; the basement of the *London Times* was said to be crammed with discarded models. Paige was the latest entrant in the typesetting sweepstakes, and Twain remained convinced, against mounting evidence to the contrary, that in backing Paige he was backing the best horse in the race. "He is a poet," Twain wrote, "a most great and genuine poet, whose sublime creations are written in steel. He is the Shakespeare of mechanical invention." Considering that Twain did not believe Shakespeare had actually written his alleged works, it was a somewhat qualified compliment. Beginning with an initial $2,000 investment, the author bankrolled the inventor with regular infusions of cash, eventually sinking more than $150,000 of his own and Livy's money into the project—some $3 million in modern terms.[4]

Paige may or may not have been a poet, but he was certainly in need of an editor. In its later—one could never say its final—state, the compositor contained a dizzying 18,000 separate parts, as outlined on 275 sheets of drawings and 123 pages of specifications. Predictably, the delicate and complicated machine broke down with dismaying regularity, even as its chief backer continued to pronounce it "flawless," "cunning," "perfect," and "sublime." Meanwhile, a presumably less poetic inventor with the lumpish name of Ottmar Mergenthaler lapped the field with his Linotype machine, which took the practical approach of imitating a mechanical typewriter rather than a human typesetter. The sympathetic but realistic Howells, himself a former newspaper printer, took a long view of the project. Twain and Paige, he said, had tried to perfect a machine "so expensive that it was practically impracticable."[5]

The financial black hole that was the Paige compositor eventually sucked in and crushed another Twain outside investment, one that, in the beginning at least, showed greater promise. Charles Webster & Company, a publishing house headed by Twain's nephew by marriage, began with a flourish in 1884–1885, publishing to great fanfare both Twain's masterpiece, *Adventures of Huckleberry Finn*, and the personal memoirs of Ulysses S. Grant. Twain had a guiding hand in both ventures. Besides writing *Huckleberry Finn*, the author somewhat less creditably served as midwife for Grant's memoirs, suborning the dying general away from his publisher of record, the Century Company, which had a verbal contract with Grant for his memoirs. After hearing inside details of the arrangement from *Century Magazine* editor Richard Watson

Gilder over Gilder's own dinner table one night in early 1885, Twain induced Grant to switch to Charles Webster & Company, offering the general an unheard-of 75 percent royalty rate. The last great battle of Grant's life commenced.

In a well-known and valorous race against death, Grant completed the manuscript mere weeks before succumbing to throat cancer in July 1885. Twain watched from the windows of the publishing company as the funeral procession for the dead hero wound its way through the streets of New York City on the afternoon of August 8. Six months later, he had the immense personal satisfaction of hand-delivering to Grant's widow, Julia, a check for $200,000, at that time the largest single royalty payment in publishing history. That was also the amount that Twain netted in profits from Grant's book (Mrs. Grant eventually received $450,000 in total royalties). Added to the strong showing of *Huckleberry Finn*, which sold 51,000 copies in the first three months after its publication in February 1885, the neophyte publishing company seemed poised to become a major figure in the industry. "I am frightened at the proportions of my prosperity," Twain bragged. "It seems that whatever I touch turns to gold." His boast would prove to be a classic case of hubris, a self-jinxing of monumental proportions.[6]

The creeping financial shadows seldom darkened the sun-filled tranquility on Farmington Avenue. Twain's three daughters grew up in a cocoon of comfort and privilege. Susy, in particular, was her father's delight. Always the most like Twain in looks and temperament, the moody, mercurial Susy showed an unsurprising precocity for words. At the age of thirteen she wrote a 19,000-word biography of her father, beginning emphatically, "We are a very happy family!" and adding, "We consist of Papa, Mama, Jean, Clara and me. It's Papa I am writing about. He is a very good man, and a very funny one; he *has* got a temper but we all of us have in this family. He is the liveliest man I ever saw, or ever hope to see." The girls and their father wrote and performed plays, sang songs, played cards, acted out charades, made up elaborate bedtime stories. Together with their mother, they functioned as an early sounding board for Twain's novels—they all favored *The Prince and the Pauper*—and provided a comfortable domestic bubble within which the presiding genius lived and wrote. The house itself seemed an active participant in their happiness. "Our house was not unsentient matter—it had a heart and a soul," Twain would later insist. "It was of us and we were in its confidence, and lived in its grace and in the peace of its benediction."[7]

The Hartford years seemed bathed in eternal late-summer twilight. The girls played together in the well-trimmed yard while Livy watched over them from the shaded front porch, knitting or reading. Twain wandered in and out, smoking cigars and sometimes an old-fashioned corncob pipe. Neighbors Joseph and Harmony Twichell, Harriet Beecher Stowe, Charles and Susan Warner, and Trinity College president George Worthington Smith frequently dropped by to visit. One perfect June evening was lovingly preserved in Livy's diary: the family shared an early dinner on the veranda, then went for carriage ride in the twinkling twilight. Fireflies blinked away in the distance like tiny stars. After the girls went to bed in their second-floor bedrooms, friends arrived to play whist, eat ice cream, and listen, inevitably, to Twain's stories. Later, while the women continued playing cards in the sitting room, the men relocated to the billiards room upstairs for more stories, beer, and cigars. It was the epitome of upper-middle-class recreation at the height of the Gilded Age. One regular dinner guest at Twain's table was the actor Joseph Jefferson, whose most famous role was Rip Van Winkle. It must have seemed to the family that their own dream life, unlike Rip's, would go on forever.

It did not. The Paige compositor continued to drain off $3,000 a month, and the publishing company, under the vacillating leadership of the increasingly ill Charles Webster, soon faltered. After the twin triumphs of *Huckleberry Finn* and Grant's memoirs, the company made a number of ill-advised gambles. Hoping to capitalize on its success with Grant, Twain and Webster brought out a two-volume set of fellow Union general Phil Sheridan's memoirs, but it didn't fare nearly as well, even after the fiery little general dropped dead right before the book was published, giving it something of a valedictory push. Other memoirs by Civil War figures George McClellan, Winfield Scott Hancock, and George Armstrong Custer's widow, Libbie, did little better; and a $5,000 advance to Henry Ward Beecher for his autobiography and *The Life of Christ*—not the same book, surprisingly—went unrewarded after Beecher died unexpectedly two months later. When Webster suggested attempting to resurrect *The Life of Christ* with another author, Twain recommended that Webster resurrect Lazarus instead, "because that had been tried once and we knew it could be done."[8]

The biggest fiasco, personally pushed by Twain, was an authorized biography of Pope Leo XIII. Twain reasoned that such a book would be required reading in every Catholic home in the world; it did not occur to him that many of the world's ten million Catholics were illiterate peasants in Third World countries. Despite Webster's private audience with the Pope in Rome and an aggressive advertising campaign that trumpeted "the Greatest Book of the Age," the venture languished with mediocre sales. All the company had to show for the Pope's book was a knighthood for Webster in the Catholic Order of Pius, which allowed him to wear an elaborate uniform of tri-cornered hat, blue tunic, gold epaulets, white cashmere pants, and a parade sword. Twain offered the withering comment that "if Charley Webster deserves to be a Papal Knight, I deserve to be an archangel."[9]

After his forced retirement in 1888, Webster continued to be the target of much of Twain's displaced anger. "I have never hated any creature with a hundred thousandth fraction of the hatred which I bear that human louse, Webster," he told Orion. As a long-time recipient of his brother's displeasure, Orion must have pitied their nephew for that dubious distinction. And to Webster's mother-in-law, Twain's sister Pamela, the author fumed that "I am not able to think of him without cursing him & cursing the day I opposed your better judgment of the lousy scoundrel & thief & sided with Annie in her desire to marry him. The thought of that treacherous cur can wake me out of my sleep." Two years later Webster died, prematurely worn out at age thirty-nine. Twain sent Orion to the funeral in his place.[10]

Belatedly, Twain shifted his disapproval to James W. Paige, though not his wonderful machine. "It is superb, it is perfect it can do 10 men's work," the author continued to believe. "It is worth billions; & when the pig-headed lunatic, its inventor, dies, it will instantly be capitalized & make the Clemens children rich." They should live that long. After a disastrous private demonstration for wealthy Nevada senator John P. Jones and other potential investors (Paige had inexplicably taken apart the compositor and left it "a crazy tangle of gears, keys, cams, wheels, springs, cogs, levers, and other hardware"), the would-be investors pulled out, leaving Twain holding a very large, very empty bag. "For a whole year you have breathed the word of promise to my ear to break it to my hope at last," Twain wrote to Jones, a friend from their old prospecting days out West. "It is stupefying, it is unbelievable." He stopped paying the inventor's bills.[11]

The family's Elysian Hartford existence began showing cracks in the fall of 1890, when eighteen-year-old Susy went away to college at Bryn Mawr, fifteen miles northwest of Philadelphia. Livy seems to have felt that the separation of high-strung daughter and high-strung father would do them both some good, but Twain was devastated by Susy's absence. Revealing rather more of his own feelings than Susy's, he described their leave-taking at the Bryn Mawr train station. "Our train was drifting away," Twain wrote to his sister, Pamela, "and she was drifting collegeward afoot, her figure blurred and dim in the rain and fog, and she was crying." So was her father. The departure of the daughter Twain called "a dreamer, a thinker, a poet and philosopher" left a void at home that the more taciturn Clara and the much younger, frequently unwell Jean could not fill. Susy, said Twain, "was full of life, full of activity, full of fire. In all things she was intense; in her this characteristic was not a mere glow, dispensing warmth, but a consuming fire." He might have been writing about himself.[12]

As for Susy, she made a determined attempt to fit in at college, winning the lead role in a student production of Gilbert and Sullivan's operetta *Iolanthe* and beginning an intense

emotional relationship with an older girl from Orange, New
Jersey, Louise Brownell, who was president of the Bryn Mawr
student body. Susy began calling herself Olivia, her first name,
to underscore perhaps her growing sophistication. She was
pulling away, but her father still loomed. In a rare incidence
of wifely sarcasm, Livy allowed that Twain would have delivered Susy's laundry if he could. In March 1891, he finagled an
invitation from Bryn Mawr's president, James E. Rhoads, to
speak to the students. Susy, sensing trouble, asked Twain specifically not to perform his melodramatic ghost story "The
Golden Arm," which she considered too unvarnished for her
refined classmates. He promised he wouldn't tell the story,
then did so anyway, driving Susy from the hall in tears. A
month later, coincidentally or not, she withdrew from school,
never to return. She missed Louise terribly.

By then, Twain's disastrous financial decisions had left him,
as someone joked, "A Connecticut Yankee in Bankruptcy
Court." Deciding that it would be cheaper to live abroad, Twain
and Livy made plans to relocate the family to Europe for a few
months. It would prove to be much longer than that. The Hartford house was closed, the staff let go. The piano and the horse
and carriage were sold off. Twain, an inveterate list maker,
jotted down final instructions to himself: "Stop street sprin-
kling, and electric lights, and publications, and clubs, 3 yr, and
pensions, stop the telephone." In early June 1891, the family
left Farmington Avenue for the last time. Livy walked through
the now-empty house, her footsteps echoing on the uncarpeted
wooden floors, peering into each room she passed as though
to imprint them forever in her memory. Clara, who was sixteen
at the time, remembered the overwhelming sadness that
affected them all. "We adored our home and friends," she
wrote. "We had to leave so much treasured beauty behind that

we could not look forward with any pleasure to life abroad. We all regarded this break in a hitherto smooth flow of harmonious existence as something resembling a tragedy." Harriet Beecher Stowe, their now-senile next-door neighbor, wandered across the lawn holding a handful of flowers and muttering impenetrable gobbledygook. "This maniac," Twain sighed.[13]

On June 6 the family, accompanied by housemaid Katy Leary and Livy's recently widowed sister, Susan Crane, sailed from New York on the French liner *La Gascogne*. So sudden was their departure that William Dean Howells had to read about it in the newspaper. "The papers say you are going to Europe for your few remaining years," a surprised Howells wrote to Twain. "I hope this is not ill health or ill luck that is taking you." Actually, it was both, but Twain responded that the trip was merely for the sake of Livy's health: "Mrs. Clemens must try some baths somewhere, and this it is that has determined us to go to Europe." He joked, a little weakly, that he hoped Howells would "get sick or sorry enough" to join them. He did not.[14]

Unlike Twain's previous trips abroad, this one was more an escape than an excursion. To defray expenses, he signed a contract with the McClure publishing syndicate and the *New York Sun* to write half a dozen letters from Europe at $1,000 apiece, but his heart wasn't in it. He had no set itinerary. As he told Howells, "I don't know how long we shall be in Europe—I have a vote, but I don't cast it. I'm going to do whatever the others desire, with leave to change their mind, without prejudice, whenever they want to." And he informed his old *Innocents Abroad* companion, Mary Fairbanks: "We are leaving for

Europe in a few days, to remain there until we shall get tired—a point which I shall reach in thirty days, Jean in sixty, Clara in ninety, Susy in a hundred, and Livy in six months." These were not the words of a noted enthusiast.[15]

Settling their daughters and companions into an apartment in Geneva, Twain and Livy spent the next several weeks touring various spas and health facilities in eastern France and Bohemia, attempting to find some relief for Livy's increasingly worrisome heart condition and Twain's chronic, exasperating rheumatism. At Aix-les-Bains, forty miles south of Geneva on the Swiss border, the couple soaked daily in the pungent waters. In his first travel letter, "Aix, the Paradise of the Rheumatics," Twain described a typical treatment: "They took me into a stone-floored basin about fourteen feet square, which had enough strange-looking pipes and things in it to make it look like a torture chamber." The attendants seated Twain on a pine stool and blasted him with thick warm-water jets while "they kneaded me, stroked me, twisted me, and applied all the other details of the scientific massage to me for seven or eight minutes. Then they stood me up and played a powerful jet upon me all around for another minute. The cool shower bath came next, and the thing was over. I came out of the bathhouse a few minutes later feeling younger and fresher and finer than I have felt since I was a boy." The salutary effects lasted about three hours. Livy's lasted no longer. She continued to be plagued by headaches, hypertension, and shortness of breath.[16]

A visit to Bayreuth for the annual Richard Wagner music festival left the author feeling "like a heretic in heaven, the one sane person in the community of the mad." The caterwauling in *Lohengrin* reminded him of "the time the orphan asylum burned down." Livy, who loved classical music, particularly

German, and encouraged musical lessons for all the girls, scheduled them for nineteen separate concerts. It was a sore trial for the novelist. The soloist in *Parsifal*, wrote Twain, "pulled out long notes, then some short ones, then a sharp, quick, peremptory bark or two—and so on and so on; and when he was done you saw that the information which he had conveyed had not compensated for the disturbance." To call the performance singing, said Twain, would be to give the wrong name to it. He quoted fellow humorist Bill Nye's remark: "Mr. Wagner's music is better than it sounds." It was a momentary return to the dryly unimpressed attitude of *The Innocents Abroad*. Livy tried to enjoy herself. "We are having a very pleasant stay here," she wrote to her friend Grace King back in America. "These lands over here are desperately interesting and charming, yet I must confess to much of homesickness."[17]

Twain felt much the same way. A two-day pilgrimage to Heidelberg for a nostalgic return to Schloss Hotel where they had stayed in 1878—"I was a skittish young thing of 42 then"— was disappointing. Two young women working at the hotel whom he remembered as mere children at the time of his previous visit did not recognize him, an oversight that marred the rest of the visit. "Hell or Heidelberg," he groused. "Whichever you come to first." Nor did a return to the glorious Alpine region around Lucerne raise his spirits. "Shrines all the way," Twain grumbled. "What you want is cussing places." At least Switzerland was a free republic. "After trying the political atmosphere of the neighboring monarchies," he wrote, "it is healing and refreshing to breathe in air that has known no taint of slavery for six hundred years."[18]

His dark mood verged on latent Bolshevism. "The first gospel of all monarchies should be rebellion," Twain wrote.

"The idiotic Crusades were gotten up to 'rescue' a valueless tomb from the Saracens; it seems to me that a crusade to make a bonfire of the Russian throne & fry the Czar in it would be some sense." For that matter, his old acquaintance from the *Innocents Abroad* tour, Czar Alexander II, had been assassinated and replaced by his son, the rather more repressive Alexander III. The third Alexander's son, Nicholas II, in time would become the last "Czar of All the Russias." He and his family, including the famously "missing" Princess Anastasia, would meet their own "great reckoning in a little room," shot down in cold blood by their Communist captors at a safe house in Ekaterinburg in 1919 before their would-be rescuers in the royalist White Army could reach them. As for surviving monarchs, "God save the king is uttered millions of times a day in Europe, & issues nearly always from just the mouth, neither higher nor lower." In other words, it was merely lip service.[19]

In late September 1891, as a way, perhaps, of avoiding the implied reproach in his family's eyes and his own sense of guilt over the financial mistakes that had taken them away from their cherished home, Twain set off on a solitary ten-day boat trip down the Rhone from Lake Bourget to Arles. Rather optimistically, he hoped to make a full-length book out of the excursion. He already had a provisional title, *The Innocents Adrift*, which harkened back to his first European adventure but might just as easily have served to describe the family's current vagabond status. The wandering life of the American expatriate, however much time was spent at luxury hotels, Wagnerian music festivals, and exclusive health spas, could not hope to replicate the simple comforts of home.

In any event, the boat trip was not nearly as much fun as he (or the reader) might have hoped. Accompanied by the boat's "admiral," Joseph Rougier, Twain cast off, determined, he said, "not to see the sights, but to rest up from sight-seeing. There was little or nothing on the Rhone to examine or study or write didactically about; consequently, to glide down the stream in an open boat, moved by the current only, would afford many days of lazy repose, with opportunity to smoke, read, doze, talk, accumulate comfort, get fat and all the while be out of reach of the news and remote from the world and its concerns."[20]

It may have been peaceful; it was not particularly interesting. Setting out from Castle Chatillon, "a rather picturesque old stack of masonry with a walled yard about it and an odd old stumpy tower in a corner," Twain drifted through the grape-growing region of southeastern France. He passed the occasional cottage, some dogs, a company of French infantry out on maneuvers, and not much else. A solitary woman paddling a boat had a face like the Mona Lisa, which put him in mind of his Hartford neighbor Noel Flagg, a fledgling artist who once made a special trip to Paris with his brother to view the painting. The brothers "exhausted their treasure of wit in making fun" of the painting, a judgment Twain concurred with, saying Da Vinci's masterpiece had always seemed to him "merely a serene and subdued face" with a bad complexion. Eventually, Twain would flog 174 pages of manuscript from the boat trip, most of them concerned with what he had to eat, what little he saw of the countryside, and how he felt about it. He tried to work up some suspense from a sudden violent rainstorm on the river—"If we were wrecked, swimming could not save us"—but the drama was undercut when Twain simply got out of the boat and waded to shore. The account ended with

Twain and the admiral eating breakfast again before getting
back under way. "The whole land looked defeated and discouraged," he wrote. "And very lonely."[21]

The same thing could have been said for Susy Clemens.
While her father was drifting aimlessly down the Rhone, Susy
was marooned in Lausanne, writing laceratingly needy letters
to Louise Brownell back at Bryn Mawr. "If I could only look
in on you," she wrote on October 2. "We would sleep together
tonight." And a few days later: "My darling, I do love you so
and I feel so separated from you. If you were here I would kiss
you *hard* on that little place that tastes so good just on the right
side of your nose." On the last day of October, she wrote:
"Louise beloved, I love you night and day with all my might.
You are so sweet, dear, so lovely! Oh, Louise if I could only see
you! I am so afraid—*Don't forget me!* "[22]

No scholarly consensus has ever been reached—or is likely
to be reached—regarding the exact nature of the relationship
Susy and Louise had shared during their comparatively brief
time together at Bryn Mawr. Using Susy's own words, it is possible to argue both for and against a lesbian component to their
friendship. Keeping in mind that Susy was a very well-
bought-up and proper young lady, it would seem unlikely that
there was any overt sexual behavior between her and Louise.
Chaste, same-sex crushes are a common occurrence at prep
schools, both male and female. Still, the modern eye pauses
when reading Susy's letters. There is certainly room to wonder
when one comes across such lines as: "Oh, my beloved I cannot
tell you how precious you are to me. I wish that when I see
you I could just slip into your room and take you in my arms."
Or, "I have wondered all along if you have seen me as I am.
I am confirmed in my fear that perhaps it would not be safe
for me to tell you as much about myself as I should like to. How

do I know you mightn't break off your relations on the spot?" What seems beyond doubt is Susy's loneliness and unhappiness, to which her parents were either innocently oblivious or else too preoccupied by their own worries to address.[23]

Clara, who liked to travel and had something of her paternal grandmother's phlegmatic frontier grit, took a more active role in socializing—not always to her father's liking. When Livy and Susan Crane went to Berlin to find an apartment for the family, Clara accepted an invitation to a military ball in Marienbad. Wearing a "slightly décolleté" pink gown, Clara attracted a good deal of attention from the spruce young Bavarian army officers. After she had spent a couple hours in the limelight, her disapproving father took her back to their hotel. The next morning one of the officers paid Clara a courtesy call and Twain gave the young man "a lofty expression that would make a mastodon shrink to a mouse." The gentleman caller left quickly enough, but when Twain caught Clara exchanging glances with the officer in the hotel dining room a bit later, he immediately marched her upstairs and locked her in her room. Katy Leary took meals to the prisoner on a tray. Clara, rather more resilient than Susy, laughed off the incident, at least in her recollection of it: "When at last Mother arrived she found a lackadaisical daughter in one room and a fiercely irritated Father in another. She brought us together and listened to our vibrating stories. I expected Mother to pour out words of indignant condemnation, when to my amazement, she burst with peals of laughter till her cheeks were bathed in tears."[24]

The family settled in Berlin for the winter. Despite his well-known struggles with "the awful German language," Twain

liked and admired the country's people and extolled the
clean, well-lit virtues of its capital city. Berlin he found "the
newest [city] I have ever seen. Chicago would seem venerable
beside it; for there are many old-looking districts in Chicago,
but not many in Berlin. The main mass of the city looks as if
it had been built last week, the rest of it looks as if it might be
six or even eight months old." The German Chicago, as he
dubbed Berlin, ran with typical Prussian efficiency. "It seems
to be the most governed city in the world," wrote Twain, intending it as a compliment. "Method and system are observable on every hand—in great things, in little things in all
details, of whatsoever size. It has a rule for everything, and
puts the rule in force. It deals with great matters and minute
particulars with equal faithfulness, and with a plodding
and painstaking diligence and persistency which compel
admiration."[25]

The family's temporary quarters, a first-floor apartment on
Kornerstrasse, a somewhat rundown neighborhood that Twain
termed "the Rag-picker's Paradise," were barely adequate.
When their short-term lease was up, they relocated to the more
suitably luxurious Hotel Royal on the Unter den Linden, which
ran "as straight as a ray of light" and emptied into a huge park.
The family, with the exception of Susy, thrived. Livy consulted
with the city's best doctors and soon felt well enough to resume her German lessons with a formidable female professor.
Jean was put under the charge of a German governess, and
Clara studied piano from a well-known teacher and embarked
on a busy social life with her fellow students and friends at
the Willard School for American Girls. When her father
learned that she had been the only young lady in attendance
at a luncheon with forty army officers, he again exploded,
warning Clara that "we want you to be a lady above reproach,

a lady always, never hoydenish." Clara, as usual, brushed it off. Only Susy, still writing regularly and forlornly to Louise Brownell, remained at loose ends.[26]

Twain's St. Louis–born cousin, Mollie Clemens von Versen, lived in Berlin with her general-husband, and through them the author received a royal summons to dine with the kaiser. On the evening of February 20, 1892, Twain found himself sitting at the right hand of the German emperor. Then in the fourth year of his reign, Wilhelm II had recently dismissed his brilliant chancellor, Otto von Bismarck, and was beginning the slow but seemingly irresistible slide toward war, an ultimately disastrous conflict that Bismarck likely would have avoided. In the first full flush of power, the forty-three-year-old monarch praised Twain's writings. Speaking English in deference to his guest, Wilhelm said that he particularly liked *A Tramp Abroad*, which included a favorable mention of the kaiser's mother, Empress Augusta, and that *Life on the Mississippi* was his favorite Twain work. Twain, flattered, broke in to offer an opinion or two of his own, starting with the quality of the potatoes at dinner, after which the kaiser seemed notably cooler. "It was half past six in the evening, and the frost did not get out of the atmosphere entirely until close upon midnight," Twain recalled, "when it did finally melt away—or wash away—under generous floods of beer." Years later, an American diplomat told Twain that the German ruler had always wondered why the writer hadn't talked more at dinner— surely one of the few times in Twain's life that such a question was raised.[27]

Advised to find a warmer climate for Livy, the family relocated to Italy in the spring of 1892. After five weeks in Rome, where Twain ran into his American compatriots John Singer Sargent and William James, they rented a villa in the Tuscan hills outside Florence. Webster & Company had just published a thin volume of Twain's sketches with the somewhat misleading title *Merry Tales*, which was notable only for Twain's semifictional Civil War remembrance, "The Private History of a Campaign That Failed." By coincidence, the editor who originally commissioned that piece for *Century Magazine*, Robert Underwood Johnson, was also in Florence. He came upon Twain one day in the Uffizi gallery, carefully studying a primitive painting of devils, monks, and bears. "Here at last I have found a picture worth looking at," said Twain.[28]

The family's residence, the Villa Viviani, a seventeenth-century building located halfway up Settignano Hill overlooking the Arno River, would be a regular stopping point for the next three years as they bounced restlessly between Florence, Berlin, and Bad Nauheim, with side trips to other European destinations. Twain vacillated in his opinion of the villa, reporting to Mary Fairbanks that "this serene & noiseless life out here, with the unimaginable beauty of the view, is heaven, & I want to stay in this one when I die." But to visiting author Grace King, who praised the Florence sunset, he scoffed, "It cannot be compared to the sun on the Mississippi River." The capacious mansion was so large that Twain suggested the family designate a particular time and place to run into each other during the day. The household staff was a virtual United Nations: the cook and butler were Italian, the housekeeper was French, and the maids were German and Irish.[29]

Clara spent a good deal of time alone in Berlin, studying music and socializing. She even missed the family Christmas in Florence. Her mother in particular felt Clara's absence sharply, bursting into tears whenever she read one of her middle daughter's heedlessly happy accounts of life in Berlin.

"Don't get used to being away from us my darling and have
such a good time in Berlin that you feel content to stay away
from us," Livy enjoined. "I cannot bear to have you so far away
from me and such a big piece of your life I am not sharing in."
How much of her life Livy was sharing with Susy is debatable.
In the drafty stone house with the green shutters, the desperately unhappy young woman marked her twentieth birthday.
Except for a few forays into Florence for voice lessons, which
were not going well (Susy had a good soprano voice but little
range or power), she spent much her time alone, reading in her
room. She was having difficulty eating and sleeping. Writing
to Clara, Susy made a troubling admission. Having been a
writer since childhood, seemingly born with a pen in her
hand, Susy now felt unable to write anything but the most
cursory letters. "Reading all day can be tiresome," she told her
sister. "As for writing I never think of that nowadays. I should
love to, but I can't now anyway, and I don't ever expect to be
able to." It might have raised some red flags, had anyone
noticed.[30]

Susy's father did not have the same problem. Somehow, between wandering around the Continent and making eight
separate trips back and forth across the Atlantic to monitor
his failing businesses, Twain found the time to complete four
novels, several short stories, and a number of essays and
travel sketches. Given his scattered lifestyle and diminished
physical and emotional resources, it is not surprising that
none of the novels ranks with his best work. The first, *The
American Claimant*, is an awkward blend of social satire and
farce, centering on Colonel Mulberry Sellers, one of the

original characters in Twain's first novel, *The Gilded Age.*
Sellers, based on Twain's uncle, James Lampton—with a
little of Twain's brother Orion thrown in—is a schemer and
dreamer, a self-proclaimed attorney at law, claim agent, ma-
terializer, hypnotizer, mind-cure dabbler, and inventor of a
board game called "Pigs in Clover." The plot, which Twain
found hilarious but most modern readers do not, concerns
Sellers's claim to be the rightful English Earl of Rossmore.
Meanwhile, the true heir has come to America to live as free
man in an egalitarian society. High jinks ensue. There are
mistaken identities, a Cherokee Strip desperado named One-
Armed Pete, a Sellers-designed "Cursing Phonograph" for
sea captains too busy to curse for themselves, and Sellers's
plan to buy Siberia and start a Russian revolution. Eventually, Sellers's daughter marries the true earl's son, uniting the
two families in peace and harmony.

The second novel Twain wrote in Europe was *Tom Sawyer
Abroad,* a short, unsuccessful attempt to capitalize on the
growing market in boys' adventure books such as Horatio Al-
ger's best-selling Ragged Dick and Tattered Tom series. Ill-
advisedly using his two most famous characters, Tom and
Huck, as cheap comic foils, along with a broadly drawn
minstrel-show Jim, the book starts off like a remake of *The
Wizard of Oz,* which it predates by a mere half-dozen years.
Tom, Huck, and Jim are in St. Louis touring a giant balloon-
like craft when the craft's pilot, a crackpot inventor called the
Professor and modeled obviously on James W. Paige, sets sail
prematurely. Heading across the Atlantic in the balloon, which
looks like a giant football with wings, the Professor gets drunk,
fights with Tom, and falls overboard—a wish-fulfilling fantasy
on the part of the author. Heading for England, the "erronorts"
drift over Africa instead. They are chased by lions, engulfed

by fleas, and shot at by Arabs. Huck and Tom spend a fair amount of time arguing over the existence of mirages, whether or not Catholic clerics curse, and why God had created something as apparently valueless as the Sahara Desert. There are more lions, tigers, sand storms, caravans, and kidnappings. They sail around the Egyptian pyramids and the Sphinx, upon whose head Jim plants an American flag. Tom sends Huck and Jim back to Missouri to fetch him a new corncob pipe, and they return with a note from Aunt Polly telling Tom to come home. They do.

Twain sold the serial rights to *Tom Sawyer Abroad* to *St. Nicholas Magazine*, whose editor, Mary Mapes Dodge, was a personal friend of his. Twain told her to use her own discretion when preparing the work for publication. Dodge, to Twain's subsequent chagrin, felt empowered to put new, sanitized words into the characters' mouths and directed staff artist Dan Beard to put shoes on their countrified feet. When Twain learned of the changes, he stormed into Dodge's office, his face red with outrage. "Any editor to whom I submit my manuscript has an undisputed right to delete anything to which he objects," spluttered Twain, "but God Almighty Himself has no right to put words in my mouth that I never used!" The original language was restored, but the characters remained respectably shod.[31]

More successful, although also flawed, is *Pudd'nhead Wilson*, the last Twain novel set in America. An uneasy blend of low comedy and such serious themes as slavery, murder, and miscegenation, the novel takes place in an altogether darker version of St. Petersburg, here renamed Dawson's Landing, a decade or so before the Civil War. The central plot concerns a one-sixteenth-black slave girl, Roxana, who switches her baby with a white baby in their cradles. The two boys grow up in parallel but unequal worlds. Ironically, Roxana's son, raised as a free white man, grows into a sullen, bitter adult who eventually murders his uncle for his money, whereas the other child, raised a slave, grows into a kind, tolerant individual. Using the new science of fingerprinting—an anachronism at the time the novel takes place—the title character is able to prove the true murderer and restore the men to their rightful places. There is a subplot involving dispossessed Italian twins from Florence, and a fair amount of foolishness of the local-color variety. The book's chief value, as far as Twain was concerned, was that it "kept my mind away from [other] things"—presumably financial matters, although he may also have been referring to worries over Livy's health and the three daughters who were growing up and away from him on foreign soil.[32]

Twain's fourth novel during their European sojourn, *Personal Recollections of Joan of Arc*, was an act of love, both real and idealized. A visit to the saint's birthplace at Domremy-la-Pucelle had rekindled the author's lifelong fascination with the national heroine of France. The book seemed almost to write itself, Twain recalled—"I merely have to hold the pen." Mixing straight history with a sentimental narrative about a flawless peasant girl whose beauty is so extraordinary that it cannot be exaggerated, the book purports to be the modern translation of a contemporary account by Joan's personal secretary, Sieur Louis de Conte. It follows the remarkable trajectory of the Maid of Orleans, from her humble upbringing and untaught military genius to her betrayal and death at the stake. Twain sidesteps the issue of Joan's religious ecstasy, neither explaining nor denying her claim to be divinely inspired. It is a very long and pious novel, and Twain and his family considered it his best. "Papa is progressing finely with his 'Joan of Arc' which promises to be his loveliest book," Susy wrote to Clara. "The character of Joan is pure and perfect to a miraculous degree. Hearing the M.S. read aloud is an up-lifting and revealing hour to us all. Many of Joan's words and sayings are historically correct and Papa cries when he reads them." So did Susy, excusing herself often to go dry her eyes. She apparently didn't suspect that her father's version of Joan was based to a great degree on her—or on the Susy she had been in her mid-teens, before she grew up and went away to college and discovered, perhaps, a secret sharer and a secret self.[33]

In June 1892, while Livy and the girls stayed behind, Twain made the first of eight separate voyages back across the Atlantic to try and salvage their finances. Belatedly, he had come to the realization that he was not much of a businessman. "Get me out of business," he told Fred Hall, who was now was running Webster & Company—or running it into the ground. "I am by nature and disposition unfitted for it." So was Hall, a stenographer by profession who had risen more or less by the Peter Principle to become head of the company. The company showed liabilities of more than $6,000 per month, and the Mount Morris Bank was threatening to foreclose on an outstanding $30,000 loan. Twain hadn't been paid any of the nearly $80,000 in royalties his books had earned over the previous year. It was all ploughed back into the publishing company, more money down a dry hole. The fall list wasn't promising; besides Twain's own second-rate novel, *The American Claimant,* the company offered such extra-literary efforts as *One Hundred Ways of Cooking Eggs, One Hundred Ways of Cooking Fish, Paddles and Politics Down the Danube,* and A *Perplexed Philosopher: Being an Examination of Mr. Herbert Spencer's Various Utterances on the Land Question.*[34]

Not all the company's problems were of its own making. In the winter of 1893, the country was struck by the worst financial panic, to that point, in American history. The initial cause of the Panic of 1893 was the failure of the Philadelphia and Reading Railroad, which in turn led to other railroad and business failures, bank closings, gold hoarding, bankruptcies, foreclosures, and rampant unemployment—more than 25 percent nationally. Wall Street teetered on the edge on collapse. The subsequent depression would last for four years, putting four million Americans out of work, shuttering fifteen thousand businesses, closing five hundred banks, and driving everyone—rich, poor, and middle class—well past the brink of desperation. The ever-jittery Twain was not immune. "I feel panicky," he wrote to Hall. "I have never felt so desperate in my life—& good reason, for I haven't got a penny to my name, & Mrs. Clemens hasn't enough laid up with Langdon to keep us two months." In the dire economic environment, profits for book publishers naturally shrank. People worrying about where their next crust of bread was coming from—many respectable women reportedly turned to prostitution to keep food on the family table—had little interest in books. Like thousands of other American businesses, Webster & Company was doomed; all that remained was the date of the funeral.[35]

Twain made a solo journey to Chicago in April 1893 to see James Paige and check on his ever-languishing compositor, but caught a bad cold and spent the next eleven days in bed, missing the World's Columbian Exposition in the newly erected White City. Eventually, Paige turned up at Twain's hotel and delivered another of his trademark lachrymose performances,

apologizing for past transgressions and assuring his benefactor that great days were coming. "Even more tears than
usual," noted Twain. "He could persuade a fish to come out
and take a walk with him. When he is present I always believe
him; I can't help it. When he is gone away all the belief evapo-
rates. He is a most daring and majestic liar." Twain returned
to New York unsatisfied, unmollified, and uncompensated.[36]

Socially at least, Twain managed to enjoy himself in New
York. He renewed ties with William Dean Howells, who had
been stung by his old friend's abrupt, unannounced departure
to Europe. The two dined together at the Hotel Glenham, and
Howells told him about his new position as editor of *Cosmopolitan* magazine. Howells's most recent novel, *A Hazard of
New Fortunes*, was far superior to anything Twain was pro-
ducing at the time. Twain also dined with Rudyard Kipling,
another writer who was working at a higher level than Twain
just then, and with the financier Andrew Carnegie, who declined Twain's offer to buy Webster & Company, offering the
unhelpful Dutch-uncle advice: "Put all your eggs in one basket,
and watch that basket." It was a little late for that.[37]

Twain would have better luck with another titan of industry,
Henry Huttleston Rogers, whom he met through their mutual friend, Dr. Clarence Rice, in September 1893. Rogers, like
Twain, was a self-made man, having risen from the coal mines
of Pennsylvania to become one of the founding partners in
Standard Oil. By the time Twain met him in the lobby of the
Murray Hill Hotel, Rogers had helped extend the vise-like
coils of that all-encircling monster into controlling interests
in gas, railroads, insurance, and copper worth somewhere in
the neighborhood of $100 million in 1893 dollars—a stag-
gering $39 billion today. His enemies, and perhaps his friends,
called him Hell Hound Rogers, the Mephistopheles of High

Finance. It was all the same to Rogers. "We are not in business for our health," he unapologetically told a congressional committee, "but are out for the dollars."[38]

Twain, Rogers, and Rice sat down for drinks in the hotel bar, and the oil man immediately charmed the author by telling him that he had attended one of Twain's Sandwich Island lectures years earlier. When Rogers heard that Twain was having financial trouble—to say the least—he set up a meeting with him and Hall the next day at Rogers's eleventh-floor office in the Standard Oil Building on Broadway. Acting quickly and decisively, as was his wont, the tycoon directed his son-in-law to purchase, for $50,000, the publishing rights to the company's ten-volume white elephant, the *Library of American Literature*. Rogers also wrote Twain a check for $4,000 to tide him over in the short term and arranged a private Pullman car for them on the Pennsylvania Railroad to visit James W. Paige's new typesetting factory in Chicago. "In just six minutes," Twain wrote to Livy, "we had the check & our worries were over till the 28th." Rogers, gushed Twain, was "the only man I care for in the world, the only man I would give a damn for."[39]

With Rogers's help, Twain negotiated a new contract with Paige, restructuring the company's stock options and providing, on paper at least, more royalties on the future sale of compositors. Rogers personally bought seven thousand shares in the company, further underpinning Twain's investment. The author immediately dashed off a letter to Livy, announcing the changes and exulting, "Our ship is safe in port." He had paced the floor for half an hour, said Twain, before the realization hit him that "I and mine, who were paupers an hour ago, are rich now and our troubles are over." Livy was wintering in Paris with the girls, minus as usual Clara, who had accompanied Twain on his most recent transatlantic voyage and was returning to the bosom of her family on a roundabout route via Berlin. Susy, depressed, unwell, and underweight, admired her sister's spunk. "I would rather be locked up in a box alone for the rest of my life than gather up courage to go out into the world and enjoy myself," she told Clara, "and so you see as I admire you and love you and am infinitely interested in you without being afraid of you—you're just everything in the world to me!"[40]

As usual, Twain's renewed confidence in financial matters was premature. Not even a businessman of Rogers's formidable abilities could salvage all the years of mismanagement and carelessness at the heart of Twain's business dealings. The national panic had seriously rattled the business community, and the new president and board of directors at Mount Morris Bank abruptly called in Twain's loan in April 1894. After only three weeks back with his family in Paris—always his least favorite city—Twain sailed back to America to sift through the wreckage. Foresightedly, he had given Rogers his power of attorney, and the tycoon managed to stave off absolute ruin by taking the arguable legal position that Livy, by virtue of her numerous loans to the publishing company, was her husband's primary creditor, not the bank. She also controlled his lucrative copyrights and owned the Hartford house. Driving a typically hard bargain, Rogers forced the bank to accept fifty cents on the dollar for Twain's outstanding debts. That was the best he could do. On April 18, the same day that *Tom Sawyer Abroad* was published in book form, Webster & Company declared bankruptcy. Fred Hall wept when he signed the papers, but Twain defiantly maintained that he had nothing to be embarrassed about, telling Livy: "As I hadn't done anything to be ashamed of, so I didn't avoid anybody, but talked with everybody I knew on the train."[41]

Livy, the daughter of a successful businessman much like Henry Huttleston Rogers, saw things differently. In a letter to her sister, Susan Crane, who had recently scraped together $5,000 to loan the couple after Twain told her frantically that "the ship is sinking," Livy lamented "the hideous news" of Webster & Company's bankruptcy. "Of course I knew it was likely to come," she wrote, "but I had great hope that it would be in some way averted. I have a perfect horror and heart-sickness over it. I cannot get away from the feeling that business failure means disgrace." Complaining that she had grown old overnight, the former belle of Elmira, New York, added: "I have wrinkled. Most of the time I want to lie down and cry. I feel that my life is an absolute and irretrievable failure." In the wake of Rogers's roaring denunciations of the bank, she insisted that "we want those debts paid and we want to treat them all not only honestly but we want to help them in every possible way. Mr. Rogers has said some caustic and telling things to the creditors. I should think it was the creditors' place to say caustic things to us."[42]

Returning to France in May 1894, Twain learned that Paige had finally signed the disadvantageous contract hammered out by Rogers months earlier. "I am glad Paige has signed," Twain wrote to Rogers. "I wish it was his death-warrant. Well, maybe it is." Seeking distraction, Twain turned his attentions to someone else who offended him, albeit on a literary rather than financial basis—James Fenimore Cooper. He had just read Cooper's novel *The Deerslayer*, said Twain, and found it "the most idiotic book I ever saw." In a devastating comic essay, "Fenimore Cooper's Literary Offenses," he enumerated nineteen rules for writing romantic fiction and charged that Cooper had violated eighteen of them. "Counting these out," Twain reckoned, "what is left is Art." Among Cooper's various offenses were failing to write dialog that sounded like real human beings were speaking it, failing to "use the right word, not its second cousin," failing to invent believable characters, and failing to "say what he is proposing to say, not merely come near it." "There have been daring people in the world who claimed that Cooper could write English," Twain concluded, "but they are all dead now. . . . I feel sure, deep down in my heart, that Cooper wrote about the poorest English that exists in our language."[43]

While Twain was back in the States, fretting over his finances, Susy Clemens had entered a period of steep decline. A long-anticipated visit with Louise Brownell, who was in England pursuing postgraduate studies at Oxford, had not gone well. Louise apparently made it clear that she did not care for Susy in the same perfervid way that Susy cared for her. Angry words were exchanged, and Louise cancelled a return visit to Susy in France. The news, said Susy, made her heart stand still. "I would not, could not dream this would happen and that I should lose you now at the moment of having you again, after all these years of waiting," she wrote to Louise in naked anguish. "It is impossible. I cannot believe it. It cannot be true. Oh no. I cannot, *cannot* bear it. Oh! I have *lost* you and can do nothing. I am so miserably helpless. I love you so. This being apart *breaks* my heart. It is a *nightmare*. It isn't true. My darling, beloved. Please come in to me and let me lie down in your arms, and forget everything but the joy of being near you."[44]

The failed reunion with Louise literally made Susy sick. Her worried parents took her to the coastal spa at La Bourboule-les-Bains, where she lay in bed with a high fever for two days.

When she was well enough to travel they headed back to Paris, but were forced to stop at Rouen, the town where Joan of Arc had been burned at the stake, after Susy's fever suddenly spiked to 104 degrees. Eventually the fever broke and they went on to Paris. Twain entertained thoughts of taking Susy back to Hartford and letting her stay with Joseph and Harmony Twichell. William Dean Howells, who five years earlier had lost his own daughter, Winifred, to the absurd pseudoscience of Dr. Silas Weir Mitchell's enforced rest cure, recommended hypnotism for Susy. A related therapy, the "mental science" of Mary Baker Eddy's Christian Science, was also tried to no particular effect. The usually skeptical Twain became an ardent admirer of the Eddy regimen, advising Susy to "stick to it; don't let anybody talk you out of it." Later he would rethink his position, denouncing Eddy as a "self-seeking and remorseless tyrant" and pointing to her rise as conclusive proof that God had a well-developed sense of humor.[45]

Clara, meanwhile, insisted on taking a mountain-climbing trip with friends through the Swiss Alps rather than settling down in Paris for the winter. "I do not at all at all like it," Livy emphatically repeated to her Hartford friend Alice Day. "I am never satisfied except when we are all together. I have told Clara that this is the last time I shall ever consent to it. I hate all this having a young girl away from her family and it is the last time, I think, except for visits." Twain took a more philosophical view. Noting Jean's fourteenth birthday on July 26, he told Livy: "14 years old, think of that. No children left—I am submerged with women." Except for Clara, they all seemed to be sinking, or at best treading water. Brief encounters with such other European wanderers as Oscar Wilde and Edward, Prince of Wales, provided momentary diversions. Literary-minded Susy was thrilled to run into the former at a restaurant in Ouchy, Switzerland, where she noted with novelistic precision his "soft brown suit with a pale pink flowered vest, a blue necktie and some strange picturesque white flower in his button hole." Twain, introduced to the prince by the English ambassador to Germany, Edward Malet, at Bad Homburg, shared dinner with the heir to Victoria's throne, judging him to be "one of the heartiest & pleasantest Englishmen I have ever seen, absolutely un-English in his quickness in detecting carefully concealed humor." It was a marked improvement from the author's previous judgment of the royal, who he had predicted years earlier "will probably make the worst king that Great Britain has ever had."[46]

Paris, as usual, held few pleasures for Twain, who remained stolidly unimpressed with the City of Light. For some reason, perhaps their casual immorality, Twain simply did not like the French. From the time of his first visit to Paris with the *Quaker City* pilgrims in 1867, he had proved resistant to the city's fabled charms. "Every man in France over 16 years of age & under 116, has at least 1 wife to whom he has never been married," Twain jotted in his notebook. "'Tis a wise Frenchman that knows his own father." And in a savagely Francophobic essay, "The French and the Comanches," he unfavorably compared America's oldest foreign allies to the much-dreaded southwestern Indian tribe that was still attacking settlers as late as 1874. "It must in candor be admitted that in one point the Comanches rank higher than the French," wrote Twain, "in that they do not fight among themselves, whereas a favorite pastime with the French, from time immemorial, has been the burning and slaughtering of each other." The average Frenchman, he judged, "is in some respects the superior of the Chinaman, in others the equal of the Turk and the Dahomian, and in hardly any particular the conspicuous inferior of the Comanche." It was a position from which he never retreated.[47]

On Thanksgiving Day 1894, Rogers reported to Twain that he had lost all faith in the Paige Compositor. It had taken the tycoon considerably less time to arrive at that verdict than the fourteen years and hundreds of thousands of dollars Twain had invested in the venture—perhaps as much as five million dollars in modern terms. Following a failed demonstration in Chicago for the *Times-Herald* newspaper, Rogers had summarily pulled the plug on the machine. In Paris the news hit Twain "like a thunderclap." They were dead broke. In February 1895, on the occasion of their twenty-fifth wedding anniversary, he gave Livy all that he had left—a silver five-franc piece. He now realized that, whatever happened, they could never move back to Hartford, "though it would break the family's hearts if they could believe it." He began making plans to rent out their residence on Farmington Avenue while he, Livy, and their daughters commenced a year-long lecture tour of the northern United States, Canada, and the far-flung "little Englands" that constituted Great Britain's remaining colonial possessions. At Livy's urging, he was determined to pay off their creditors, dollar for dollar. A new speaking tour seemed to offer the best approach. Twain told Rogers that the tour was merely an excuse to get Livy away from the "heavy nervous strains" of the past few months. The Wall Street maven probably saw it for what it was—a purely money-making venture. Whatever the case, Rogers approved wholeheartedly of the scheme.[48]

In March 1895, Twain recrossed the Atlantic to oversee the renting of the Hartford house. At least it would stay more or less in the family: their good friends John and Alice Hooker Day had agreed to rent the house for two hundred dollars a month. Alice Day was a niece of Henry Ward Beecher and Harriet Beecher Stowe; Livy had been a bridesmaid in her wedding twenty-five years earlier. Katy Leary, the family's old housemaid, was put in charge of undraping the furniture, re-laying the carpets, dusting the mantle, fluffing the drapes, and clearing away the cobwebs inside the long-vacant house. Twain had not wanted to go near their old home, he told Livy, "but as soon as I entered this front door I was seized with a furious desire to have us all in this house again & right away, & never go outside the grounds any more forever—certainly never again to Europe." Walking through the house where their daughters had played as children "almost took my breath away. Katy had every rug & picture and ornament & chair exactly where they had always belonged, the place was bewitchingly bright & splendid & homelike & natural, & it seemed as if I had burst awake out of a hellish dream, & had never been away, & that you would come drifting down out of those dainty upper regions with the little children tugging after you."[49]

But in a way he had not awakened, and the truly hellish part of the dream was yet to come.

CHAPTER FOUR

STOWAWAYS WILL BE
PROSECUTED

U nlike his previous trips abroad, Mark Twain's yearlong
lecture tour of the English-speaking colonies of Australia, New Zealand, Ceylon, India, and South Africa was to
be strictly a working trip. Little in the way of casual tourism,
sightseeing, resting, or vacationing was planned. Pleasure was
unanticipated. Twain dreaded "the hard travel and broken rest
inseparable from lecturing," he told his nephew and namesake
Samuel Moffett. Still, in his current financial state, it was un-
avoidable. With Livy urging him to pay their debts in full, a
speaking tour was his best available option. "I could have
supported myself comfortably by writing," Twain said, "but
writing is too slow for the demands that I have to meet; therefore I have begun to lecture my way around the world." He was
blunter with the plain-spoken Rogers. "I've got to mount the
platform next fall or starve," he said.[1]

In formulating his plans for an around-the-world tour,
Twain was encouraged personally and professionally by his
fellow celebrity Henry Morton Stanley. The two men were

much alike. Each had started out dirt-poor, made his way through the world at an early age, and worked as a cub newspaper reporter in Missouri. Each had served in, and deserted from, the Confederate Army, although Stanley had gone Twain one better by also serving in the Union Navy. Each was an accomplished lecturer, bon vivant, and much-sought-after dinner guest. Each had a generous view of himself. Returning from America in early 1895, Twain stopped off in London for two days to confer with Stanley about the upcoming tour. While he was there, Stanley hosted a gala dinner in Twain's honor at his magnificent house off Downing Street. "He had an extraordinary assemblage of brains and fame there to meet me—thirty or forty (both sexes) at dinner, and more than a hundred came in after dinner," Twain reported. "There were cabinet ministers, ambassadors, admirals, generals, canons, Oxford professors, novelists, playwrights, poets, and a number of people equipped with rank *and* brain. I told some yarns and made some speeches." More concretely, Stanley put Twain in touch with the explorer's personal travel promoter, Australian impresario Carlyle Greenwood Smythe, who had also managed speaking tours for Sir Arthur Conan Doyle and Roald Amundsen. Smythe would handle the grand colonial part of Twain's tour. American agent James B. Pond, who had put together the "Twins of Genius" tour for Twain and George Washington Cable a decade earlier, would handle arrangements for a preliminary tour across the upper Midwest, Pacific Northwest, and Canada.[2]

The family received the news of Twain's travel plans with some regret. "After a long period of homesickness," Clara later recalled, "my sisters and I had become attached to life abroad" and were therefore "aghast at the prospect of leaving" Europe. That was probably true for Clara, but less true for Susy and

Jean, each of whom had her own reasons for wanting to return to the United States. Susy wanted to see Louise Brownell again; Jean wanted to attend her mother's old finishing school in Elmira, New York. Livy, for her part, remained hopeful that once the tour was over, "we shall be able to settle down in our own home and live there." Twain didn't have the heart to tell her otherwise. The family sailed for home on May 11 on the S.S. *Paris,* having last touched American soil together almost exactly four years earlier. After a brief layover in New York City, they went to Susan Crane's farm in Elmira for the next two months. Twain, tortured by gout and carbuncles, spent much of his time in bed, planning his worldwide tour while flat on his back.[3]

The tour would begin with a twenty-three-city tour of the Great Lakes region and follow a northern route along the American-Canadian border, ending with a series of appearances in British Columbia. From there the party would sail to Honolulu, stopping over in Twain's beloved Hawaii before continuing on to Australia. Pond and his wife, Margaret, would accompany them on the North American part of the tour; Smythe would pick up the party in Sydney, Australia, for the rest of the journey. The North American route would follow the well-grooved byways of the Lyceum circuit. The heyday of the self-educating movement had passed, but remnants of the mid-century craze still remained, and Twain hoped to tap into them during the opening phase of his tour. Most of the best-known lyceum orators had passed from the scene, including Twain's one-time inspiration, Henry Ward Beecher, but the indefatigable Mary Baker Eddy was still carrying the flag for a variable assortment of faith healers, spirit knockers, temperature lecturers, abstinence promoters, health food advocates, foreign traveloguers, and outright

charlatans—all of which she was herself. Experienced performer that he was, Twain brought his own set of preoccupa-
tions to the stage. He was playing a heightened version of
himself—the American Vandal in late middle age.

From his sickbed, where he reported that he was "perishing
with idleness," Twain carefully planned his stage performance.
As usual, he would not give a formal lecture or reading, but
present a seemingly casual after-dinner discussion among
friends. He billed the show "Mark Twain at Home." He would
vary the talks depending on his mood and his reading of the
audience on any particular night, but he expected to deliver
variations of such dependable crowd favorites as "The Celebrated Jumping Frog of Calaveras County," "The Golden Arm,"
"Jim Baker's Blue Jay Yarn," "The Genuine Mexican Plug," "The
Awful German Language," selections from *Huckleberry Finn*,
and, as a special treat, quotations from the as-yet-unpublished
Personal Recollections of Joan of Arc.

While Pond and Smythe finalized the touring schedule,
family members made their own travel plans. Susy and Jean
would stay in Elmira with their Aunt Susan, but the ever-ready
Clara would accompany her parents on the trip. "Livy & Clara
go with me around the world, but Susie refuses because she
hates the sea," Twain told Orion, adding that Jean was scheduled to enroll at her mother's alma mater and could not spare
the time from school. There may have been another, unstated
reason for leaving Jean behind. Despite being something of a
tomboy—she loved hiking and riding horses—Jean had been
in delicate health for much of her life. She had contracted
scarlet fever when she was two, and a serious but undiagnosed
illness had felled her when she was ten. While in Europe, her
parents had noticed alarming changes in Jean's behavior. The
previously good-natured girl had grown increasingly sullen

and withdrawn. Without knowing what, exactly, was wrong with her, it was decided for everyone's sake to leave her behind. It would prove to be a wise choice: Jean suffered the first of a series of epileptic convulsions while her parents and Clara were abroad. She would never be entirely well again.[4]

As for Susy, her supposed hatred of sea travel provided a convenient excuse for her to escape, at age twenty-three, the familial prison. Despite their recent unspecified quarrel, she was looking forward to reuniting with Louise Brownell, who was also back in the States, taking postgraduate studies at Bryn Mawr. When her parents and Clara pulled out of the Elmira train station on the evening of July 14, bound for Twain's first scheduled appearance in Cleveland, Susy waved good-bye from the platform beneath the glare of electric lights. "She was brimming with life and the joy of it," her father recalled a year later. "That is what I saw; & it was what her mother saw through her tears." There would be more, and bitterer, tears to come.[5]

The world into which Twain, his wife, and their twenty-one-year-old daughter were venturing in mid-1895 was very different from the orderly world he had encountered during the *Innocents Abroad* tour three decades earlier. While Europe itself was relatively peaceful, storing up energy for the self-inflicted cataclysm to come in the summer of 1914, other parts of the world were increasingly unstable. In South Africa, their final destination, the discovery of gold in the Transvaal region had brought English fortune-hunters pouring into the country, angering the native Boers and quickening the pace for the second war in fourteen years between Great Britain and the stolid burghers. There had even been harsh words between the United States and Great Britain over a boundary dispute in Venezuela. Because his world tour amounted to an extended transit of the British Empire's distant colonial corners, Twain may have entertained doubts about the friendliness of his reception. If so, he kept them to himself.

Before departing, the author tried out his act on two literally captive audiences. The first came during a brief visit to New York City to testify in a creditor's suit in the state supreme court. On July 12, Twain appeared before seven hundred inmates at the Randall's Island House of Refuge, a glorified reform school. His comic lecture on moral regeneration did not go over well with the miscreant youths, Twain reported to Rogers. "Oh, but wasn't it a comical defeat," he said, "delivering a grown-folks' lecture to a sucking-bottle nursery!" Two nights later, back in Elmira, Twain appeared before the inmates at the local reformatory, where he got a slightly better reception, perhaps because he was well-known locally to the boys. He may even have recognized some of the hardened apple-stealers, window-breakers, truants, and petty sneak thieves among the upturned faces in the crowd.[6]

Twain's first formal tour appearance was a nostalgic return engagement in Cleveland, hometown of his old *Innocents Abroad* companion Mary Fairbanks, where he had debuted his American Vandal tour in 1868. Mother Fairbanks wasn't on hand for his new performance; she and her newspaper publisher husband, Abel, had moved to Omaha, Nebraska, several years earlier after Abel had undertaken a series of misconceived financial investments and lost control of the *Cleveland Herald*. It was just as well that Fairbanks wasn't there that night—the performance at the Stillman Music Hall was a fiasco. Someone had the bright idea of putting two hundred local newsboys on stage behind Twain (the performance was billed as a benefit for the boys' home). Predictably, the cheeky crowd of Ragged Dicks and Tattered Toms stole the show, squirming and mugging in the ninety-degree heat as uncomfortably as Tom Sawyer had fidgeted in Sunday school. "I got *started* magnificently," Twain told Rogers, "but inside of half an hour the scuffling boys had the audience's maddened attention and I saw it was a gone case; so I skipped a third of my program and quit." The announced crowd of 4,200 seemed to find the show hilarious, even if the boys didn't. The *Cleveland Plain Dealer* reported the next day that the audience had been "convulsed" by his moral regeneration theme.[7]

From Cleveland the company, including the Ponds, headed northwest by steamer across Lakes Erie and Huron to Michigan, where Twain made four appearances at the exclusive Mackinac Island summer resort. Decked out in a flat-topped, black-visored captain's hat—he would wear the hat invariably throughout his journey—the old riverboat pilot enjoyed the onboard luxury of the *Northland,* a luxury vessel that he said made its European counterparts seem like "a garbage barge by comparison." Passing through the narrows at Port Huron, Twain was hailed from shore by "groups of summer-dressed young people, waving flags and handkerchiefs, and firing cannon—our boat replying with four toots of the whistle and now and then a cannon." The young people, outlined against the green-and-brown countryside and the sinking sun, made for "the perfection of voyaging," he said. They were the direct forebears of Ernest Hemingway's vacationing "summer people" up in Michigan, and Twain even made an appearance in Petoskey, not far from the Hemingways' future vacation cottage, Windemere, on Traverse Bay.[8]

It was an unusually hot summer in the Great Lakes region, but Twain appeared before gratifyingly large crowds in Minneapolis, St. Paul, and Winnipeg. A Canadian reporter for the *Winnipeg Daily Tribune* gave readers a good description of the world-famous writer at age fifty-nine: "A short, slightly built man, with a heavy mass of iron gray hair, a fierce looking mustache, wide, open, massive forehead, bushy eyebrows, under which scowl at you a couple of fierce eyes, firm looking chin, but alas, with the fatal droop thereto so common with impulsive, easy-going natures." It was tribute to Twain's acting ability—few people had ever described him as easygoing.[9]

Arriving in Duluth at nine in the evening of July 22 after an unexpected delay at the locks between Lakes Huron and Superior, Twain and Pond rushed directly from gangplank into a carriage, bound for the First Methodist Church, where a crowd of 1,250 fans had been waiting for more than an hour in 100-degree heat. Hurrying onto stage, Twain deadpanned, "I am very glad, indeed, that my strenuous efforts did succeed in getting me here just in time." Ordinarily, Twain avoided performing in churches, where he found audiences reluctant to laugh. That wasn't a problem the next night at the Grand Opera House in Sault Sainte Marie, where a woman in the audience suffered a minor heart attack brought on, it was said, by convulsive laughing. Sharp-eyed Clara carefully noted the effect her father had on the audience. "Father knew the full value of a pause and had the courage to make a long one when required for a big effect," she wrote. "And his inimitable drawling speech, which he often lost in private life, greatly increased the humorous effect on the stage. People in the house, including men, got hysterical. Cries that resembled the cries of pain could often be heard."[10]

Everywhere he went along the U.S.-Canadian border, Twain found large, affectionate crowds. His travel notes brimmed with pleasure at his reception: "Beautiful audience. Compact, intellectual & dressed in perfect taste," he noted from Butte, Montana. "Splendid house full to the roof," he said of Portland, Oregon. "Big house & great time," he said from Tacoma. "Splendid house most splendid time," he reported from Seattle. From Crookston, Minnesota, he wrote to Rogers: "Thus far I have had more people in three opera houses than they've ever had in them before, winter or summer, & they swelter there with admirable patience; they all stay & see me through." At Fort Missoula he was met by an honor guard of the all-black Twenty-fifth U.S. Infantry and serenaded by a thirty-piece band. At Victoria, British Columbia, the Canadian governor-general and his family came to see him. The band played "God Save the Queen," which Twain chose to interpret as a tribute to him. Not even a series of heavy forest fires blanketing Washington and British Columbia fazed him. "I don't mind," he told an apologetic delegation of city fathers in Olympia, Washington. "I am a perpetual smoker myself." And to a reporter in Tacoma, he joked, "Really, your scenery is wonderful. It is quite out of sight."[11]

Scores of Americans, touched by Twain's gallant vow to repay his debts, had begun sending him letters of support and condolence, some containing dollar bills that he sent back, regrettably, with his thanks. "My eyes have been opened by this lecture trip across the continent," he told relatives. "I find I have twenty-five friends in America where I thought I had only one. I shall be out of debt a long way sooner than I was supposing a month ago." He added, "In my preliminary run through the smaller cities on the northern route, I have found a reception the cordiality of which has touched my heart and made me feel how small a thing money is in comparison to friendship."[12]

Occasionally the other, less attractive side of Twain showed through in flashes of anger directed at Major Pond. At Crookston, Minnesota, the morning after a well-received performance, Twain and his family rose before dawn to catch the scheduled four a.m. train to Great Falls, Montana. They arrived at the railway station to find a note pinned to the bulletin board informing them that the train was running eighty minutes late. Twain growled that he was paying Pond to arrange their travel, not to wait around railway stations at four o'clock in the morning. He insisted that Pond fulfill his contract to the letter by wheeling Twain around the station on a baggage truck. Clara, using the 1888 model Kodak box camera that Pond had brought along to record the great man's tour, snapped a photo showing the major doing just that, pushing the cart while Twain, overcoat drawn up to his ears, dangled his feet over the end. In the surviving photo Livy looks on, hand to her face, in seeming embarrassment, and Mrs. Pond, seen from a distance, appears rigid and unamused. The ghostly shadow of Clara falls across the foreground.

Twice more, as reported by Pond, the talent exploded at the handler. In Anaconda, Montana, outside Butte, the manager of the Evans Opera House found himself short by sixty dollars of the amount he had contracted to pay Twain. Pond, in his role as agent, "took what he had, and *all* he had." When Twain learned what Pond had done, he exploded. "And you took the last cent that poor fellow had!" he roared. "Send him a hundred dollars, and if you can't afford to stand your share, charge it all to me. I'm not going around robbing poor men

who are disappointed in their calculations as to my commer-
cial value. I'm poor, but I don't want to get money in that way."
At a subsequent show in Seattle, Twain uncharacteristically
walked off the stage when the audience kept filing into the the-
ater after his performance had begun. Thinking he was ill,
Pond rushed over to Twain, who was white-faced with anger.
"You'll never play a trick like this on me again," said Twain.
"Look at that damned audience. It isn't half in yet." Pond explained that the city trolleys ran only every half hour, which
mollified Twain enough to get him back on stage.[13]

Whether or not Twain realized it, he was in the presence of a
legitimate war hero. Three years later Pond would be awarded
a very tardy Medal of Honor for his actions as a young lieutenant in the Third Wisconsin Cavalry at the Battle of Baxter
Springs, Kansas, in October 1863. (His brother George would
also receive the Medal of Honor, making them one of only
five pairs of brothers to share the nation's highest military
honor.) At Baxter Springs, in the extreme southeastern corner
of the state, Pond had run athwart of William Clarke Quantrill's pitiless guerrillas, who were fresh from their sack of
Lawrence, Kansas. The guerrillas, commanded by longtime
Quantrill lieutenant Dave Poole, fell on Pond's men as they
were assembling for breakfast outside the walls of their
earth-and-log fort. As the terrified Federals broke and ran,
the guerrillas rode them down, shooting many of them in the
head after they had surrendered. Only Pond's quick action in
wheeling out a howitzer and firing several rounds into the
horsemen's ranks prevented an absolute massacre. Twain had

gone West to avoid this sort of warfare in 1861, and it is possible that the Confederate raiders that day included some of his old Marion Rangers compatriots.

Despite the outbursts, Pond retained a genuine fondness for Twain, recording his adventures with the novelist in a number of black-and-white photographs and a 1900 reminiscence, *Eccentricities of Genius*. Pond also seems to have had something of a crush on Clara, whom he somewhat generously described as "the loveliest girl I ever saw." She was not quite that, but she was undoubtedly the prettiest of Twain's three daughters, with her mother's dark good looks and heart-shaped face. Pond took a number of photographs of the traveling party with Clara featured prominently in the middle, invariably wearing a straw boater and a glittering smile. She was enjoying herself greatly. In Spokane, Pond dined with Clara and Livy in the dining room of Spokane House, the largest hotel in the state. As they passed through the parlor, Clara impulsively sat down at the piano and began playing a Chopin nocturne. Her long years of European studies came to the fore. Like a proud stepfather—Twain had remained in his room, resting—Pond described the young woman's triumph: "Stealthily guests came in from dinner and sat breathlessly in remote parts of the boundless room listening to a performance that would have done credit to any great pianist. Never did I witness a more beautiful sight than this sweet brunette unconsciously holding a large audience of charmed listeners. If it was not one of the supreme moments of her mother's life, who saw and heard her, then I have guessed wrong."[14]

On August 15 the party arrived at Vancouver, jumping-off point for their Pacific crossing. They were chagrined to learn that their ship, the Canadian-Australian mail packet *Warrimoo*, had run aground while passing through Juan de Fuca

Strait near Victoria. Repairs would take a week. Pond took advantage of the delay by booking another engagement for Twain in Victoria, where he performed for the Canadian governor-general. At one point the audience laughed in the wrong place, momentarily throwing Twain off his game. He learned later that a kitten had walked across the stage behind him. Pressed by Rogers, who had been hearing some grumbling from the author's creditors in New York, Twain released a statement to the *New York Times* denying that he was lecturing for his own benefit. "The law recognizes no mortgage on a man's brains, and a merchant who has given up all he has may take advantage of the rules of insolvency and start free again for himself," said Twain, reiterating his intention to repay all his debts "as fast as I can." He had already sent Rogers five thousand dollars in tour profits to put toward his bill.[15]

Twain's nephew Samuel Moffett, then working as an editorial writer on William Randolph Hearst's *San Francisco Examiner*, ran up the coast to see them off. Taking the pen literally out of his nephew's hand, Twain addressed an open letter to the newspaper. In it he engaged in a little good-natured, spirit-lifting braggadocio. "Perhaps it is a little immodest in me to talk about paying my debts, when by my own confession I am blandly getting ready to unload them on the whole English-speaking world," Twain wrote. "Lecturing is gymnastics, chest-expander, medicine, mind healer, blues destroyer, all in one. I am twice as well as I was when I started out. I have gained nine pounds in twenty-eight days, and expect to weigh six hundred before January. My wife & daughter are accumulating health & strength nearly as fast as I am. When we reach home a year hence I think we can exhibit as freaks."[16]

On August 23 the repairs were completed and the *War-rimoo* prepared to sail into the sunset toward Honolulu and Australia. In preparation for departure, Pond reported, Twain had purchased three thousand Manila cheroots and four pounds of Durham smoking tobacco to tide him over on the month-long crossing. "If perpetual smoking ever kills a man," Pond wrote, "I don't see how Mark Twain can expect to escape." At this point the Ponds left the traveling party. Despite some private reservations about the agent, Twain gave him a copy of *Roughing It*, which was inscribed: "Here ends one of the smoothest and pleasantest trips across the continent that any group of five has ever made." Pond took a last photo of the family posed at the rail of the ship above a posted notice: "ALL STOWAWAYS WILL BE PROSECUTED AT HONOLULU AND RETURNED TO THIS PORT." In the picture, Twain is smoking a long pipe, Livy is smiling tightly like the small-town librarian she increasingly resembled, and Clara is beaming delightedly between her parents, whom she has all to herself for the duration of the voyage.[17]

The prospect of an extended sea cruise rallied Twain's spirits. "We moved westward about mid-afternoon over a rippled and sparkling summer sea," he would remember in the book he wrote about his tour, *Following the Equator*. "The voyage would furnish a three-week holiday, with hardly a break in it. We had the whole Pacific Ocean in front of us, with nothing to do but do nothing and be comfortable." That was something of a stretch. The *Warrimoo* was a long step down from the luxurious transatlantic steamers Twain and his family were used to taking. An overabundance of rats and cockroaches swarmed the decks, and the haughty British stewards were slow to respond to passengers' requests. The family's bathroom flooded. Meals were typical shipboard fare, "furnished by the Deity and cooked by the devil." The captain's little dog, with full run of the ship, freely left its calling card strewn about the decks.[18]

As it was, the ship's captain was sailing home under a cloud. Thirty-four-year-old R. E. Arundell, on his maiden command voyage, had nearly sunk the *Warrimoo* five miles south of Vancouver Island when he ran onto a reef in the dark. Only the comparatively calm seas and winds had prevented a disaster of the first magnitude. As a result, Arundell was facing a maritime hearing once they reached Sydney. The looming legal proceedings did not influence the captain's mood, and Twain found the handsome young Englishman "polite and courteous even to courtliness." The captain had no vices, said Twain, neither drinking nor smoking, and spent most of his down time in the ladies' saloon, singing and playing the piano or sharing a friendly game of whist. "The captain, with his gentle nature, his polish, his sweetness, his moral and verbal purity, seemed pathetically out of place in his rude and autocratic vocation," wrote Twain, who as a former Mississippi River pilot presumably had not labored under such gentlemanly constraints.[19]

One week out from port the *Warrimoo* steamed into Honolulu harbor. It was shortly before midnight, and the lights of the city sparkled across the water. Spectral Diamond Head loomed, announcing to Twain "those islands which to me were Paradise, a Paradise which I had been longing all those years to see again. Not any other thing in the world could have stirred me as the sight of that great rock did." Memories of long horseback rides and "pictures—pictures—pictures" rose in Twain's mind. He thought that he "might go ashore and never leave." Much to his chagrin, a cholera outbreak had struck the island, and *Warrimoo*'s passengers were quarantined aboard ship. Five people already had died on shore. In the end the epidemic, mild by Hawaiian standards, claimed a total of sixty-two victims, most of them native Kanakas. Twain's previously scheduled appearance was cancelled, and five hundred dollars in advance ticket sales was refunded. The author consoled himself with happy thoughts of sharks playing around the boat, "laying for Christians." After two fruitless days of waiting, the ship steamed out of port, bound for the Fiji Islands. Twain would never come that close to paradise again.[20]

On September 5, the *Warrimoo* crossed the equator. "I think I would rather see it than any other thing in the world," Twain joked. A photo presumably taken by a fellow passenger shows the author and an avid-looking Clara gazing at the blue ribbon of the equator. Livy sits behind them by the rail. Twain noted with relief that there were none of the customary equator-crossing high jinks. "We had no fool ceremonies, no fantastics, no horseplay," he wrote. "All that sort of thing has gone out. In old times a sailor, dressed as Neptune, used to come in over the bows, with his suite, and lather up and shave everybody who was crossing the equator for the first time, and then cleanse the unfortunates by swinging them from the yard-arm and ducking them three times in the sea. This was considered funny. Nobody knows why."[21]

Nine days out from Honolulu the *Warrimoo* made landfall at Suva, capital of the Fiji Islands, which reminded Twain of Hawaii. His arrival in Suva, Twain said, put him in mind of "a pleasant book" he had recently read by a South Seas captain named Wawn describing the practice of "recruiting" workers for Australian plantations from Fiji and surrounding islands. Twain called it "plain simple manstealing." At a price of twenty pounds per man, the recruiters grabbed young islanders and transported them to Queensland, where they typically served three years of more or less involuntary servitude, with an option to work another term. "One can understand why the recruiter is fond of the business," Twain observed. "The thing that is not clear is, what there is about it all to persuade the recruit. He is young and brisk; life at home in his beautiful island is one lazy, long holiday to him. . . . In Queensland he must get up at dawn and work from eight to twelve hours a day in the canefields—in a much hotter climate than he is used to—and get less than four shillings a week for it." The answer, said Twain, could be found in a missionary's pamphlet: "When he comes from his home he is a savage, pure and simple. He feels no shame at his nakedness and want of adornment. When he returns home he does so as well dressed, sporting a Waterbury watch, collars, ruffs, boots, and jewelry." The recruit had also learned how to swear, Twain added, an art form in itself—"and art is long, as the poet says."[22]

On September 16, the *Warrimoo* steamed into the harbor at Sydney, Australia. An enterprising journalist named Herbert Low from the *Sydney Morning Herald* commandeered a launch and puttered out to interview the famous author before he made it to shore. Bobbing alongside the ship, Low hollered up at Twain, who leaned over the rail to respond. Low wanted to know what Twain thought about Australia. "I don't know," said Twain. "I'm ready to adopt any [ideas]

that seem handy. I don't believe in going outside accepted
views." He announced that he was planning to write a book
about the country and was going to get started right away,
since "you know so much more of a country when you haven't
seen it than when you have." Low's enterprising interview,
published the next day, was mostly fiction, as the journalist
admitted several years later. "After a few attempts at questions, I gave it up," said Low. "I could neither be heard nor
hear. I bawled out, 'Mr. Twain, I'll have to imagine this interview,' to which he screamed, 'Go ahead, my boy; I've been
there myself!'"[23]

The family, greeted by tour promoter Carlyle Greenwood
Smythe, checked into the ornate, seven-story Australia Hotel.
Smythe had papered the town with photos of the author and
had sent so many floral arrangements to the hotel that Clara
jokingly wondered if someone had died. Inadvertently, Twain
immediately found himself embroiled in a series of controversies, all of his own making to one degree or another. The first
involved a standing challenge to a duel from French journalist
Leon Paul Blouet, who wrote for Australian newspapers under
the Anglicized nom de plume Max O'Rell. Blouet had issued
the challenge after reading Twain's unfavorable review of
fellow Frenchman Paul Bourget's book *Outre-Mer*, about his
travels in America. In his essay, "What Paul Bourget Thinks
of Us," Twain had let his simmering Francophobia show
through, claiming that the French had nothing to teach Americans, either railroading or steamboating or novel writing. As
for government, he said, the French system merely stood for
"Liberty, Equality, Fraternity, Nobility, Democracy, [and]
Adultery."[24]

Blouet, answering for his countrymen, reported that France
could teach America "all the higher pursuits of life, and there

is more artistic feeling and refinement in a street of French workingmen than in many avenues inhabited by American millionaires." Furthermore, said Blouet, making a direct, unsubtle personal attack on Twain, "In France, a man who had settled his fortune on his wife to avoid meeting his creditors would be refused admission in any decent society. Many a Frenchman has blown his brains out rather than declare himself a bankrupt." It was a low blow, particularly since Twain had come halfway around the world to pay off his creditors. Nevertheless, he declined to duel with Blouet. "I can disgrace myself nearer home, if I felt so inclined, than by going out to have a row with a Frenchman," Twain told reporters. "The fact of the matter is I think Max O'Rell wanted an advertisement, and thought the best way to get it was to draw me. But I'm far too old a soldier for that sort of thing." That was true, but when Twain continued to rail against the Frenchman as "a writer of no rank whatever," Livy gently interceded by placing "a delicate hand" over her husband's mouth.[25]

Unfortunately for Twain, Livy was not around when he made his next gaffe. Asked what he thought about Bret Harte, Twain teed off on his old California friend and companion. "His forte is pathos," Twain told a correspondent for the *Melbourne Argus*, "but there should be no pathos which does not come out of a man's heart. He has no heart, except his name, and I consider he has produced nothing that is genuine. He is artificial." The two had become friends soon after Twain had arrived in California from Nevada in 1864, but later had clashed over their planned collaboration on a play based on Harte's popular poem, "The Heathen Chinee." Besides creative differences, Harte had angered Twain by drinking heavily during a visit to the refined homestead in Hartford and inadvertently insulting Livy (or at least her furnishings). Twain, in turn, angered Harte by refusing to loan him money, then loaning exactly the same amount to another friend. In one of his best-known witticisms, Twain would say of his erstwhile collaborator: "Bret Harte was one of the pleasantest men I have ever known. He was also one of the unpleasantest men I have ever known." Twain may not have been aware that Harte's work remained enormously popular in Australia, where numerous dramatic versions of his stories were regularly performed before large, admiring crowds. Outraged editorials and letters followed Twain's off-the-cuff remarks, and one journalist hoist Twain on his own petard by speculating that the author, in criticizing Harte, had been motivated by "a mild form of advertising." Livy suggested that she sit in on her husband's interviews and read them in proof before they were set in print.[26]

A third controversy was political in nature. Opposing party leaders in Sydney and New South Wales were locked in an electoral feud involving the knotty issue of free trade versus protectionism. Sir Henry Parkes of New South Wales, the grand old man of Australian politics, had long supported free trade, but lately had reversed his position. Henry Reid, representing the shipping interests of Sydney, had won a narrow victory by arguing against trade barriers. Twain for some reason felt compelled to comment on the issue. Applying his best financial wisdom to the subject of free trade, he observed, "Surely it is wrong that on the west coast of the United States they should be compelled to bring their iron from the east when they might get it landed at a much lower price direct from foreign ships at their own door." He found it "hard to believe that [Parkes] could make the bitter speeches that he had heard attributed to him." Parkes, showing no hard feelings, later hosted Twain and his family for lunch, but the *Australian Star*, Sydney's leading protectionist newspaper, observed tartly that Twain, in his eternal struggle for international copyright enforcement, "wants plenty of protection for his own books."[27]

The various controversies did not hurt Twain at the box office, and he made four well-attended performances in Sydney. One of the best descriptions of Twain in action on stage was provided by the local correspondent for the *London Sketch:*

> Mark Twain steals unobtrusively onto the platform, dressed in the regulation evening-clothes, with the trouser-pockets cut high up, into which he occasionally dives both hands. He bows with a quick dignity to the roaring cheers which greet him at every "At Home." Then, with natural, unaffected gesture, and with scarcely any prelude, he gets underway with his first story. He talks in short sentences, with a peculiar smack of the lips at the end of each. He speaks slowly, lazily, and wearily, as of a man dropping off to sleep, rarely raising his voice above a conversational tone; but it has that characteristic nasal sound which penetrates to the back of the largest building. With the exception of an occasional curious trot, as when recounting his buck-jumping experiences, Mark Twain stands perfectly still in one place during the whole of the time he is talking to the audience. He rarely moves his arms, unless it is to adjust his spectacles or to show by action how a certain thing was done. His characteristic attitude is to stand quite still, with the right arm across the abdomen and the left resting on it and supporting his chin. In this way

he talks on for nearly two hours; and, while the audience is laughing uproariously, he never by any chance
relapses into a smile.[28]

From Sydney the party proceeded to Melbourne, on the
country's extreme southern coast, traveling seventeen hours
by train through sheep-raising farms that seemed to Twain
to be the size of Rhode Island. Changing cars at Albury,
Twain saw in the hazy distance the Blue Mountains, which a
local resident told him were not really mountains at all, but
piles of dead rabbits. It might well have been true. The long-
eared rabbits had been imported to Australia years earlier,
along with the various pickpockets, cutpurses, strong-arm
men, and confidence tricksters who comprised the majority
of the nation's first transported settlers. Despite the best
efforts of the Australian government, the pernicious rabbits
had overrun millions of acres of sheep- and cattle-grazing
countryside. Bounty hunters killed twenty-seven million rabbits per year, always careful to leave enough alive to quickly
repopulate and thus preserve the hunters' livelihood. When a
member of the ruling legislature called for a formal proposal
outlawing rabbits, another member said they might just as
well propose a bill for the extermination of fleas. In New
South Wales, a 15,000-mile rabbit-proof fence had recently
been erected, but proved inefficient. Twain sympathized, but
told a local reporter that "I don't like to see the distinctive
animals of a country killed off." He had personally spent several hours trying to make the distinctive Australian bird, the
kookaburra, laugh. "It sat on a tree, and I stood looking at it,"
Twain recounted. "But it wouldn't laugh for me. I tried to

make it laugh; indeed I did, but it respectfully declined." Livy, watching the efforts, observed mildly, "Probably it didn't think you were funny."[29]

Twain gave five performances in Melbourne, the last one added by popular demand. The reception was gratifying but exhausting, and Twain developed a new carbuncle on his leg that had to be lanced and dosed with opium. Two planned appearances in Bendigo were cancelled, and the author spent the next eight days in bed in his hotel room, where—shades of Oscar Wilde—he found that "the study of wall-paper patterns, even if they are various, is not hilarious enjoyment." Livy and Clara maintained a busy social schedule, serving as guests of honor at a high-society tea party at which Clara charmed everyone with two piano solos. Twain's middle daughter was interviewed by a reporter from the *South Australian Register,* who found her "a lively, self-possessed, frank, chatty young lady." Clara allowed that she preferred horses to bicycles. Publicity-shy Livy was startled to see their likenesses on display in a Melbourne shop window. Twain personally wrote the proprietor and asked that the photos be taken down. "My wife," said Twain, "is so troubled by the exhibition of her & our daughter's photographs that for her sake I wrote to ask you to remove it. She is not used to publicity & cannot get reconciled to it."[30]

From Melbourne the family moved on to Adelaide, riding the last several miles in an open carriage with American consul A. C. Murphy, who helpfully described the flora and fauna along the way despite "knowing nothing whatever about them." Twain reported that everything he saw on the ride was unfamiliar to him except grass, which he had seen before. He professed admiration for the religious variety of southern Australia, counting (he claimed) some 89,271 members of the

Church of England, 47,179 Catholics, 23,328 Lutherans, 18,906 Presbyterians, 17,547 Baptists, 299 Muslims, 100 Quakers, 59 Agnostics, 53 Buddhists, 14 Deists, 258 Free-thinkers, 30 Pagans, 9 Infidels, 3 Pantheists, 2 Zoroastrians, a Shaker, a Hussite, and 398 Christians.[31]

Everyone flourished in Australia, said Twain, except aborigines, whose population had declined by 80 percent in twenty years. One creative stationmaster, noted Twain, had recently fed some unsuspecting aborigines an arsenic-laced plum pudding on Christmas Day. "The poisoned pudding," said the author, "smirches the good names of our civilization, whereas one of the old harsher measures would have had no such effect because usage has made those methods familiar to us and innocent." He enumerated such methods as chaining and starving natives to death, burning them at the stake, hunting them with dogs and guns "for an afternoon's sport," enslaving and working them to death. The poisoner, said Twain, "is almost the only pioneering representative of civilization in history who has risen above the prejudices of his caste and his heredity and tried to introduce the element of mercy into the superior race's dealings with the savage." In a conclusion that would become famous in his post-colonial writings, Twain observed, "There are many humorous things in the world; among them the white man's notion that he is less savage than the other savages."[32]

Twain double-backed to Melbourne through sheep-raising, gold-mining country, giving a series of lectures in little towns along the way. By the time the family left Australia for Tasmania and New Zealand on October 31, he had given twenty-two performances in ten separate locations, netting another seventy-five hundred dollars to send to Rogers to pay back creditors. Boarding the Union Line steamship *Mararoa*,

Twain met with reporters in his pilot's cap, smoking his invariable cigar. He was "downright sorry to leave Australia," he said, "because all my impressions of this country and of the people are of a pleasant sort." When one of the journalists referred to *The Innocents Abroad*, its author sighed: "That was a splendid trip. Everything was fresh and new then: everything is old now." The newness of travel had long since worn off.[33]

Brushing past the coast of Tasmania, the family spent a pleasant few hours in the island capital of Hobart. Livy and Clara shared "a glass of wine & a piece of cake (or kike as the Australians say)" with a local hostess, while Twain indulged his lifelong fascination with jails and convicts, visiting a refuge for the indigent. Reflecting the fact that Tasmania had been a "convict-dump," the refuge included 263 ex-convicts, 81 of them female. The brief glimpse of Tasmania induced Twain to decry the total extermination of the island's native population by "fugitive gangs of the hardiest and choicest human devils the world has seen." The local convict-hunters, called "blackgrabbers," had managed to reduce Tasmania's aborigine population to three hundred men, women, and children, and the government herded them behind a sort of human rabbit-proof fence in an isolate corner of the island. Civic leaders, noted Twain, had spent thirty thousand pounds to contain a grand total of sixteen tribesmen. "These were indeed wonderful people, the natives," wrote Twain. "They ought not to have been wasted. They should have been crossed with the Whites. It would have improved the Whites and done the Natives no harm." The last surviving Tasmanian aborigine, a woman named Truganini, died and was buried

with great ceremony in 1876. A year later members of the
Royal Society of Tasmania dug up her skeleton and exhibited
it in a museum. In 2002, hair and skin samples from the un-
fortunate woman were discovered in the collections of the
Royal College of Surgeons in London. They were returned.[34]

Moving on to New Zealand, the party landed at Bluff, on
the extreme southern end of South Island, and proceeded up
the east coast. They made landfall on Guy Fawkes Day, November 5, when England and her colonies traditionally celebrate the foiling of a plot by Catholic militants to blow up the
House of Lords and assassinate King James I. Twain wondered about the absence of a similarly grand celebration in
America. "In America we have no annual supreme day; no day
whose approach makes the whole nation glad," he wrote. "We
have the Fourth of July, and Christmas, and Thanksgiving.
Eight grown Americans out of ten dread the coming of the
Fourth, with its pandemonium and its perils, and they rejoice
when it is gone—if still alive. The approach of Christmas brings
harassment and dread to many excellent people. They have
to buy a cart-load of presents, and they never know what to
buy to hit the various tastes; they put in three weeks of hard
and anxious work, and when Christmas morning comes they
are so dissatisfied with the result, and so disappointed that
they want to sit down and cry." As for Thanksgiving, he observed, "The Thankfulness is not so general. Two-thirds of the
nation have always had hard luck and a hard time during the
year, and this has a calming effect upon their enthusiasm."[35]

In New Zealand, Twain found himself in a land of "Junior
Englands," towns that competed with each other to be the
most English. Christchurch, home to a famous boys' school,
was said to be the most Anglicized city outside the Mother-
land, while Dunedin was Scottish to the core. "The people are

Scotch," wrote Twain, confusing the citizens with his favorite drink. "They stopped here on their way from home to heaven—thinking they had arrived." Much of the New Zealand scenery, as glimpsed from his train, was similarly celestial: six thousand-foot-high mountains, called the Southern Alps, lakes, waterfalls, fjords, and the greenest countryside in the world, all snowed over with sheep. The entire country, he said, was English to the core. "If it had an established Church and social inequality it would be England over again with hardly a lack."[36]

As usual, Twain, Livy, and Clara were well received by the local aristocracy. In Dunedin their hosts were Dr. and Mrs. Thomas Moreland Hocken and their eleven-year-old daughter, Gladys, to whom Twain joked upon meeting, "My how you've grown since I last saw you." Not only was Hocken the city's leading medical practitioner, he was also the discoverer, or re-discoverer, of a national treasure—the 1840 Treaty of Wait-angi between the Crown and the native Maori chieftains—a discovery that Twain scholar Robert Cooper likens to a modern-day American uncovering the original Declaration of Independence. Through Hocken, Twain was introduced to the glories of Maori culture, including their ritualized facial tat-toos. Unlike the native Australian and Tasmanian tribesmen, said Twain, the Maori had "nothing of the savage in the faces . . . these chiefs looked like Roman patricians." The tat-toos themselves were "so flowing and graceful and beautiful that they are a most satisfactory decoration. It takes but fifteen minutes to get reconciled to the tattooing, and but fifteen more to perceive that it is just the thing. After that, the un-decorated European face is unpleasant and ignoble."[37]

The Maoris had an even more important distinction from their Australasian cousins: unlike the aborigines, they had not been hunted and harried to extinction. "It is a compliment to them that the British did not exterminate them, as they did the Australians and Tasmanians, but were content with subduing them, and showed no desire to go further," Twain noted. Instead, the government allowed the Maoris to keep their choicest land, protected them from rapacious land-sharks, and even accorded them representation in the legislature and universal suffrage—half a century before American women finally acquired the right to vote.[38]

Two war monuments in Moutoa Gardens attracted Twain's attention. The first, the Weeping Woman monument, personified Grief, in this case grief over the deaths of fifteen loyalist Maori warriors who fell at the Battle of Moutoa Island in May 1864 fighting against guerrillas aligned with the Pai Marire freedom movement. Twain objected to the honoring of Maoris who had died fighting other Maoris. "It is an object-lesson to the rising generation," he fumed. "It invites to treachery, disloyalty, unpatriotism. Its lesson, in frank terms, is 'Desert your flag, slay your people, burn their homes, shame your nationality—we honor such.'" The second monument, called the Sleeping Lion, commemorated slain members of the Eighteenth and Fiftieth British regiments who had died at the Battle of Nukumanu in June 1865. This provoked another outburst of anticolonialism in Twain, who quibbled with the description of Pai Marire members as fanatics and barbarians. "Patriotism is Patriotism. Calling it Fanaticism cannot degrade it; nothing can degrade it," he wrote. "The presence of that word detracts from the dignity of their cause and their deeds, and makes them appear to have spilt their blood in a conflict with ignoble men, men not worthy of that costly sacrifice. But the men were worthy. It was no shame to fight them. They fought for their homes, they fought for their country; they bravely fought and bravely fell; and it would take nothing from the honor of the brave Englishmen who lie under the monument but add to it, to say that they died in defense of English and laws and English homes against men worthy of the sacrifice—the Maori patriots." Twain felt that only dynamite could rectify the situation.[39]

Two boat trips from South Island to North Island were included in the family's New Zealand itinerary, and each was memorable for the wrong reason. The first, aboard the Union Line packet *Flora*, took them from Christchurch to Wellington. The *Flora* was badly overcrowded with junketeers returning from the nation's Anniversary Day. "The people who sailed in the *Flora* that night may forget some other things if they live a good while," Twain recalled, "but they will not live long enough to forget that." The men and women were divided by sex and crammed into common sleeping rooms without pillows or bed linen, separated by calico curtains. "I had a cattle-stall in the main stable," Twain wrote. "The place was as dark as the soul of the Union Company, and smelt like a kennel." Had the ship gone down, he said, half the 200 passengers would have drowned. Jumping ship at Wellington, Twain, Livy, and Clara booked passage on the *Mahinapua* to complete the coastal journey to Auckland. The new boat was "a wee little bridal-parlor of a boat," Twain remembered, "clean and comfortable; good service; good beds; good table, and no crowding. The seas danced her about like a duck, but she was safe and capable." Clara remembered it differently. Riding into a storm immediately out from Wellington, the *Mahinapua* was "as helpless as a cork on the water," she wrote. Everyone had to retreat to their beds. Twain, for one of the few times in his life, became seasick himself and slept through the ship's subsequent temporary grounding on a sandbank outside of Nelson, a failure that Clara never ceased to bring up to her exasperated father.[40]

Three weeks of performances on North Island completed their New Zealand tour. During that time, Twain celebrated his sixtieth birthday, Livy her fiftieth. (Clara, born in June, was between birthdays.) "Livy and Clara enjoy this nomadic life pretty well; certainly better than one could have expected they would," Twain wrote to Joseph Twichell. "They have tough experiences, in the way of food and beds and frantic little ships, but they put up with the worst that befalls with heroic endurance that resembles contentment." Livy, dissenting a bit from that rosy evaluation of their travels, complained to Susy that the New Zealand leg of the journey had not included a single day set aside for sightseeing. "Imagine," she wrote, "visiting Lucerne without traveling to Interlaken, especially if you knew that you would never again be so close to it. But we are traveling to pay our debts, not to enjoy ourselves." She expressed the hope that they would eventually be able to live again in their Hartford home, "but it is a long way"—longer indeed than she anticipated.[41]

Returning to Australia for a final round of lectures, Twain and the women spent the holidays in Melbourne. A simmering border dispute between Venezuela and British Guiana had flared up, leading to a brief war scare in the United States, Great Britain, and their client colonies. President Grover Cleveland, the only Democrat Twain had ever backed for president, had sided with Secretary of State Richard Olney's view that the Monroe Doctrine entitled the nation to intervene in any dispute involving South American nations and Europe. Great Britain disagreed. Cleveland went before Congress and got authorization to defend "by any means necessary" American interests in the Southern Hemisphere. War clouds roiled in the distance. Twain was worried enough about the crisis to break character at one of his final Australian appearances and walk to the edge of the stage to address the audience directly. "In bidding the audience good night," the *Sydney Morning Herald* reported the next day, "he wished to express his belief, as well as his earnest hope, that the 'little war cloud' that had been lowering over England and America during the last few days would be quickly blown away under the influence of colder and calmer counsels. (Loud cheers.) He trusted sincerely that the fruitful peace that had reigned between the two nations for 80 years would not be broken—(cheers)—and that the two great peoples would resume their march shoulder to shoulder, as before, in the an of the world's civilization. (Prolonged cheering.)" In subsequent interviews, Twain ventured to suggest that Cleveland's interpretation of the Monroe Doctrine was probably strained. In the end, the crisis blew over. The British tacitly accepted America's controlling interest in the region, while winning most of their boundary claims in arbitration.[42]

After a fourteen-day voyage from Australia, Twain, Livy, and Clara arrived in Bombay, on India's western coast, on January 18, 1896. Checking into Watson's Esplanade Hotel, reputedly the best hotel in the country, they were startled by the actions of the German-born manager, who unceremoniously punched a porter in the face for a minor offense. It

instantly took Twain back fifty years to his prewar days in
Hannibal. "It flashed upon me . . . that this was the *usual*
way of explaining one's desires to a slave," he recalled, noting
that his father, "a refined and kindly gentleman," periodically
cuffed one of his slaves, a boy named Lewis, "for trifling little
blunders and awkwardnesses." He also remembered the time
when a townsman threw a lump of iron-ore at a slave, fatally
striking him in the head. "I knew the man had a right to kill
his slave if he wanted to," recalled Twain, "and yet it seemed
a pitiful thing and somehow wrong." No one complained
about it at the time.[43]

Soon after checking into the hotel, Twain was struck by another of the upper respiratory infections that plagued him regularly during the tour. He stayed indoors for the next five days
while Livy and Clara enjoyed a fresh round of parties and en-
tertainments, including a luncheon at the government residence of Bombay's English governor, Lord Sandhurst, and an
evening reception for Kumar Bahadur, the newly knighted
prince of Palitana. Livy pronounced Bombay "the most fasci-
nating place" she had ever seen. Twain's convalescence ended
on January 24 with the first of three performances at Bombay's Novelty Theatre. The next day he ventured into the city,
which he found "a bewitching place, a bewildering place, an
enchanting place—the Arabian Nights come again!" Accompanied by Livy and Clara, he toured a Jain temple, wandered
the bazaars, watched jugglers and snake charmers, and felt
himself overwhelmed by the sheer native color of the place. "It
is all color, bewitching color, enchanting color—everywhere,"
Twain gushed. "This is indeed India! the land of dreams
and romance, of fabulous wealth and fabulous poverty, of
splendor and rags, of palaces and hovels, of famine and pesti-
lence, of genii and giants and Aladdin lamps, of tigers and

elephants, the cobra and the jungle, the country of a hundred nations and a hundred tongues, of a thousand religions and two million gods."[44]

Their tour of Bombay included a private luncheon at the hillside mansion of Prince Kumar, who customarily went about swathed in long ropes of pearls and emeralds. Following lunch the prince clapped his hands and had several piles brought out of what Twain defined vaguely as "rich stuffs" and "beautiful things"; he invited his guests to take what they liked. They did. As was their wont, the family mingled with other prominent society figures, including Lord and Lady Sandhurst and the Maharajah of Baroda, Sir Sayaji Rao III, whom Twain entertained at a private performance for three hundred of the ruler's closest friends. In return, the guests received complimentary elephant rides. The sight of her father atop a howdah-wearing Indian elephant was too much for Clara, who dissolved into laughter. "What are you laughing at, you sassmill?" Twain demanded grumpily. If he could learn not to be afraid of them, he said, he would take one of the elephants home with him when no one was looking.[45]

The family traveled back and forth from Bombay to Baroda by rail. Twain never tired of the multifarious sights at Indian train stations. "Inside the great station, tides upon tides of rainbow-costumed natives swept along, this way and that, in massed and bewildering confusion," he wrote. "Here and there, in the midst of this hurly-burly, and seemingly undisturbed by it, sat great groups of natives on the bare stone floor,— young, slender brown women, old, gray wrinkled women, little soft brown babies, old men, young men, boys; all poor people, but all the families among them, both big and little, bejeweled with cheap and showy nose-rings, toe-rings, leglets, and armlets, these things constituting all their wealth, no doubt."[46]

Besides taking in the local color, Twain indulged some darker speculations. The scurrying rats in the alleyways and the mounds of sleeping beggars in the streets of Bombay reminded him of the ever-imminent threat of disease, particularly the Black Death of bubonic plague that emptied the city a year later and killed an estimated 12.5 million Indians over the next three decades. "We can all imagine, after a fashion, the desolation of a plague-stricken city," Twain noted, "but I suppose it is not possible for us to realize to ourselves the nightmare of fear and dread that possesses the living who are present in such a place and cannot get away." As it was, Twain, Livy, and Clara missed the plague's arrival in Bombay by mere months from its starting point in rural China. A Bombay doctor, Russian-Jewish immigrant Waldemar Hoffkine, developed the world's first plague vaccine one year later and was knighted by the queen for his life-saving discovery.[47]

The heartless murder of a twelve-year-old lower-caste Hindu girl in the city caught Twain's attention, but it was the organized cult of roving murderers known as the Thugs that truly captured his morbid imagination. The cult of Thuggee, worshiping the dread goddess Kali, was prevalent in India for centuries before finally coming to official English attention in 1839 after the capture of a leading Thug chieftain named Feringhea, "a mysterious and terrible Indian who was as slippery and sly as a serpent, and as deadly." Feringhea's subsequent, almost unbelievable account of his cult's ritualized depredations was printed in pamphlet form by British Major Henry Sleeman of the Indian Service in 1840, which is where Twain first encountered their mention. Thugs were estimated to have killed a staggering two million people, mostly lone travelers killed one at a time, over the course of three centuries. The most prolific murderer, one Behram, supposedly claimed 931 victims before being hanged by the Crown in 1840.[48]

Modern scholars are divided about the extent, or even existence, of the cult. Some, like Martine van Woerkins, have argued that alleged Thuggee depredations were largely an invention of British authorities to justify their ongoing colonial repression. Others, including Kim Wagner, Mike Dash, and Kevin Rushby, have concluded that the Thugs did indeed kill countless thousands of travelers, but that the primary motive for their crimes was simple robbery, not religious adoration of Kali. (Muslims and Sikhs were also members of the cult, as well as at least one renegade British soldier named Creagh.) Because the vast majority of their victims were poor, rootless, and largely unmissed, and because the crimes generally took place in remote areas of a vast country, it is impossible to place an accurate figure on the total number of Thug murders.[49]

Using the ritual yellow cloth, or *pangori,* which could be worn as a turban or cummerbund, Thugs were trained to dispatch their victims without warning or mercy. "No half-educated strangler could choke a man to death quickly enough to keep him from uttering a sound," Twain observed, "a muffled scream, gurgle, gasp, moan, or something of the sort; but the expert's work was instantaneous: the cloth was whipped around the victim's neck, there was a sudden twist, and the head fell silently forward, the eyes starting from the sockets; and all was over." The cult killed without discrimination during an annual eight-month-long hunting season that stretched from autumn through spring. Ingratiating themselves with victims, they would travel alongside them, sometimes for hundreds of miles, before the time was considered right to strike. A code phrase, "Bring the tobacco," was uttered,

at which point four Thugs would seize the victim's wrists and
ankles and hold him down while a fifth came up behind him
with the *pangori*. One account in particular caught Twain's
eye: "After murdering 4 sepoys, going on toward Indore, met
4 strolling players, and persuaded them to come with us, on
the pretense that we would see their performance at the next
stage. Murdered them at a temple near Bhopar. At Deohuttee,
joined by comedians. Murdered them eastward of that place."
Thanks to Sleeman and his special force of investigators, the
Thugs were more or less eradicated by the mid-1840s, and it
was now safe to travel the Indian countryside again.[50]

In late January 1896 the family journeyed by train from
Bombay to Allahabad, a distance of 750 miles. It was, Twain
noted, "a sorrowful land—a land of unimaginable poverty
and hardship." After another sold-out performance, he and
the ladies visited the three hundred-year-old fort of Emperor Akbar, India's first Mogul ruler, and watched a winding
stream of pilgrims descend on the confluence of the Jamuna
and Ganges Rivers, which together formed the mystical
Saraswati, the Hindu river of enlightenment. The annual religious fair, the Magh Mela, was taking place, and Twain
noted that "if we had got to the Mele this morning, we might
have seen a man who hasn't sat down for years; another who
has held his hands above his head for years and never trims
his nails or hair, both very long; another who sits with his
bare foot resting upon a lot of sharp spikes—and all for the
glory of God." The name itself, Allahabad, meant City of
God, although Twain favored the concise English translation,
Godville.[51]

The next morning they went to the holy city of Benares, eighty-five miles southeast of Allahabad, on the Ganges. Benares was one of the oldest cities in the world, and looked it. "Benares is older than history," wrote Twain, "older than tradition, older even than legend, and looks twice as old as all of them put together." As the holiest city in India, where time was said literally to have begun, Benares attracted a constant stream of penitents. Never notably religious himself, Twain was not much moved by the city. "All the aspects are melancholy," he noted. "It is a vision of dusty sterility, decaying temples, crumbling tombs, broken mud walls, shabby huts." As for the holy river, Twain, like most Westerners, was horrified. "At one place where we halted for a while, the foul gush from a sewer was making the water turbid and murky all around, and there was the random corpse slopping around in it that floated down from up country. Ten steps below that place stood a crowd of men, women, and comely young maidens waist deep in the water—and they were scooping it up in their hands and drinking it. Faith can certainly do wonders."[52]

A seventeen-and-a-half-hour train ride took the travelers to Calcutta, 430 miles away, for Twain's next scheduled appearance. Between dining with Bengal's newly arrived lieutenant governor, Sir Alexander MacKenzie, and giving three sold-out performances at the Theatre Royal before the usual elite dinner-jacketed crowds, Twain took time to tour the infamous Black Hole of Calcutta—or what was left of it, literally a black hole and a small plaque, subsequently removed, honoring the 123 British and colonial victims of the 1756 atrocity. Now synonymous with sweltering heat, the Black Hole of Calcutta was a fourteen-by-eighteen-foot prison cell at Fort William, a British stronghold that was overrun by the forces of Bengal's native ruler, Siraj ud-Daulah. Siraj threw 146 prisoners into the Black Hole; all but twenty-three were dead by morning of suffocation, thirst, or heat exhaustion. The incident led to the triumph of the British East India Company's armed forces one year later at the Battle of Plassey, which led in turn to a century of British sovereignty in India. Twain was glad he had visited the Black Hole of Calcutta during India's "cold weather," he said, since the phrase was merely a conversational aid "to distinguish between weather which will melt a brass door-knob and weather which will only make it mushy." For that matter, said Twain, "When a person is accustomed to 138 in the shade, his ideas about cold weather are not valuable."[53]

Twain, Livy, and Clara left Calcutta on February 14 for a side jaunt to Darjeeling, the romantic British outpost in the foothills of the Himalayas in extreme northeastern India. It would prove to be one of the most memorable visits of their tour. Darjeeling was famous chiefly for its tea—so famous, in fact, that much of the country's exported tea was labeled "Darjeeling," although only a fraction of the tea actually came from there. Darjeeling was also famous for the view. Seven thousand feet above sea level, the city gives onto the broad Indian flood plain in one direction and the cloud-wrapped Himalayas in the other. En route, said Twain, exaggerating a bit, they stopped at a way station for a brief tiger hunt. "It was my first hunt," said Twain. "I killed thirteen tigers." He was reminded of a famous telegraph message a railway manager was said to have sent to Calcutta a few years earlier: "Tiger eating station-master on front porch; telegraph instructions." Seven wild elephants also crossed the tracks, but they got away, Twain said, before he could catch them.[54]

From the Darjeeling station they were transported to their hotel in a conveyance known as a dandy, a box chair balanced on poles and carried by four men. A few hours later, playing to "a fairly good house" at the old Town Hall, Twain took pains to praise the town's narrow-gauge railroad as "the most remarkable forty miles of railroad in the world," and joked that he had been warned so often about the cold weather in Darjeeling that he was currently wearing nine separate suits. After the lecture he went to the local gentlemen's club, the Planters, where the *Darjeeling Standard* reported that visiting celebrity had "kept the billiard-room so jolly" that members couldn't make their shots, which was probably his intention in the first place.[55]

The next morning Clara and Livy went by horseback and rickshaw to view the Himalayas from Observatory Hill. Twain stayed back at the hotel—"It was very cold, and I was not acquainted with the horses, anyway." Wrapped in several blankets, he watched the sun rise over twenty-eight thousand-foot-high Mount Kinchinjunga. From his vantage point he couldn't make out Mount Everest, but that was all right, since "I think that mountains that are as high as that are disagreeable." They departed the next morning, taking the same narrow-gauge railroad back down to the plains, a thirty-five-mile descent in a six-person, canvas-covered handcar that rode so close to the ground that it made them feel as though they were sledding in a toboggan. "That was the most enjoyable day I have spent in the earth," Twain gushed. "For rousing, tingling, rapturous pleasure there is no holiday-trip that approaches the bird-flight down the Himalayas in a hand-car."[56]

Returning briefly to Calcutta, they went next to Lucknow and Cawnpore, fabled sites of the Indian Mutiny of 1857. "No doubt all these native grayheads remember the Mutiny," Twain noted, looking about. The mutiny had been sparked by the introduction of Enfield rifles to the British East India Company's troops. In a move of remarkable cultural insensitivity, the company issued its soldiers cartridges coated with cow fat (taboo to Hindus) and pig fat (taboo to Muslims). When word got out, the native troops revolted and butchered the English garrisons at Lucknow and Cawnpore. Twain, visiting the "sacred" sites, mused that by successfully putting down the mutiny, the English had demonstrated once and for all their resolution and devotion to duty. Between three performances in the siege towns, the family found time to visit another famous Indian site, the Taj Mahal, at nearby Agra. Twain pronounced himself disappointed in the palace. "I knew all the time, that of its kind it was *the* wonder of the world, with no competitor now and no possible future competitor," he complained, "and yet, it was not my Taj. My Taj had been built by excitable literary people; it was solidly lodged in my head, I could not blast it out." He amused himself by quoting other travel writers on the Taj Mahal and counting up their common phrases. "Language," he mused, "is a treacherous thing, a most unsure vehicle, and it can seldom arrange descriptive words in such a way that they will not inflate the facts."[57]

At Jaipur, Twain fell ill with exhaustion, and Clara and Smythe were stricken with a mild form of malaria. They spent two weeks recuperating, and Twain was forced to cancel several planned appearances. The rash of cancellations created something of a sensation in the world press, which reported that the famous writer was seriously ill. It would be nearly three weeks before he was well enough to perform in public

again, at Lahore, on March 18. "Mark Twain at Last!" proclaimed the *Lahore Civil and Military Gazette*, which went
on to describe the lecturer as "looking a trifle pale and worn
after his recent illness." His final Indian appearance was two
days later at Rawalpindi, 160 miles northwest of Lahore. The
family had been warned against staying in India during the
hot season. "It was always summer in India," Twain wrote to
Rogers. "Of course we never saw any of the real summer; they
do say that when that comes Satan himself has to knock off
and go home and cool off." Two hundred people a day were
reportedly dying of cholera in Calcutta, and the Black Death
was on the way.[58]

On March 24 they boarded the British East India Company
liner *Wardha*, steamed into the Bay of Bengal, and set sail for
Ceylon and Mauritius. They had spent two full months in
India, traveling some five thousand miles while Twain gave
twenty performances and cancelled that many more. In the
end, due to the cancellations, lengthy travel times, and smallish
performance halls, they barely covered their travel expenses,
but Livy assured her sister, Susan, that they had enjoyed their
stay immensely. Clara was particularly entranced by India,
pronouncing the country "the most interesting by far." Years
later, in his autobiography, Twain would call India "the only
foreign land I ever daydream about or deeply long to see
again."[59]

After a two-day stop in Ceylon, they proceeded to the French-
controlled island of Mauritius, five hundred miles east of
Madagascar, where their ship was quarantined for two weeks
after a passenger came down with chicken pox. The family

spent the time resting and reading. There were no Jane Austen novels aboard the *Wardha,* said Twain, an omission that in itself "would make a fairly good library out of a library that hadn't a book in it." He delved into Jacques-Henri Bernardin de St-Pierre's 1787 novel, *Paul et Virginie,* about a pair of young lovers raised in a state of Rousseauesque innocence. "It was that story that made Mauritius known to the world," Twain wrote, adding that the island's actual location remained unknown. "It is the greatest story that was ever written about Mauritius, and the only one."[60]

Switching ships to the *Arundel Castle,* "the finest boat I have seen in these seas," they resumed their voyage to Africa, making landfall at Portuguese-controlled Lourenco Marques (now Maputo, Mozambique) on May 4. Two days later they hopped southward to Durban, South Africa, where Twain left Livy and Clara behind while he and Smythe undertook a seven-week tour of the southern tip of Africa, through Natal, the Transvaal, the Orange Free State, and Cape Colony—territory that within a few years' time would be contested again when the simmering conflict between native-born Boers and English colonists erupted into the Second Boer War. A few months before Twain's arrival, an armed gang of Anglo adventurers led by Leander Starr Jameson had invaded the Transvaal in an attempt to foment armed insurrection against the Boer government. Jameson was a close associate of Cecil Rhodes, the trouble-making prime minister of Cape Colony, and it was widely accepted that Rhodes was behind the plot. The Jameson Raid failed ignominiously, and the raiders and many suspected supporters were jailed. Twain found the political situation in South Africa "an inexpressible tangle," but his sympathies, as usual, were with the British. Terming the Jameson raiders "reformers," he criticized the tactics—but not the motives—of the raid, which he viewed as a sort of mounted version of the Boston Tea Party.[61]

Twain was acquainted slightly with one of the jailed conspirators, an American mining engineer named John Hays Hammond. At the intercession of Hammond's wife, whom he had met on one of his various transatlantic voyages, Twain agreed to visit the prisoners in Pretoria, where he managed to annoy both sides simultaneously. The Boers were angry that the famous American writer saw fit to involve himself in their personal business, and the prisoners were angry that Twain, in a misguided stab at humor, had treated them to a lengthy discourse on the advantages of being in jail. "Explained to the prisoners," he noted later, "why they were better off in the jail than they would be anywhere else; that they would eventually have gotten into jail anyhow, for one thing or another; that it would be better all around if they remained quietly where they were and made the best of it; that after a few months they would prefer the jail and its luxurious indolence to the sordid struggle for bread outside." He promised to meet with Transvaal president Paul Kruger and "do everything I could, short of bribery, to get the government to double their jail terms." No one laughed. A few days later, Twain paid a call on Kruger to ask for leniency for his fellow Americans. Kruger assured Twain that "he felt friendly toward America and that it was his disposition to be lenient with the American captives." Ultimately, the prisoners, including Hammond, were released from jail with stiff fines and stiffer warnings to leave the Transvaal immediately. They did.[62]

Despite his amicable meeting with Kruger and his well-attended performances in Boer-dominated cities, the author retained a harsh opinion of the typical Boer. "He is deeply religious, profoundly ignorant, dull, obstinate, bigoted, uncleanly in his habits," Twain wrote. "He cannot read, he cannot write; he has one or two newspapers, but he is, apparently not aware of it; until latterly he had no schools, and taught his children nothing; news is a term which has no meaning to him, and the thing itself he cares nothing about." All in all, said Twain, the Boers had "stood stock-still in South Africa for two centuries and a half, and would like to stand still till the end of time." Two years later, after war had broken out, Twain had a change of heart, praising the Boers for their "honesty, kindliness, hospitality, love of freedom and limitless courage to fight for it, composure and fortitude in time of disaster, patience in time of hardship and privation, absence of noise and brag in time of victory, contentment with a humble and peaceful life void of insane excitements—if there is a higher and better form of civilization than this, I am not aware of it."[63]

On July 15, one year and one day after his initial tour appearance in Elmira, New York, Twain, Livy, and Clara sailed for England from Cape Town aboard the S.S. *Norman*. They left South Africa with a sense of relief. The colorless countryside, humorless natives, and festering political intrigue had bored and depressed them all. "Africa seemed a colorless country after India," Clara recalled, "and we were glad to embark on our last voyage." All things considered, the year-long tour had been a remarkable feat of endurance by all of them, particularly the sixty-year-old author. Frequently ill, physically exhausted, and financially anxious, he nevertheless had traveled 53,000 miles and given more than 120 lectures in seven countries. "I seemed to have been lecturing for a thousand years," Twain wrote, "though it was only a twelvemonth." In the end, he cleared only about one-fourth of the funds needed to pay off his outstanding debts, but he confidently expected his next travel book to make up the difference. In the meantime, as he wrote to William Dean Howells: "We hope to get a house in some quiet English village away from the world and society, where I can sit down for six months or so and give myself up to the luxury and rest of writing a book or two after this long fatigue and turmoil of platform-work and gadding around by sea and land. Susy and Jean sail from New York today and a week hence we shall all be together." Soon—too soon—those plans would change.[64]

CHAPTER FIVE

THIS EVERLASTING
EXILE

A fter a restorative sixteen-day cruise up the western
coast of Africa, during which time Twain luxuriated in
Scotch, books, and cigars, the family docked at Southampton,
England, on July 31, 1896. They were momentarily undecided
about whether to stay in England or return immediately to
America. Twain, worn down by his many public performances,
favored the latter; Livy did not want to go home again until
they had paid off the remainder of their debts. As usual, she
won on the domestic front, and the trio settled into a rented
cottage in Guildford, Surrey. Meanwhile, back in Elmira, ever-
loyal housemaid Katy Leary arranged passage across the Atlantic for Susy, Jean, and herself. They were due to sail from
New York City on August 5.

Katy went to Hartford to collect Susy, who had been living
there for several months, first with John and Alice Day in the
old family house before moving in next door with Charles and
Susan Warner after the Days gave up their lease. The Farmington Avenue home was still partly furnished with their old

furniture, and Susy haunted the house like a wraith, singing and playing the piano, her voice carrying out the open windows and across their neighbors' well-trimmed lawns. Sometime around the first of August she suddenly became ill. When Katy Leary arrived, she found the young woman feverish and unwell, and hastily postponed their departure. On the advice of doctors, she moved Susy back into her childhood bedroom to recuperate. The first diagnosis was inconclusive. Susan Crane first cabled Susy's parents that there would be an unexpected delay in the girls' departure, then that Susy was slightly ill. Understandably, Twain and Livy were frantic with worry. Charley Langdon, Livy's brother, cabled Guildford on August 12 to report that Susy's recovery would be "long but certain." That same day Livy and Clara decided to sail to America to be with Susy. A second diagnosis, too late to reach them before they left—or to do much good for the desperately ill young woman languishing back home—confirmed the worst: Susy had spinal meningitis.[1]

While her mother and sister steamed west across the Atlantic on the S.S. *Pavia* and her desperate father waited in Guildford for a follow-up message, Susy burned with fever. Too restless to remain in bed, she paced incessantly through the empty house, her footsteps echoing on the uncarpeted hardwood floors, listening to the trolley cars rumble past on the street outside. "Up go the trolley cars for Mark Twain's daughter," she murmured. "Down go the trolley cars for Mark Twain's daughter." Her mind wandered. She scribbled page after page of incoherent notes, imagining herself a dead Parisian opera singer. "God bless the shadows as I bless the light," she wrote. "I see that even darkness can be great. To me darkness must remain from everlasting to everlasting." She found an old gown of Livy's hanging in the closet; thinking her mother dead, she kissed the dress and wept. On August 16 she suddenly went blind. Touching Katy Leary's face, she cried, "Mamma, mamma, mamma." They were her last words. She lapsed into a coma and died two days later. Twain, still waiting in his rented English cottage, opened another telegram from his brother-in-law. "Susy could not stand brain congestion and meningitis and was peacefully released today," it read. Years later, Twain would still marvel: "It is one of the mysteries of our nature that a man, all unprepared, can receive a thunder-stroke like that and live."[2]

When their ship arrived in New York harbor on August 22, the captain sent a crewman for Clara. Entering his stateroom, Clara was handed a copy of the day's newspaper, with the headline: "Mark Twain's Eldest Daughter Dies of Spinal Meningitis." She went back to tell her mother, who took one look at her stricken face and burst out, "I don't believe it!" As with everything surrounding the tragedy, the family doctor Twain had cabled to meet the ship was too late. The author sent a heartbroken telegram to Livy. "I wish there were five of the coffins, side by side," he told her. "How lovely is death; & how niggardly it is doled out." Whether or not that message was a comfort, Susy's lone coffin was laid out in the same drawing room in Elmira where her parents had been married twenty-six years earlier. Joseph Twichell, who had assisted at the wedding, now presided at the funeral. Susy's tombstone featured lines from a poem by an obscure Australian poet named Robert Richardson that Twain had read once and liked: "Warm summer sun, shine kindly here, / Warm southern wind, blow softly here, / Green sod above, lie light, lie light, / Good night, dear heart, good night, good night."[3]

Too far away to return in time for the funeral (Louise Brownell didn't make it either, although years later she did name one of her daughters Olivia in honor of Susy), Twain bore up alone in the grotesquely beautiful English countryside, playing game after game of solitary billiards in his rented cottage until he dropped from exhaustion. William Dean Howells, who had lost his own daughter, Winifred, five years earlier, could offer little in the way of consolation. "There is really nothing to say to you, poor souls," he wrote. "We suffer with you. As for the gentle creature who is gone, the universe is all a crazy blunder if she is not somewhere in conscious blessedness that knows and feels your love." Twain was unreconciled. The loss of Susy, he told Howells, was "bitter, bitter, bitter. It would bankrupt all vocabularies of all the languages to put it into words." He had no doubt they would see Susy again, he said, "if it can furnish opportunity to break our hearts again." And to Henry Huttleston Rogers, he wrote, "It kills me to think of the books that Susy would have written, and that I shall never read now. This family has lost its prodigy."[4]

With Susy buried and her husband alone and crazed with grief, Livy hurried back to England with the others immediately after the funeral. There was no thought of staying in America; well-meaning friends would have kept Susy's loss an open wound. Instead, as Twain told Hartford businessman Frank Whitmore, the family would remain in England, "not to live in public there, but to hide from men for a time & let the wounds heal." In November they moved from Guildford to London, taking a minimally furnished apartment on Tedworth Square, midway between King's Road and Royal Hospital Road in Chelsea. For the next nine months, they pulled the drapes, literally and figuratively, on their lives, a family in deepest mourning. The intensity of her parents' grief made Clara aware, perhaps for the first time, that Susy had been their favorite. "It was a long time before anyone laughed in our household," she wrote. "Father's passionate nature expressed itself in thunderous outbursts of bitterness shading into rugged grief. He walked the floor with quick steps and there was no drawl in his speech now." Livy was inconsolable, spending all day in her bedroom—Twain aptly termed it a "submergence"—reading and rereading Susy's copy of Tennyson's *In Memoriam*, the English laureate's extended threnody on the premature death of his friend Arthur Hallam at the age of twenty-two. "Let Love clasp Grief lest both be drowned," Tennyson advised, and Livy was doing her best to stay afloat. "We are a broken-hearted family," she wrote to Mary Mason Fairbanks, "and such I think we must always remain."[5]

Thanksgiving and Christmas went by without notice. Occasionally Twain and the girls went for walks along the Thames or in Regent's Park. "It was on such days that Father created the habit of vituperating the human race," Clara remembered. "What started in formless criticism grew into a sinister doctrine. There was no hope for the human race because no appreciable improvement was possible in any individual." His sandy hair turned mostly white; his walrus mustache went untrimmed. Once he reduced Livy to tears by raging against a universe "governed by some sort of malign thug." After the outburst was over, he stroked her hair and said, "Don't mind anything I say, Livy. Whatever happens, you know I love you." It was cold comfort at best.[6]

To escape his own grief, Twain threw himself into his work, spending the next seven months writing an extended account of their world tour. He wrote obsessively, even grimly, beginning work after breakfast and continuing without pause until seven at night. As with his other travel books, he used both his own notes and quotations from other sources—some thirty in all. He gave the book the provisional titles *Another Innocent Abroad* or *The Surviving Innocent Abroad,* as if the earlier book's joyous luck and exuberance could rub off on the new one. In general, it did not. *Following the Equator,* as it was somewhat inaccurately titled (the journey followed more closely the tropics of Cancer and Capricorn than the equator), eventually grew into two volumes, seventy chapters in all. Inevitably for a writer of Twain's ability, there were flashes of insight, if not always brilliance, but the book as a whole was largely uninspired. "I would rather go hang myself than do the like again," he told his friend Wayne MacVeagh. "It was a contract, & couldn't be helped. But that slavery is over."[7]

Sheer grief was not the only reason why *Following the Equator* was difficult for Twain to write. In the three decades between his first and last travel books, the world had changed—and not necessarily for the better. Lacking, for the time being, a war at home, the great European powers were fighting a proxy war in the developing world, colonizing madly and extending all the unwanted "appliances of civilization" to native peoples from India to South America. Twain, for all his joking facade, was a keen and sensitive observer, and his recent world tour had brought him face to face with the myriad horrors of power politics. Long after his first glimpse of the comparatively mild colonization of Hawaii in 1866, he had seen the brutal, often murderous, advance of European imperialism in the Third World: "In many countries we have chained the savage and starved him to death," he noted. "In many countries we have burned the savage at the stake. . . . In many countries we have taken the savage's land from him, and made him our slave, and lashed him every day, and broken his pride, and made death his only friend."[8]

Twain's travels through what cultural critic Mary Louise Pratt has termed the "contact zone" between imperialist and indigenous cultures caused him to question not only his own cultural assumptions, but the very act of travel itself. As Jeffrey Alan Melton notes, *Following the Equator* is Twain's "most ethically conflicted travel book. He is forced to grant his readers a tour of the world through the eyes of the tourist, as he has for thirty years, while also for the first time becoming acutely conscious that the tourist is by no means a harmless if indulgent visitor who enters, roams, and departs from a landscape and culture without leaving a lasting trace. . . . If *The Innocents Abroad* heralded the beginning of the Tourist Age, complete with obnoxious but relatively harmless Americans, *Following the Equator* announces the end of its first phase. The vandals have evolved into oppressors." He is not sure he can, or even wants to, write about it any more.[9]

Twain turned the completed manuscript over to Frank Bliss at the American Publishing Company, which would sell the book by subscription, like Twain's other travel books. Chatto & Windus gave the British edition the prosaic title, *More Tramps Abroad*, which inexplicably begged comparison with the author's poorly received 1880 book. Both editions of *Following the Equator* were published in November 1897. The cover featured an African elephant and an Indian temple on a pastel-pink background, with filigreed oriental panels on either side, suggesting a rather more exotic text than the one inside. There were 193 illustrations, including the first use of photographs in any of Twain's books. Reflecting his growing celebrity status, there were approximately thirty-six images of Twain (it is sometimes hard to tell), including a full-page author's photo on the frontispiece of the author reading a newspaper—an ironically relaxed image for what had been, all things considered, a physical and mental grind.

One silver lining for Twain was that the international copyright situation for authors had improved dramatically in recent years. From the time of his first public forays against piratical English publisher John Camden Hotten in the early 1870s, Twain had intermittently joined the efforts to extend copyright protection for writers. In 1885 he had taken part in a mass reading at Madison Square Garden sponsored by the American Copyright League, and he had met privately with President Grover Cleveland at the White House later that same year to discuss changes in the law. How much impact Twain had personally on the situation is debatable, but in 1891 Congress had passed the International Copyright Act, extending copyright protection for the first time to foreign authors in the United States. The thinking behind the act was to encourage reciprocal protection for American authors in other countries, which had long looked askance at America's refusal to offer foreign authors such protection. Twain would continue to take an interest in the issue, appearing as late as December 1906 before a Joint Congressional Committee on Patents that was looking into extending copyright protection in perpetuity, an appearance that marked the public debut of his famous white suit.[10]

Privately, Twain continued to have doubts about the overall quality of *Following the Equator*. "I am very glad you like the book," he told Rogers. "It pretends to an interest in its subject—

which was mostly not the case. It pretends that it was freely spouted out of a contented heart—not the forced work of a rebellious prisoner rotting in chains." Sales were respectable—thirty thousand in the first three months—and helped go a long way toward retiring the remainder of Twain's debts, but reviews, particularly in England, were less than rapturous. "Hardish reading," "No longer the fresh fun of youth," "Not always at his best," "Too long," "Too diffuse," and "A failure" were some of the milder comments. Twain did not disagree. He would later tell Howells: "I wrote my last travel-book in hell; but I let on, the best I could, that it was an excursion through heaven. Some day I will read it, & if its lying cheerfulness fools me, then I shall believe it fooled the reader." Given the circumstances in which it was written, perhaps the greatest accomplishment of *Following the Equator* is merely that it got written at all.[11]

Twain produced another relatively uninspired work that summer, a specially commissioned newspaper article on Queen Victoria's Diamond Jubilee. Publisher William Randolph Hearst had engaged the author to write the piece for Hearst's *New York Journal* and *San Francisco Examiner*. On the morning of June 22, 1897, Twain took his seat outside the Cecil Hotel at one of the many observation stands up and down the Strand to witness the sixty-year anniversary celebration of Queen Victoria's reign. The seventy-eight-year-old queen, still the longest-serving female monarch in history (King Sobhuza II of Swaziland reigned for almost eighty-three years before his death in 1982), was scheduled to proceed from Buckingham Palace to St. Paul's Cathedral and then to make a winding six-mile detour through the crooked streets of London before ending back where she had started. Because the ceremonial head of the Church of England was too lame from rheumatism to climb the steps at the church, the Church came to her, with the archbishop of Canterbury offering curbside felicities while the queen remained seated in her carriage.

For some reason Twain, an experienced journalist, chose to begin his account with a fanciful digression on the supposed victory parade following King Henry V's historic triumph at Agincourt on October 25, 1415. It amused Twain, if not Hearst, to posit his account as a report from a "spirit-correspondent" looking down on the proceedings from his home in heaven. Twain followed this labored three-page fancy with a long catalogue of the many modern advances Victoria had witnessed during her lifetime, from newspapers and labor unions to anesthetics and women's rights, concluding with the expansion of British dominion to the four corners of the globe and, by the author's careful count, over four hundred million subjects. The procession itself, Twain decided, "could not be described. There was going to be too much of it, and too much variety in it, so I gave up the idea. It was to be a spectacle for the Kodak, not the pen." Hearst must have wondered, with some justice, what exactly he was paying for.[12]

Earlier that same month, Twain inadvertently made news of his own when reports surfaced in the *New York Herald* that he was gravely ill or even dead. Hearst, always looking to discredit his competitors, dispatched a reporter to the author's front doorstep to verify the accuracy of the report. Knocking on the door, Frank Marshall White showed Twain a cable from Hearst: "If Mark Twain dying in poverty, in London, send 500 words. If Mark Twain has died in poverty send 1000 words." Twain, smiling grimly, responded with a matter-of-fact observation that somehow struck readers as a delightful quip: "The report of my death was an exaggeration." (Actually, it was his cousin, London-based Dr. James Ross Clemens, who was sick.) Of course he was dying, Twain added, "But I do not know that I am doing it any faster than anybody else." The second part of his statement was a good deal funnier than the first, but it was the comment about the exaggeration of his death that entered the lexicon, the public for the first time perhaps supplying the humorist's punchline for him.[13]

The worldwide clamor surrounding Twain's reported death reflected both his status as the world's most famous American writer and the inexorable rise of his native country to a position of global power. If Queen Victoria had given her name to the British-dominated nineteenth century, a new generation of American leaders would come to define the twentieth. Perhaps fittingly, democracy-reared Americans would not name the coming era after a particular president, even though the two most prominent were both named Roosevelt, but the next hundred years would become known collectively as the American Century. And Mark Twain, born in the geographical center of America, would come to embody the cultural ascendance of his country as unmistakably as Charles Dickens, another low-born, self-made man, had personified the England of his birth.

In July the family left London for Weggis, Switzerland, on the north shore of Lake Lucerne at the foot of Rigi-Kulm, which Twain had climbed with Twichell in happier days. "This is the charmingest place we have ever lived in, for repose," he told Twichell. "Sunday in heaven is noisy compared to this quietness." The family spent the next two months there, a period that coincided with the first anniversary of Susy's death. Livy, wordlessly grabbing her hat and coat,

went off alone to spend the day on a steamboat cruising Lake
Lucerne. Her husband passed the time sitting under a tree
and writing a mawkish poem, "In Memoriam," eulogizing
Susy as "a poet whose song died unsung" and proving conclu-
sively that his own great gifts did not extend to poetry.[14]

The two-month stay at Weggis freed something in Twain's
mind, and he produced a number of interesting, if incomplete,
works on the shores of Lake Lucerne. The best is "Villagers
of 1840–3," a fragmentary but revealing account of his old
Hannibal neighbors that presages Edgar Lee Masters' *Spoon
River Anthology* in its despairing look at small-town life on
the American frontier. "Villagers" tersely reworks Tom Sawyer's heavenly river town into a sort of midwestern *Book of the
Dead*. Writing plainly and without affect, Twain name checks
various villagers and their fates: "Jim Wolfe. The practical
jokes. Dead"; "Clint Levering, drowned"; Mary Moss, whose
"thigh was broken and badly set. She got well with a terrible
limp, and forever after stayed in the house and produced children"; "Bill League. Married the gravestone-cutter's daughter.
Children. Died"; "Blankenship. The parents paupers & drunk-
ards; the girls charged with prostitution—not proven. These
children were never sent to school or church. Played out & dis-
appeared." Tom Blankenship, it should be remembered, was
the real-life model for Huckleberry Finn.[15]

A second fragmentary story, "Hellfire Hotchkiss," features
a transparently Susy-like heroine who rides around town on
a big black horse, lugging a handy life preserver and a baseball bat, rescuing oddly feminized boys from ice floes and
school bullies and functioning as "the only genuwyne male
man in this town." There are elements in Hellfire of Twain's
eccentric young San Francisco friend Lillie Hitchcock, who
chased after fire engines as a girl, smoked cigars, played poker

with the men, and cross-dressed in denim blue jeans and plaid miner's shirts. Both Lillie and Hellfire (Christian name, Rachel) were adopted as mascots by volunteer fire companies, and in the climax of the story, Hellfire clambers across collapsing rooftops to rescue a family trapped in a burning house. Modern critics have found traces of latent lesbianism in the title character's boyish energy, and perhaps this was as near as Twain could come to recognizing that side of Susy's developing nature.[16]

"Tom Sawyer's Conspiracy," the third uncompleted manuscript dating from his stay in Weggis, represents a failed attempt on Twain's part to reunite Tom, Huck, and Jim in a new adventure. Opening a year or so after the events in *Huckleberry Finn*, the story concerns another harebrained scheme by Tom to work up excitement in their sleepy hometown. He dresses in blackface to fool a nearsighted slave trader named Bat, then engineers an escape in order to fool the townsfolk into believing that a dreaded abolitionist group, the Sons of Freedom, is at work in St. Petersburg. When the slave trader is murdered, Jim, now a free man working for the Widow Douglas, is arrested and charged with the crime. There is talk of lynching. At the trial Jim is found guilty, but the real culprits conveniently turn up at the last moment—the King and the Duke from *Huckleberry Finn*. Tom proves their guilt by displaying a drawing of the King's footprint made at the murder scene and a set of false teeth stolen from the victim. Jim goes free. The story is not as much fun as it sounds.

In September 1897 the family moved from Weggis to Vienna, taking a four-bedroom corner suite at the luxurious Hotel

Metropole. (The hotel, eager to advertise itself as Mark Twain's home away from home, offered them a cut-rate deal.) They had come to the Austrian capital primarily for Clara to study piano with the famed music teacher Theodor Leschetizky, who had taught, among others, Ignacy Jan Paderewski. Clara was not remotely as gifted a pianist as Paderewski; for one thing, her hands were too small to span all the keys. But Leschetizky took her on, perhaps recognizing, like the hoteliers, the inherent publicity value in being associated with Mark Twain. There was an unexpected bonus for Clara in her music lessons. At a dinner party hosted by her parents for Leschetizky, she met a nineteen-year-old fellow student named Ossip Gabrilowitsch, a Russian-born Jew who traveled in more exalted musical circles than Clara, counting Gustav Mahler as a personal friend. Clara and Ossip began a tempestuous, off-and-on romance that would carry over for the next twelve years.

Vienna was the artistic and intellectual center of the late-flowering Austro-Hungarian Empire. Freud was there, and so were the musicians Johann Strauss, Gustav Mahler, Antonín Dvořák, Arnold Schoenberg, and Anton Bruckner; the painters Gustav Klimt and Maximilian Kurzweil; and Zionist homeland adherent Theodor Herzl. Vienna was also home to 175,000 Jews, a wealthy, hard-working minority that already was causing serious strains in the Austrian body politic. Twain, visiting the Viennese city council and the lower house of parliament, witnessed a number of tumultuous debates over the Jews and their rightful place in Austrian society. From these visits came two early political essays, "Stirring Times in Austria" and "Concerning the Jews." Clara, whose boyfriend was one of the comparatively few people, Jew or Gentile, whom Twain consistently liked, noted that her father was "always a great admirer" of the Jewish race. "Arguments as the virtues or non-virtues of the Jews were often the topic of discussion in our drawing-room," she said, "and Father always grew eloquent in defense of Christ's race." He was, in fact, so eloquent in his defense of the Jews that some Austrians, noting that his first name was Samuel, speculated darkly that Twain was Jewish himself.[17]

The two essays depicted a city and country on the cusp of virulent anti-Semitism. (Vienna's newly elected mayor, Karl Lueger, later became a role model for Adolf Hitler, who spent six years living in the city less than a decade after Twain left it.) In "Stirring Times in Austria," Twain described a tumultuous thirty-three-hour debate over the concept of *Ausgleich,* the formal linking of Austria and Hungary that began in 1867 and had to be renewed every ten years. Amid much booing and name-calling—"infamous louse-brat," "East German offal tub," "cowardly blatherskite," "pimp," "brothel knight," "Polish dog"—the leading spokesman for the union, Dr. Otto Lecher of Brunn, undertook a twelve-hour-long filibuster on behalf of the measure and its effect on the Fatherland. The debate eventually came to blows, and Twain noted "a surging, struggling, shoulder-to-shoulder scramble" similar to a bench-clearing baseball brawl. About the only thing the delegates could agree upon, he said, was that "they all hate the Jews." After the parliamentary debate, several days of rioting broke out across Germany and the Austro-Hungarian Empire. "The Jews and Germans were harried and plundered, and their houses destroyed," noted Twain. "In some cases the Germans [were] the rioters, in others the Czechs—and in all cases the Jew had to roast, no matter which side he was on." It was modern European history in a nutshell.[18]

Twain's follow-up article, "Concerning the Jews," was a well-intentioned, if somewhat condescending, attempt to clarify his own feelings about the much-persecuted race. In response to a letter from a Jewish New York attorney, Twain addressed the question that within a generation would linger mutely in the smoke and ash above the Nazi crematoriums: "Will you kindly tell me why, in your judgment, the Jews have thus ever been, and are even now, in these days of supposed intelligence, the butt of baseless, vicious animosities?" Twain began by pointing out that another Jewish reader had noted years earlier that there were no disparaging references to Jews in Twain's books. This was because, the author said, "I am quite sure that (bar one) I have no race prejudices." The exception was Native Americans, a group toward whom Twain retained a lifelong antipathy dating back to his 1861 trip to Nevada, when he first saw Indian "sit-arounds" loitering outside western forts begging for handouts of food and whiskey. "I can stand any society," he noted. "All that I care to know is that a man is a human being—that is enough for me; he can't be any worse." He was not even prejudiced against Satan—"We never hear *his* side." Twain ventured the opinion "that in Russia, Austria, and Germany nine-tenths of the hostility to the Jews comes from the average Christian's inability to compete successfully with the average Jew in business." Not to worry, said Twain. "The Jew need not stand in any fear of being robbed and raided. Among the high civilizations he seems to be very comfortably situated indeed." Subsequent events would prove him tragically wrong in that assumption.[19]

The family was summering at the Austrian resort town of Kaltenleutgeben in September 1898 when word arrived of the assassination of Empress Elisabeth in Geneva. The empress, a melancholy beauty who dieted and exercised constantly and visited mental hospitals for amusement, was stabbed to death by an Italian anarchist, Luigi Lucheni, while strolling to the train station with her lady in waiting. Lucheni had come to Geneva intending originally to assassinate the Duke of Orleans, pretender to the French throne, but the duke had already left town. It didn't matter much to Lucheni who he killed, as long as his victim was a royal. Approaching the sixty-year-old empress from behind, he stabbed her once in the heart with a four-inch-long needle. Her heavy corset limited the bleeding by naturally compressing the wound, and the empress at first did not even realize she had been wounded—much less mortally. When her husband, Emperor Franz Joseph I, heard the news, he feared at first that she had committed suicide. Her assassin later did just that, frustrated that Switzerland had no capital punishment law that would have allowed him to die a martyr.

In a posthumously published essay, "The Memorable Assassination," Twain angrily decried the stabbing of "that good and unoffending lady the Empress," as he termed her in a letter to Joseph Twichell. Her assassin, Twain said, was nothing more than "a soiled and patched young loafer, without gifts, without talents, without education, without morals, without character, without any born charm or any acquired one . . . an unfaithful private in the ranks, an incompetent stone-cutter, an inefficient lackey; in a word, a mangy, offensive, empty, unwashed, vulgar, gross, mephitic, timid, sneaking, human polecat." Besides ordinary human sympathy, Twain's intense response to the empress's murder may have been occasioned by the knowledge that Elisabeth, too, had lost a child (to suicide) a few years before her own death.[20]

Twain's identification with the empress reflected perhaps the high regard in which he himself was held by Viennese society. City policemen commonly cleared the riffraff from the street while Herr Twain passed. "I confess," Twain told Clara, "that I rather like it." Asked his opinion of Russian Czar Alexander II's proposal for world disarmament, Twain joked—one hopes—that "the Czar is ready to disarm; I am ready to disarm. Collect the others, it should not be much of a task now." As a further indication of his status, Twain was granted a private audience with the emperor. The two conversed in a mixture of English and German, with the emperor translating for them. "I had prepared and memorized a very good speech but had forgotten it," said Twain. "He was very agreeable about it. He said a speech wasn't necessary." At the end of their visit, Twain made the modest proposal that Franz Joseph eliminate the human race by withdrawing oxygen from the air. He didn't explain how this would be in any way advantageous to the Austro-Hungarian crown.[21]

The family stayed for twenty months in Vienna, relocating from the Hotel Metropole to the even more lavish Hotel Krantz on Neuer Markt. There they entertained so many important artists, politicians, and diplomats that Clara dubbed their suite "the second U.S. Embassy" and Twain took to calling himself the "self-appointed Ambassador at Large of the U.S. of America—without salary." Father and daughter attended plays, dinner parties, and concerts together, while Livy remained at home with Jean and her nurse. Clara, as usual, was the target of flirtatious young men, both Austrians and Americans. The American ambassador to Vienna, the grandly named Charlemagne Tower, took a special interest in Twain, appointing him guest of honor at various diplomatic open houses. They sat in Johann Strauss's private box at the opera, dined with Clara's master, Leschetizky, and were taken up by the reigning doyenne of Viennese society, Countess Misa Wydenbruck-Esterhazy, at whose vacation villa they were

staying when they heard the news of Empress Elisabeth's assassination. After one charity reading, Twain met and shook
hands with Sigmund Freud.[22]

It wasn't all wining and dining for Twain during his stay
in Vienna. He also found time to produce a series of surprisingly dark works, reflecting both his own increasingly morbid
state of mind and the simmering Austrian political milieu.
Along with the essays "Stirring Times in Austria" and "Concerning the Jews," Twain wrote several new fictional works,
including his last unquestioned masterpiece, "The Man That
Corrupted Hadleyburg," an icy fable about a wronged traveler
who exposes a narrow little town's innate corruption. He also
worked on an extended fantasy called "The Chronicle of Young
Satan," detailing the apprentice demon's seven hundred-year
mission trip to Earth, where his uncle the Archfiend functions
as "spiritual head of 4/5 of the human race, and political head
of the whole of it." Twain felt particularly qualified to relate
the fantastic happenings, he said, since Satan was also an
uncle of his. The chronicle purports to be the memoir of an
aged Austrian, Theodor Fincher, who meets and befriends the
angel during his youth. In this version, the second of four
"Mysterious Stranger" manuscripts concerning Satan's visit to
Earth, the young demon is a charming but casually brutal
being who amuses himself by interfering with, and sometimes
crushing, the lives of mere mortals. "You would think he was
talking about flies," the narrator says, echoing Gloucester's lament in *King Lear:* "As flies to wanton boys are we to th' gods;
/ They kill us for their sport." Twain would continue playing
with the story, off and on, for the next ten years, always giving
the Devil the best lines.[23]

Most revealing of Twain's Vienna stories is "The Great
Dark," an unfinished novella about a devoted family man who
goes to sleep one afternoon after playing with his daughters

in their comfortable home and awakens to find himself in the midst of a nightmare voyage aboard a ghost ship in a steaming, unquiet sea. The girls in the story are exactly the ages of Susy and Clara in 1880, eight and six respectively, and other details correspond precisely to their lives that year, including their first trip abroad. The father, Henry Edwards, had been showing the girls a drop of water in a microscope, a gift for the oldest girl. It is her birthday (March 19, the same as Susy's). The sinister, omnipresent Superintendent of Dreams explains that Edwards and his family are sailing across that same drop of water. "We were in no way prepared for this dreadful thing," Twain writes, speaking as much for his own family as for the fictional Edwardses. "We were a happy family, we had been happy from the beginning; we did not know what trouble was, we were not thinking of it nor expecting it." In the course of their journey the family experiences various disasters, from giant sea creatures to mutinous sailors. The Superintendent intrudes from time to time to explain that Henry has lived his entire life aboard ship, and that his other life, in "dream homes," was just that—a dream. The older girl dies. Henry awakens to find that he can't remember his wife or daughters. His happy home life has been the dream.[24]

"The Great Dark" is not perhaps first-rate Twain, but it reflects accurately the impact the long years of exile were having on the author's philosophy. "We are strangely made," the narrator notes. "We think we are wonderful creatures. Part of the time we think that, at any rate. And during that interval we consider with pride our mental equipment, with its penetration, its power of analysis, its ability to reason out clear conclusions from confused facts, and all the lordly rest of it; and then comes a rational interval and disenchants us. Disenchants us and lays us bare to ourselves, and we see that intellectually we are really no great things; that we seldom really know the thing we think we know; that our best-built certainties are but sand-houses and subject to damage from any wind of doubt that blows." Increasingly, in the wake of his repeated business failings, the sudden loss of their Hartford house, the long years of restless wandering across Europe, and the unassuageable death of Susy, those winds were gusting ever more fiercely about the family.[25]

The nightmares bled over into real life. In December 1897, Twain's brother Orion died as he had lived, quietly and humbly, sitting in a chair alone in his upstairs bedroom in Keokuk, Iowa, the victim of a massive heart attack. Twain told Orion's widow, Mollie, a little callously perhaps, that he rejoiced for her dead husband—"He has received life's best gift." Two months later, the writer's old *Virginia City Territorial Enterprise* mentor, Dan De Quille (William Wright), died in obscurity in West Liberty, Iowa, and later that same year Twain's *Innocents Abroad* soul mate, Mary Mason Fairbanks, died in Providence, Rhode Island, at the age of seventy. The circle of life was getting smaller by the day.[26]

About the only good news Twain received in Vienna—and it was excellent news indeed—was a letter from Henry Huttleston Rogers's personal secretary, Katharine Harrison, in February 1898 reporting that the author's finances were finally back in the black. Thanks to his royalties from *Following the Equator*, the continuing sales of his collected works, and most importantly a series of canny investments by Rogers on his behalf, Twain was able to pay off all his remaining creditors. "Mrs. Clemens has been reading the creditors' letters over and over again," he reported to Rogers, "and says this is the only really happy day she has had since Susy died." Rock-solid stock holdings in such surefire companies as Brooklyn Gas and

Federal Steel insured that the stream of money would continue flowing. "I have been out and bought a box of 6 cent cigars," Twain bragged to William Dean Howells. "I was smoking 4½ before."[27]

The start of the Spanish-American War in April 1898 had a negative impact on Twain's Viennese popularity. There was a large Spanish community in Vienna, centered on the country's foreign embassy, and Europeans in general had grave reservations about America's forcible entry into the great game of international power politics. Twain initially supported the war, telling Joseph Twichell back in Hartford: "I have never enjoyed a war as I am enjoying this one. For this is the worthiest one that was ever fought, so far as my knowledge goes. It is a worthy thing to fight for one's own freedom; it is another sight finer to fight for another man's. I think this is the first time it has been done." He would soon have cause to reconsider his opinion.[28]

For all its myriad social pleasures, Vienna began to wane as a base of operations for Twain and his family. The worsening of Jean's epilepsy, first diagnosed when she was fifteen, depressed and frightened them all. On the advice of Jean's New York doctor, M. Allen Starr, her parents had been treating her with heavy doses of potassium bromide, a powerful sedative and antiepilepsy drug. For more than a year her seizures abated, only to return with a vengeance in the summer of 1897. Viennese doctors increased the dosage, and for the next two years Twain and Livy kept an obsessively close watch on their youngest daughter, alive to the merest twitch or change of expression. "It was," said Twain, "like watching a house that was forever catching fire & promised to burn down if you ever closed an eye." Despite their best efforts the seizures continued, and after a particularly terrible episode on March 19, 1899—perhaps not coincidentally Susy's birthday—they sought outside help, contacting the renowned Swedish epilepsy specialist Jonas Henrik Kellgren, who had his headquarters in London. It was Twain's intention to have Kellgren treat Jean throughout the summer, then return to America in the fall.[29]

On May 31, 1899, the family arrived in London, and Livy took Jean to her first consultation with Kellgren. He immediately recommended a six-month-long schedule of treatment, which he termed "movement therapy," before Jean could even think about returning to the United States. Treatment would begin with a summer-long stay at the Sweden village of Sanna, on the southern tip of Lake Vattern, 175 miles southwest of Stockholm, where Kellgren operated a research clinic and sanitarium. "It was our purpose to remain in London till the end of July," Twain informed Henry Rogers in late June, "but I want to turn the family loose on the Swedish Movement Cure for a change; so [our] passage is booked in a ship which leaves London for Gottenborg, Sweden, about 2 weeks hence. The sanitarium is all alone by itself on a lake 4 hours from there. We expect to be there three or four months, then return to London, and finally leave for America in the winter or toward spring. It is a radical change of all the plans."[30]

Kellgren's treatments amounted to little more than extreme chiropractics. The daily regimen called for strenuous exercise, regular massages, careful dieting, and plenty of fresh air. He took Jean off potassium bromide, which instantly improved her condition by not aggravating it. The entire family, including the ever hale and hearty Clara, took treatments alongside Jean, and Twain credited the stringent exercise routine for a marked improvement in his chronic arm pain and bronchitis. "Jean is in good spirits and brisk health," Twain reported. He was doubly wrong. Although for a time her epilepsy was controlled, Jean remained deeply depressed. Neither as pretty as Clara nor as talented as Susy, she felt herself both unlovely and unloved. "Is it going to be my miserable lot never to really love & be loved?" she wondered. "That would be too dreadful, and would offer another fair reason for suicide." It is unclear whether her parents recognized the true depth of Jean's despair, although they clearly understood that she, and they, were increasingly unhappy. "Hell (Sanna Branch)," Twain jotted in his notebook.[31]

That October they returned to London, where Jean continued her treatments at Kellgren's Knightsbridge clinic. Clara, for her part, switched her musical dreams from piano to voice, intending to restart her performing career as a concert singer. Meanwhile, the family experienced vicariously England's long-brewing war with the Boers, which had begun in May of that year. Three straight shocking defeats in December 1899—at Stormberg, Magersfontein, and Colenso—shook British confidence to the core, and black mourning crepe swathed the capital. Restaurants and theaters were empty, and newsboys shouted out the latest terrible news from the front. "Our national life and thought never were the same again," English editor J. L. Garvin observed. Twain sympathized. "It's awful here," he told Katharine Harrison. "Half of our friends are in mourning, and the hearts of the other half stop beating when they see a newsboy." The dismal weather and attendant illnesses contributed to another lackluster Christmas. Privately, Twain fumed to Howells, "This is a sordid & criminal war, & in every way shameful & excuseless." Still, he said, "England must not fall; it would mean an inundation of Russian & German political degradations which would envelop the globe & steep it in a sort of Middle Age night & slavery which would last till Christ comes again." As it was, he had missed running into Adolf Hitler by a few short years.[32]

Thanks in large part to her newest military innovation, the concentration camp, Great Britain managed to withstand the initial Boer successes in South Africa and win a negotiated victory in May 1900. "London wild with joy and noise all day until two hours after midnight," Twain noted when the armistice was signed. A few days later he reported to Twichell: "London is happy-hearted at last. The British victories have swept the clouds away and there are no uncheerful faces." But the war had worn on everyone, even the noncombatant American visitors. "I should not want to live those 5 months over again," Twain confessed to Rogers, "even at an advance of wages."[33]

With the end of the war and the stagnation of Jean's recovery in London, it was time to end what Twain termed "this everlasting exile." Much to his exasperation, he discovered that the widely ballyhooed Kellgren treatment was, in reality, the same sort of common osteopathic treatment currently being practiced all over America. "If only I had found this out in September, instead of yesterday," he told Rogers, "we all should have been located in New York the 1st of October." Instead, they had wasted the better part of a year in London, during which time Twain had done a good deal of socializing but little writing, dropping in at the Savage Club, where he now had

member's privileges, spending a long weekend at Henry M.
Stanley's country estate, and attending a ball in honor of King
Oscar II of Norway and Sweden. He felt confident enough in
his finances to turn down a ten thousand dollar offer from his
old promoter James B. Pond for ten nights of new American
lectures and an equally remunerative offer from *Punch* magazine for one hour of editing work per week. They were going
home, Twain said, although none of them could decide exactly
where home was anymore. "It looks as if we shall go to Hartford," Twain wrote to Rogers, "but we can't make up our minds.
Half of the friends there are dead, and we sort of shudder at
the prospect." Practical-minded Clara summed up the family's quandary: "None of us felt able to face the old Hartford
home without Susy." It had become a mausoleum.[34]

With no final destination in mind, the family returned to
American shores on October 15, 1900, having been away
from the country for the better part of nine years. A large
crowd of reporters was on hand when their ship, the S.S. *Min-
nehaha*, docked in New York harbor. As the canny Rogers had
foreseen years earlier, Twain's worldwide tour and highly
publicized repayment of his debts had only increased his popularity with the American public. Newspaper headlines trumpeted his return: "Mark Twain Comes Home," "Mark Twain
in America Again," and giddiest of all, "Mark Twain Wants
to Be President." The author wasn't ready to go that far, but
he did admit that "if I ever get ashore I am going to break
both of my legs so I can't get away again." Asked to recount
his globe-circling experiences, Twain demurred, saying he

had put them all in his book, and "there aren't enough of them to go 'round."[35]

Not all the questions were so lightweight. A reporter from the *New York Herald* wanted to know what Twain thought about "the grave question of imperialism." Twain admitted that he had initially supported the war with Spain, but said he drew the line when President William McKinley, soon to be reelected, turned the army on the very Filipino rebels who had helped the United States defeat Spain in the first place. "I left these shores, at Vancouver, a red-hot imperialist," Twain told the *New York Herald*. "I wanted the American eagle to go screaming into the Pacific. But since then my eyes have been opened. I have read carefully the treaty of Paris, and I have seen that we do not intend to free, but to subjugate the people of the Philippines. We have gone there to conquer not to redeem. And so I am an anti-imperialist. I am opposed to having the eagle put his talons on another land."[36]

In that same interview, Twain allowed that he and his family would be moving back to Hartford in the spring, "after nine years of wandering up and down the earth." They never did. Five days after their arrival, Twain's old Hartford neighbor Charles Dudley Warner, coauthor of *The Gilded Age*, died. Twain went alone to attend the funeral, mordantly telling a reporter from the *Hartford Courant* that "the Monday Evening Club was assembling in the cemetery." He went by the Farmington Avenue house, which he took "a pathetic pleasure" in seeing again, but the melancholy visit confirmed in Twain's mind the feeling that the family could never live there again. Susy's death had changed things permanently; the house was now well and truly haunted. Eventually it was sold, at a loss, to Richard M. Bissell, president of the Hartford Fire Insurance

Company. Instead, they moved into a brownstone on West 10th Street near Union Square, and Twain became a familiar daily presence in the city, strolling the streets with his instantly recognizable tousled hair and ever-present stump of cigar.[37]

With the melancholy exception of an eight-month-long stay in Italy in 1903–1904, Twain would spend the next four years in New York City, heavily involved, along with William Dean Howells and other prominent Americans, in the burgeoning anti-imperialist movement. Among those enrolled in the local chapter of the Anti-Imperialist League were such strange bedfellows as industrialist Andrew Carnegie and American Federation of Labor president Samuel Gompers. Other members included naturalist John Burroughs, philosopher William James, magazine editor E. L. Godkin, former U.S. Secretary of the Interior Carl Schulz, and Unitarian Church minister Henry White Chadwick. Howells was chapter president, Twain was vice president. In a remarkable burst of crystalline anger, he produced such masterpieces of political invective as "To the Person Sitting in Darkness," "The Czar's Soliloquy," "King Leopold's Soliloquy," and "The War Prayer," each reflecting, in its way, the darkening of Twain's worldview after his eye-opening experiences abroad. He was no longer an innocent.

Twain's brave stand against American adventurism still strikes a resonant chord with modern readers in the post–9/11 world, but it brought him into conflict with a number of his fellow citizens at the time, including Joseph Twichell, who continued to preach muscular Christianity from his pulpit at the

Asylum Hill Congregational Church in Hartford. "I'm not expecting anything but kicks for scoffing at McKinley, that conscienceless thief & traitor," Twain wrote to Twichell, but for the life of him he could not understand how Twichell, "a public guide & teacher," could counsel his worshippers "to hide their opinions when they believe their flag is being abused & dishonored. How do you answer for it to your conscience?"[38]

Assassin Leon Czolgosz would shortly remove McKinley from the world's concerns, but the slain president's replacement, Theodore Roosevelt, would prove to be even more aggressive in the pursuit of American foreign policy. Attending a ceremony at Yale University at which Twain received an honorary degree, Roosevelt went out of his way to say within Twain's earshot that he wanted to skin the author alive for his criticism of foreign policy. Another larger-than-life figure had a milder response to Twain's antiwar views. Winston Churchill, then twenty-five, came to New York in December 1900 to promote his book about his exploits in the Boer War, which had already made him a celebrity in Great Britain. Introducing Churchill at a reception held in the Waldorf-Astoria hotel, Twain noted the visitor's Anglo-American bloodlines: "Mr. Churchill by his father is an Englishman; by his mother he is an American," said Twain, "no doubt, a blend that makes the perfect man." The two countries had always been kin, he noted, and now they were related again. "I think that England sinned when she got herself into a war in South Africa which she could have avoided, just as we have sinned in getting into a similar war in the Philippines," Twain said. "Yes, we are kin, and now that we are also kin in sin . . . the harmony is complete." Churchill accepted the criticism with good grace and got Twain to sign for him all thirty volumes of Twain's collected works.[39]

The American intervention in the Philippines continued to
gnaw at Twain's conscience. "We were to relieve them from
Spanish tyranny to enable them to set up a government of their
own, and we were to stand by and see that it got a fair trial,"
he had said in an interview with the *London World* in October
1900. "It was not to be a government according to our ideas,
but a government that represented the feeling of the majority
of the Filipinos, a government according to Filipino ideas. That
would have been a worthy mission for the United States. But
now—why, we have got into a mess, a quagmire from which
each fresh step renders the difficulty of extrication immensely
greater. . . . I wish I could see what we were getting out of it,
and all it means to us as a nation." Generations of Americans
would find themselves asking the same questions in the century to come, as the nation became bogged down in one quagmire after another in Korea, Vietnam, Iraq, and Afghanistan.
Earlier than most, Twain recognized the intrinsic absurdity
of attempting to force democracy on others by purely military
means.[40]

Despite his late-blooming radicalism, Twain continued to
vacation with Henry Huttleston Rogers and other rich
friends aboard Rogers's 227-foot yacht, *Kanawha*. The yacht,
said to be the fastest private vessel then plying American
waters, had been named for the Kanawha River in West Virginia, along whose banks Rogers had secretly bought up
thousands of acres of prime coal-mining land and constructed
two railroads to link his mines to the eastern seaboard. In
March 1902, Twain joined Rogers and a bevy of high rollers
including former Speaker of the House Thomas Reed, who
had earned Twain's respect by resigning from Congress in

protest of the war with Spain. For three weeks the party sailed the Caribbean, island-hopping from Miami to the Bahamas to Cuba and Jamaica. In Havana harbor, they saw the rusting skeleton of the battleship *Maine*, which reminded Twain of a giant tarantula in its death throes.

In May 1902, Twain returned to Hannibal for the last time, detouring one hundred miles north from the University of Missouri in Columbia, where he received an honorary doctor of letters degree. It was a bittersweet homecoming. The town itself had thrived in recent years, thanks in no small part to its famous native son, and Twain was feted at a number of events during a jam-packed four-day visit. He posed for photographs at his old boyhood home at 206 Hill Street, climbed Holliday's Hill with his now elderly schoolmates, and visited Mount Olivet Cemetery, where his parents and brothers were buried and "almost every tombstone recorded a forgotten name that had been familiar and pleasant to my ear when I was a boy." He handed out diplomas to the graduating class at the high school and gave a final appearance at the Labinnah Club (Hannibal spelled backwards), where he startled the five hundred assembled guests by dissolving into tears and sobbing helplessly for several moments. "I realize that this must be my last visit to Hannibal," he explained, "and in bidding you hail I also bid you farewell." He left by train the next morning, never to return. Despite his long decades of world travel, in his inmost heart he would always be the barefoot boy whitewashing his mother's picket fence and watching the steamboats coming up the river.[41]

In August 1902, Livy suffered a combination asthma attack, panic attack, and heart palpitations while they were vacationing in Maine. Both she and her husband thought she was dying. Physicians diagnosed her condition as heart disease, and the family returned to their rented mansion in Riverdale, New York, for Livy to recuperate. Clara, who had begun touring professionally as a singer, suspended her career to care for her mother. Jean was little help, contracting double pneumonia in December and nearly dying herself. Hoping to keep Livy calm, doctors discouraged her excitable husband from seeing her, which only increased their patient's unease. Twain took to pushing handwritten notes under her door. Eventually Livy was permitted to visit her sister's farm in Elmira, but she spent most of the time lying in a bed on the porch. It would be her last visit to her old hometown. Twain went alone to Woodlawn Cemetery to place flowers on Susy's grave.

After Livy expressed a desire to see Florence again, Twain quickly made it happen, going to New York in late September 1903 to book passage for them on an ocean steamer. While staying at the Grosvenor Hotel, his favorite haunt in the city, he sent Livy a note apparently intended to ease her mind. "Dear, dear sweetheart," he wrote, "I have been thinking & examining, & searching & analyzing, for many days, & am vexed to find that I more believe in the immortality of the soul than misbelieve in it." The conditional syntax revealed Twain's still unresolved doubts about immortality, but it meant a lot to Livy. "I am truly thankful that you 'more believe in the immortality of the soul,'" she wrote back, adding the wifely codicil, "You don't need to bother about it, it will take care of itself."[42]

On October 24 they sailed for Europe with Clara, Jean, and the ever faithful Katy Leary aboard the S.S. *Princess Irene*. Landing at Genoa, they went by train to Florence, where they moved into the Villa di Quarto, a draughty, fifty-room mansion owned by an Italian-American widow, the Countess Massiglia, born Frances Paxton of Philadelphia. From the start the countess and the family feuded over rent, utilities, telephone service, and property access (the countess insisted on keeping the gates locked, which in turn kept Livy's doctors waiting to see their patient). The weather was uncommonly cold for Florence, and the mood was further darkened by the news that Orion Clemens's widow, good-hearted, eternally optimistic Mollie, had died in Keokuk at the age of sixty-nine. The news was kept from Livy to avoid upsetting her.

Inside "Calamity House," as Twain called it, the family did their best to carry on. While Clara worked herself into a nervous breakdown—the first of several she would suffer in the next few years—caring for her mother, Twain toiled desultorily on a handful of magazine sketches, as well as a new short story, "The $30,000 Bequest," that was a pale copy of "The Man That Corrupted Hadleyburg." In the new story, a happy couple, Saladin and Electra Foster, are promised the inheritance from a distant relative. The couple spends years imagining their windfall and investing in equally imaginary stocks. By the time the bequest is revealed to be a cruel practical joke, they have ruined their lives with anticipatory greed—in essence corrupting themselves. It was a parable of sorts for Twain's own financial undoing.

While her sister cared for their mother and their father worked on his writings, Jean was left largely to her own devices, taking lonely walks in the woods and looking in on the villa's various animals, including a donkey that was as mean-spirited as their landlady, on one occasion biting off the thumb of an unlucky farmhand. "Satan," as Twain took to calling the countess, was cheap and stingy, "a male in everything but sex." In an unpublished piece of dictation, he flayed the troublesome landlady as an adulteress and divorcee, a fading beauty who painted her face and dyed her hair in an unsuccessful attempt to conceal her inner ugliness. She was, said Twain, "excitable, malicious, malignant, vengeful, unforgiving, selfish, stingy, avaricious, coarse, vulgar, profane, obscene, a furious blusterer on the outside and at heart a coward. . . . I think she is the best hated person I have ever known, and the most liberally despised." To get back at her, Twain became party to a number of lawsuits, including one filed on behalf of the thumbless farmhand.[43]

The countess, by all existing testimony, was a supremely unpleasant woman, but at least part of Twain's enmity toward her stemmed from displaced anger over Livy's unarrestable decline. Plagued by shortness of breath, night sweats, and high temperatures, she had to sleep sitting up in bed. Her American and Austrian doctors could do little more than inject her with morphine and brandy and limit her distraught husband's visits to a few minutes a day. One night, to cheer her, Twain sat at the piano in the parlor and banged out several of Livy's favorite spirituals, including "In the Sweet By and Bye," which an organ grinder had been playing outside the St. Nicholas Hotel in New York City on the night they first met, December 27, 1867, while she was visiting the metropolis with her family. She had struck him then as "sweet, timid, and lovely," and she remained so for all the ensuing years he was privileged to know her.[44]

After more than seven months in Florence, during which time she was confined almost exclusively to bed, Livy died at 9:20 p.m. on Sunday, June 5, 1904. Katy Leary was at her side; the others were asleep in their separate rooms. Twain kept a solitary bedside vigil with Livy's body throughout the night and the next day, telling Joseph Twichell later, "In all that night & all that day she never noticed my caressing hand." As Livy had wished, Katy dressed her in a lavender-colored silk dress and matching slippers she had bought but had never gotten to wear. Livy's brother, Charley Langdon, received Twain's telegram announcing her death on the thirty-seventh anniversary of the *Quaker City's* departure from New York—the cruise that had brought them all together in the first place. With Livy gone, Twain told another friend, "My life has lost color & zest, & I do not value it."[45]

Twain and his daughters returned from Italy on June 28 aboard the Italian ship *Prince Oscar*, and Livy was buried in Elmira in the family plot next to Susy. An empty plot on the other side was reserved for her husband. At the funeral Clara cried out and swooned into her father's arms. The next month Twain's only surviving sibling, his sister Pamela, died in Greenwich, Connecticut, at the age of seventy-six. Clara suffered a nervous collapse and spent the next year in and out of various New England sanitariums. Jean received a broken ankle and concussion after her horse collided one day with a trolley car, throwing her fifty feet through the air. It was yet another depressing mishap in a seemingly unbroken line of mishaps afflicting Twain's ill-starred daughters. Jean's seizures continued, and once or twice she struck Katy Leary in the face while Katy was attempting to comfort her. Eventually, at the urging of Twain's new personal secretary, Isabel Lyon, Jean was institutionalized. She and her father saw little of each other for the next five years.

As biographer Ron Powers has observed, the final six years of Mark Twain's life were the history of an old man, "which is to say, the history of every old man." He rented a brownstone at 21 Fifth Avenue in New York City and installed Lyon, then thirty-seven, as his chief housekeeper, accountant, and factotum. Lyon was unmarried, ambitious, and completely devoted to Twain, whom she had first met a dozen years earlier while working as a governess for one of his Hartford neighbors. Hired initially as Livy's secretary, she had accompanied the family to Florence in 1902 and never left. She called Twain "King" and he called her "Lioness." Increasingly she supplanted Clara and the absent Jean as the preeminent female in the household, sleeping in a bedroom next to Twain's and closely monitoring all aspects of his life, to the point of watching him shave in the morning. Twain, as always, enjoyed the attention, but he had no desire to take matters any further—particularly with someone who was barely older than his daughters. Another new presence in the author's life was Albert Bigelow Paine, a Massachusetts-born writer and editor who first met Twain while researching a biography of famed illustrator Thomas Nast. Twain invited Paine to serve as his amanuensis for his newly conceived autobiography. In time Paine would parlay his connection with Twain into a decades-long role as his literary executor.[46]

Clara, in isolation in a Manhattan sanitarium, sent her father a somewhat barbed message in November 1904. "I feel like sending you one more fluttering goodbye before the bars are bolted," she wrote. "You are a cunning little man and very touching with all your thoughtfulness. I hope that soon I shall hear you are beautifully situated with companionable friends about you." What her father, a genius with words, made of the word *cunning* is unknown. Meanwhile, Lyon redecorated Twain's brownstone with furniture retrieved from the vanished Hartford home. It was a mistake. The first time Twain saw the familiar sitting room pieces, he told Livy's sister, Susan, "It broke my heart." Declining an invitation to dine with Andrew Carnegie, the author responded, "I expect to stay [in bed] till the whiskey runs out, for I read, smoke, write, & am very comfortable & seldom sober."[47]

He continued to be a fascinated observer of the one American who was as famous as he was: Theodore Roosevelt. Despite his deep reservations about Roosevelt's bellicose foreign policy and flamboyant personal behavior, Twain refrained from criticizing the president publicly. In this he was motivated by his gratitude for Roosevelt's thoughtful order to port officials, upon learning of Livy's death, to clear the grieving family's way through customs. The president's act, said Twain, was "a deeply valued, gratefully received, unasked for favor; & with all my bitter detestation of him I have never been able to say a venomous thing about him in print since." In private, though, he considered Roosevelt a preening ass and an incessant publicity hound, "the Tom Sawyer of the political world." The president, said Twain, "would go to Halifax for half a chance to show off, and he would go to hell for a whole one."[48]

Setting aside their political differences, Twain and Roosevelt dined in the White House in the spring of 1905. It was a success, as was the festive gathering at Delmonico's restaurant on December 5 of the same year that was sponsored by Twain's friends on the occasion of his seventieth birthday. A forty-piece orchestra from the Metropolitan Opera House serenaded diners in the restaurant's exclusive Red Room, where the dinner fare included kingfish filet, Baltimore terrapin, saddle of lamb, and redhead duck, accompanied by various fine wines, champagne, and brandy. The chief organizer was George Harvey, Twain's editor at *Harper's Weekly* and the *North American Review,* and the distinguished list of attendees included William Dean Howells, Henry Huttleston Rogers, Andrew Carnegie, Joseph Twichell, George Washington Cable, Willa Cather, Emily Post, and Peter Finley Dunne. Howells introduced his old friend with a special sonnet that concluded, "I will not say; 'Oh, King, live forever,' but 'Oh, King, live as long as you like.'"[49]

Twain was in fine form that night, treating admirers to a thirty-minute speech filled with anecdotes and wisecracks, laughter and tears. He began by saying that he remembered well his first birthday in "a little hamlet in the backwoods of Missouri, where nothing ever happened. . . . I came the nearest to being a real event that happened in that village in more than two years." That birthday had occasioned his first after-dinner speech, said Twain; this one would be his swan-song. "I have achieved my seventy years in the usual way," he joked, "by sticking strictly to a scheme of life which would kill anybody else. I have made it a rule to go to bed when there wasn't anybody left to sit up with; and I have made it a rule to get up when I had to." He ate only those foods that disagreed with him, smoked only one cigar at a time, never smoked in bed, never refrained from smoking while awake, and drank only when it helped others feel comfortable about drinking in his presence. His only exercise, he said, was sleeping and resting. Twain concluded his remarks on a wistful note: "When you in your turn shall arrive at pier No. 70 you may step aboard your waiting ship with a reconciled spirit, and lay your course toward the sinking sun with a contented heart."[50]

From time to time, the lure of travel still arose. Twain's favorite foreign destination in his twilight years was the coral-

tipped island of Bermuda, which he had first visited with his
Quaker City shipmates in 1867. He made half a dozen trips to
the island between 1907 and 1910, with a variable roster of
traveling companions that included Joseph Twichell, Henry
Rogers, Albert Paine, and Isabel Lyon. Usually he stayed at
the Princess Hotel in Hamilton, although after becoming
friends with American vice-consul William Allen and his
family, Twain was a frequent houseguest at their official residence, Bay House. Bermuda, which he invariably pronounced
"Burmooda," was a welcome respite from the harsh New York
winters. Twain found the island "the tidiest country in the
world. There are no harassments; the deep peace and quiet
of the country sink into one's body and bones, and give his
conscience a rest." Sounding a bit like a tourist brochure, he
proclaimed, "In Bermuda a sick person gets well in 3 days, &
strong in a week. You only need the Bermuda air to make you
weller than ever you were in your life before." There were
no intrusions, no crime, no noise, no politics—"no follies but
church, & I don't go there."[51]

In Bermuda, Twain devoted much of his time to a new ob-
session, one that worried his daughter Clara at the time and
has caused biographers a certain amount of queasiness ever
since: his "Angelfish." The Angelfish, named after the flashing,
silvery little fish common to Bermudan shallows, were a ho-
mogeneous group of pretty young girls between the ages of ten
and sixteen whom the author encountered in New York or on
his voyages and visits to and from Bermuda. These girls fulfilled, at least subconsciously, a desire on Twain's part to have
grandchildren—something Clara and Jean were unwilling or
unable to do. Having attained what he termed "the grandpapa
stage of life," Twain set out to handpick his own substitute
granddaughters. "We are all collectors," he maintained. "As for

me, I collected pets—young girls from ten to sixteen years old, girls who are pretty and sweet and naïve and innocent—dear young creatures to whom life is a perfect joy and to whom it has brought no wounds, no bitterness, and few tears." As such, they were unlike his own star-crossed daughters.[52]

In time there would be thirteen Angelfish in Twain's collection, all formally inducted by the author into his Aquarium Club and presented with shiny enamel lapel pins in the shape of their namesake. In June 1908, after Twain moved into a new, eighteen-room mansion in Redding, Connecticut, that had been constructed for him by William Dean Howells's architect son John, he hung a sign over the billiards room designating it "the Aquarium" and appointing himself "the Admiral." There he entertained the girls, always carefully chaperoned by their mothers or Isabel Lyon. Much as he had done with his own daughters when they were that age, Twain amused his young visitors with funny stories, card games, charades, and billiards. Marion Schuyler Allen, the mother of his favorite Angelfish, Helen Allen, explained the club's appeal for Twain. "Young people attracted and inspired him," she wrote. "He could be himself with them, a simple lovable man, child-like in his ingeniousness; also they were the best of shields from the too demanding grown-ups." It was probably no coincidence that thirteen-year-old Helen Allen bore a striking resemblance to Susy Clemens.[53]

Much scholarly attention has been paid to Twain and the Angelfish, and the prevailing opinion is that there was nothing improper about their interactions. Nevertheless, when Clara returned in 1908 from one of her frequent trips to Europe, she quietly put an end to the club and convinced Albert Bigelow Paine and other early biographers to say nothing about her father's unconventional hobby. Certainly, to hypersensitized modern eyes, the many photographs of the white-haired, seventyish author with pretty little girls sitting on his lap, clinging to his arm, hugging his neck, or frolicking with him in bathing suits strike a disquieting note. As scholar Karen Lystra observed in her 2004 book, *Dangerous Intimacy:* "This was no ordinary hobby. Sexually innocent though it almost certainly was, treating children as collectibles is neither charming nor benign." (It should be noted that the title of Lystra's book refers not to the Angelfish but to Twain's equally troubling relationship with Isabel Lyon, whom he eventually dismissed in 1909 for alleged financial improprieties.)[54]

Besides the Angelfish, there were other autumnal diversions for Twain. In June 1907 he traveled to England for the last time to receive an honorary degree from Oxford University. The valedictory trip was a highlight of his life. During his stay Twain was treated to a series of ovations, both formal and spontaneous. Dock workers cheered him when he landed at Tilbury, and two dozen leading literary lights, including Arthur Conan Doyle, Anthony Hope, and the current British poet laureate, Alfred Austin, attended a banquet in his honor at the American embassy. He toured Parliament, where he was permitted to observe the debate in the House of Lords from the private gallery reserved for foreign ambassadors and heads of state, and he was received personally by Prime Minister Henry Campbell-Bannerman. The *London Daily Express* hailed Twain's visit as well worth celebrating: "He is just as much a national institution on this side of the Atlantic as he is in his native country," said the newspaper. "The fact that he was born in America merely constitutes him a citizen of the United States for voting purposes. Otherwise he is a citizen of the English-speaking world."[55]

A special treat for the lowborn scion of a scraggly Mississippi River town was a gilded invitation to a royal garden party at Windsor Castle. Eschewing his trademark white suit for the custom-mandated frock coat and top hat, Twain nevertheless attracted much attention. As the London correspondent of *Harper's Weekly* recorded with pardonable pride: "Mark Twain was admittedly the most popular man present. As he drove from the station to the castle he was kept incessantly bowing in response to the delighted cheers of the crowds." During the festivities, Twain was invited into the royal pavilion, where he had a lengthy conversation with King Edward VII and Queen Alexandra. The king reminded Twain that they had met years before, in Bad Homburg, Germany, when Edward was the prince of Wales. Forgetting—or disregarding—protocol, Twain impulsively shook hands with the king and tapped him on the arm several times during their chat. He made a friendly offer to buy the castle, which the king rebuffed with a smile. Afterward Twain lunched with George Bernard Shaw, Max Beerbohm, and James M. Barrie, whose eternally youthful Peter Pan vies with Huckleberry Finn as the most recognizable boy in English literature.[56]

At Oxford, Twain joined the formal procession from Magdalen College to the Sheldonian Theatre on Broad Street. The glittering parade of scholars was led by the newly installed college chancellor, Lord George Nathaniel Curzon, former viceroy of India, who was festooned in a heavy, gold-bedecked cloak, ruffled neckerchief, knee breeches, silk stockings, and silver-buckled slippers. Twain, walking a proper six places behind, wore the college's familiar gray-and-scarlet gown and a graduation-day mortarboard. He looked, modern bi-

ographer Michael Shelden has observed, very much like that
other Connecticut Yankee in England, Hank Morgan. All
things considered, it was an impressive group. Other hon-
orees included Prime Minister Campbell-Bannerman, Prince
Arthur of Connaught, Salvation Army founder General William Booth, British Field Marshal Sir Evelyn Wood, sculptor
Auguste Rodin, composer Camille Saint-Saens, and Foreign
Secretary Edward Gray, who nine years later would observe
memorably that "the lights are going out all across Europe.
They shall not be lit again in our lifetimes."

Trailing a few steps behind Twain was fellow author Rudyard Kipling. The chronicler of India and the White Man's
Burden had known Twain for twenty years, ever since showing
up uninvited on his doorstep in Elmira to pay his respects.
Now, keeping back to let the older man savor his moment in
the sun, Kipling recorded Twain's reception. "All the people
cheered Mark Twain," he wrote. "And when they weren't
cheering and shouting, you could hear the Kodak shutters
click-clicking like gun locks. The streets literally rose at him—
men cheered him by name on all sides." Smiling and waving,
Twain took off his mortarboard and bowed. Inside the the-
ater he again received the loudest applause. Twain, noted the
New York Times, was "the lion of the occasion. Everyone rose
when he was escorted up the aisle and he was applauded for
a quarter of an hour." Lord Curzon bestowed on Twain, in
Latin, the university's official doctor of literature degree. It was
a long way from the Hannibal, Missouri, elementary school.[57]

Twain liked the ceremonial gown and tasseled cap so well
that he wore them often, on the least provocation, even at

the long-delayed wedding in October 1909 of Clara and Ossip Gabrilowitsch. Two previous engagements between the couple had been called off, and when Clara told him of the latest, Twain responded, "What! Again!" before adding a less than effusive paternal blessing, "Well, anyway, any girl would be proud to marry him." The ceremony, held in Redding at the mansion Twain christened Stormfield after his novella *Captain Stormfield's Visit to Heaven,* was officiated, as so many other notable family occasions had been, by Joseph Twichell. At Clara's request, Twichell omitted the word "obey" from her wedding vows. Jean, newly returned home after years of hospitalization, stood with her sister as maid of honor.[58]

Tragedy soon preempted joy. On Christmas Eve 1909, a mere two months after Clara's wedding, Jean suffered an epileptic attack at Stormfield and drowned in the bathtub. (She may have had a heart attack first.) She was not yet thirty. Twain was working in his study when Katy Leary burst through the door and shouted, "Miss Jean is dead!" "Possibly I know now what a soldier feels when a bullet crashes through his heart," Twain would write. All that night and the next morning he worked on a final essay, "The Death of Jean," which served as a formal farewell to both his youngest daughter and the profession of writing itself. He would never publish anything else. Like Prospero, he had broken his staff. "I lost Susy thirteen years ago," Twain wrote. "I lost her mother—her incomparable mother!—five & a half years ago; Clara has gone away to live in Europe; & now I have lost Jean. How poor I am, who was once so rich!" Jean was buried in the white silk gown she had worn at Clara's wedding. Having vowed never to watch another of his loved ones being put into the ground, Twain did not attend the funeral.[59]

Not wanting to spend another winter at Stormfield, Twain returned to Bermuda, where he stayed again with Helen Allen and her parents. It would be his last trip abroad. While there he played miniature golf with New Jersey governor Woodrow Wilson, who was two years away from being elected to the presidency and seven years away from reneging on his promise to keep the United States out of war. From Bermuda, Twain exchanged letters with Clara, now living with her husband in Germany. Father and daughter had quarreled frequently in recent years, usually over the subject of Isabel Lyon or Clara's abortive singing career, which Twain dismissed as so much "warbling around the countryside." Now he assured his only surviving daughter that "you are nearer and dearer to me now than ever. Of my fair fleet all my ships have gone down but you; but while I have you I am still rich." He added, "I don't know why you should love me. I have not deserved it."[60]

Suffering from increasingly severe chest pains brought on by a lifetime of smoking, Twain cut short his visit with the Allens and prepared to sail home from Bermuda on April 12, 1910, telling Albert Paine that he did not wish to die abroad and have to lie in an undertaker's cellar or a ship's hold—"It is dark down there & unpleasant." His last scrap of writing, appropriately enough, was "Etiquette for the Afterlife," a brief note to Paine in which he jocosely advised him that "in hell it is not good form to refer, even unostentatiously, to your relatives in heaven, if persons are present who have none there." While in heaven, he said, one should avoid overdressing. "A pair of spurs & a fig-leaf is a plenty. For evening dress, leave off your spurs."[61]

The return voyage was less heavenly than hellish for both men, with Twain fighting for breath as Livy had done six years earlier, and Paine watching helplessly from the bedside, administering regular doses of morphine in a futile attempt to ease the old man's pain. Twain expected to die at any moment, wondering aloud at one point if there wasn't something he could sign to "be out of all this." Paine urged him to hold on until Clara could arrive from Europe. "It is a losing race," said Twain, "no ship can out-sail death." But somehow he did.[62]

The final photograph of Mark Twain, one of the most photographed men of his era, shows him being carried in a wheelchair off his ship in New York harbor on the afternoon of April 14. He is swathed head to toe in a striped blanket and is wearing a black bowler hat, as are his attendants. His head is tilted a little to one side and he is regarding the camera with an unreadable, hawk-like expression. One week later he died at Stormfield, with the just-returned Clara at his side. "Goodbye," he whispered to his daughter. "If we meet—" They were the last in the incomparable torrent of words—written, spoken, quoted, and performed—that had tumbled nonstop out of Mark Twain over the course of his seven and a half decades on earth. Improbably, his nearly sixty years of restless and rewarding travel ended where they had begun, at home and in bed. Outside his window, completing its lonely transit, Halley's Comet, his celestial familiar, winked westward across the darkling sky.[63]

AFTERWORD

In one of his last conversations with his daughter, Clara, a few days before his death, Mark Twain expressed a doubt common to many writers: that his work would not long outlive him. That, of course, has not been the case. In the roster of nineteenth-century American novelists, Twain surely ranks, in critical stature, with or just slightly below Henry James. In terms of reader enjoyment and name recognition, he far outdistances James and every other American writer of the era. Among British novelists of the time, only Charles Dickens clearly overtops him. Twain's popularity around the world remains undiminished more than a century after his death, and his name recognition is virtually universal. Everyone knows Mark Twain. No less a judge than Ernest Hemingway flatly declared that "all modern American literature comes from one book by Mark Twain called *Huckleberry Finn*." And George Bernard Shaw, no slavish Twain acolyte, told the author in 1907 that "the future historian of America will find your works as indispensable to him as a French historian finds the political tracts of Voltaire." So it still seems today.[1]

The scope and quality of Twain's travel writing has contributed greatly to his posthumous reputation, as indeed it contributed to his personal popularity and financial well-being during his lifetime. *The Innocents Abroad, Roughing It,* and *Life on the Mississippi* remain three of his best-known and best-loved works; and *Following the Equator,* a book about which the author had many doubts, has grown in stature over the years for its prescient depiction of the modern evils of racism, militarism, and imperialism, and the uneasy collision between the First and Third Worlds. Even *A Tramp Abroad,* the least impressive of his five travel books, contains many scattered pleasures, most involving the reader's happy sense of tramping vicariously alongside the author, sharing his amused exasperation with the ever-perplexing locals encountered along the way. As Richard Bridgman points out, Twain's background as a newspaper reporter stood him in good stead in his travel writing by "permit[ting] him to use his special literary gifts, which displayed themselves best in the short bursts of pointed observations, anecdotes, episodes, and tales . . . minimally linked at best and without any synthesizing conclusion." It was, says Bridgman, "a license to react to whatever caught his fancy and be paid for it." Being paid was good.[2]

The heart of Twain's most successful writing, fiction or nonfiction—his drawling, droll, companionable voice—is a feat of written ventriloquism that first revealed itself in *The Innocents Abroad.* There, two decades before *Huckleberry Finn* canonized the use of vernacular English in high literature, Twain somehow hit upon the perfect conversational tone for an American writer talking, figuratively, to other Americans. It was the voice of the unadorned, unintimidated "freeborn sovereign," an uncommonly intelligent, uncommonly entertaining, but always recognizably *common* man. "My books are like water," Twain wrote. "Those of the great geniuses are wine. Everybody drinks water."[3]

The nineteenth century was a great era for travel, and Mark Twain in his time was a great traveler. His curiosity, stamina, and lifelong ability to be surprised and delighted by what he saw on his journeys are among his most admirable and attractive traits. The sheer brio with which he confronted the outside world comes through clearly in his travel writing, as does his creditable disinclination—usually—to take himself too seriously. Twain may well have been, as someone said, *the* American, but he was never the Ugly American. He generally made a good impression on foreign peoples, both for himself and for his country. As with other elements of his personality, it was something of an act; he was an exceptionally complicated man. The people who knew and loved him best—his wife and daughters, his mother, brother, and sister, his great friends William Dean Howells, Joseph Twichell, and Henry Huttleston Rogers—often found it exhausting to be in his company, but they seldom found it boring.

Twain did not set out to become a travel writer—at first it was simply a means by which he could subsidize his visits to pleasant and exotic places, beginning with his move to San Francisco from Virginia City in 1864 and his months of "luxurious vagrancy" in Hawaii two years later. Writing travel letters, and then full-length travel books, enabled him to pay for his foreign excursions and also provided him with the raw material for a lucrative second career as a stage performer. The runaway success of his first public lecture, "Our Fellow Savages of the Sandwich Islands," allowed Twain to start getting paid for what he heretofore had done for free: talk. In due time he would talk his way completely around the world. "In

October, 1866," he would say, with only slight exaggeration, "I broke out as a lecturer, and since then I have not had to do any honest work."[4]

The last part was not entirely true. There was, in fact, a good deal of work involved in Twain's travels: rough seas, poor ships, crowded railcars, variable weather, bad food, strange germs, uncomfortable beds, incomprehensible languages, confusing customs—all the myriad difficulties associated with foreign travel, then and now. And yet, through it all, Twain (and his long-suffering wife and daughters) soldiered on. He became, as Jeffrey Alan Melton notes, "the prototypical modern tourist." In a way, Twain's entire life was an extended act of tourism. He was always moving, literally or figuratively. His fiction, no less than his nonfiction, frequently revolves around the act of traveling. Huck Finn floats down the Mississippi River; Prince Edward wanders the byways of England; Hank Morgan, the Connecticut Yankee, traverses both time and space; Satan pays a visit to Earth. Even Tom Sawyer, fully at home in lark-filled St. Petersburg, stays in such perpetual motion, both physically and mentally, that he almost seems a tourist of his own crowded life.[5]

Twain's remarkable life journey from a hardscrabble riverfront village in Missouri to the marbled palaces of imperial Europe was a towering personal accomplishment. And as the living embodiment of the American character, Twain in his rise mirrored the progress of his ever-advancing fellow countrymen, who eagerly followed in his footsteps to swarm the storied byways of Old World Europe and the developing outposts of the New. His writings and his personal example helped lead Americans into the twentieth century; and his open, smiling face, with its alert, unblinking eyes deep-set above the familiar drooping mustache, remains one of the most recognizable faces in the world. The advertising slogan that accompanied his image on a box of five-cent cigars in 1913 sums up Twain's enduring personal appeal and global reach: "Mark Twain—Known by everyone; liked by all."

Inevitably, for Twain and other American travelers following in his wake, extensive exposure to a world beyond their own national borders led to disappointment and disillusionment. The three decades between Twain's *Innocents Abroad* trip and the around-the-world tour chronicled in *Following the Equator* marked the end of the first great wave of American travel. As Melton concludes, "In the beginning, the Tourist Age promised that one could escape his or her part of the world, explore the rest of the world, and enrich him- or herself, but . . . ultimately he has no place to go, no reality wherein he can hide from his civilization. . . . All journeys must end. The tourist must go home." It was a homecoming that Twain, for various reasons, found difficult to manage. Like another great American artist, Bob Dylan, whose compulsion to perform has kept him riding a tour bus for decades on a never-ending musical tour, Twain was always happiest on the road, where he could continue his lifelong need to "move—move—Move!" Both, perhaps, epitomized the advice of a third unique native-born artist, Satchel Paige, who memorably cautioned, "Don't look back; something might be gaining on you."[6]

Mark Twain, tourist and traveler, lived for seventy-four years, four months, and three weeks. Nearly a dozen years, or some 16 percent of his life, was spent abroad. He seemed always to be crossing or recrossing the ocean. In the summer of 1877, Twain became fascinated by the case of a real-life *Flying Dutchman*, a Bermuda-based schooner seen drifting helplessly, seaweed-encrusted and sails drooping, in the Gulf

Stream waters off Cape Fear, North Carolina. The *Jonas Smith* had been sold piecemeal for scrap and then taken out to sea one last time by her owner. No one knew what had become of the captain or her thirteen-man crew, said to be bound for Savannah, Georgia. The ship's star-crossed journey set Twain to thinking about his own life of travel. "I have heard of a good many dismal pleasure trips, but this case leads the list," he wrote to the editor of the hometown *Hartford Courant*. "And if ever the tired old tramp is found, I should like to be there to see him in his sorrowful rags & his venerable beard of grass and seaweed, & hear those ancient mariners tell the story of their mysterious wanderings through the solemn solitudes of the ocean." Perhaps, at last, it is useful to ask if Mark Twain himself was ever truly at home anywhere, or if, like Coleridge's Ancient Mariner and his own American Vandal, he was merely a visitor to foreign shores, a mysterious stranger—innocent or not—with a carpetbag in one hand and an unsheathed tomahawk in the other.[7]

ABBREVIATIONS

NOTES

INDEX

ABBREVIATIONS

Auto   Mark Twain, *The Autobiography of Mark Twain*,
            ed. Charles Neider (New York: Harper & Row, 1959)

FE   Mark Twain, *Following the Equator* (New York:
            Oxford University Press, 1996)

Ganzel   Dewey Ganzel, *Mark Twain Abroad: The Cruise of
            the "Quaker City"* (Chicago: University of Chicago
            Press, 1968)

IA   Mark Twain, *The Innocents Abroad* (New York:
            Oxford University Press, 1996)

LLMT   *The Love Letters of Mark Twain*, ed. Dixon Wecter
            (New York: Harper and Brothers, 1949)

Melton   Jeffrey Alan Melton, *Mark Twain, Travel Books,
            and Tourism* (Tuscaloosa: University of Alabama
            Press, 2002)

MFMT   Clara Clemens, *My Father, Mark Twain* (New York:
            Harper & Bros., 1949)

MTHHR   *Mark Twain's Correspondence with Henry Hud-
            dleston Rogers, 1893–1909*, ed. Lewis Leary
            (Berkeley: University of California Press, 1969)

MTHL   *Mark Twain-Howells Letters: The Correspondence
            of Samuel L. Clemens and William Dean Howells,*

ed. Henry Nash Smith and William M. Gibson,
2 vols. (Cambridge: Harvard University Press, 1960)

MTL   *Mark Twain's Letters:* vol. 1, *1853–1866*, ed. Edgar
           Marquess Branch, Michael B. Frank, and Kenneth
           Anderson; vol. 2, *1867–1868*, ed. Harriet Elinor
           Smith and Richard Bucci; vol. 3, *1869*, ed. Victor
           Fischer and Michael B. Frank; vol. 4, *1870–1871*,
           ed. Victor Fischer and Michael B. Frank; vol. 5,
           1872–1873, ed. Lin Salamo and Harriet Elinor
           Smith; vol. 6, *1874–1875*, ed. Michel B. Frank and
           Harriet Elinor Smith (Berkeley: University of
           California Press, 1988–2002)

MTMF   *Mark Twain to Mrs. Fairbanks*, ed. Dixon Wecter
           (San Marino, CA: Huntington Library, 1949)

MTN   *Mark Twain's Notebook*, ed. Albert Bigelow Paine
           (New York: Harper & Brothers, 1935)

MTP   Mark Twain Papers, Bancroft Library, University of
           California, Berkeley

N&J   *Mark Twain's Notebooks & Journals:* vol. 1,
           1855–1873, ed. Frederick Anderson, Michael
           B. Frank, and Kenneth M. Sanderson; vol. 2,
           1877–1883, ed. Frederick Anderson, Lin Salamo,
           and Bernard L. Stein; vol. 3, *1883–1891*, ed. Robert
           Pack Browning, Michael B. Frank, and Lin Salamo
           (Berkeley: University of California Press,
           1975–1979)

Rodney   Robert M. Rodney, *Mark Twain Overseas* (Wash-
           ington, DC: Three Continents Press, 1974)

TA   Mark Twain, *A Tramp Abroad* (New York: Oxford
           University Press, 1996)

NOTES

INTRODUCTION

1. MTL, 2:49–50.

2. Arthur L. Scott, "Mark Twain Looks at Europe," *South Atlantic Quarterly* 52 (1953): 399.

3. Henry James to William James, October 29, 1888, quoted in Michael Gora, *Portrait of a Novel: Henry James and the Making of an American Masterpiece* (New York: Liveright, 2012), xvi; Henry James, *The American* (New York: Scribner's, 1907), 45.

4. IA, xii; "The American Vandal Abroad," in *Mark Twain's Speeches,* ed. Albert Bigelow Paine (New York: Harper and Brothers, 1923), 30.

5. Mark Twain, *Life on the Mississippi* (New York: Penguin Putnam, 2001), 166, 246.

6. Auto, 111.

7. Mark Twain, *Roughing It* (Berkeley: University of California Press, 1993), 396.

8. For Twain's time in Hawaii, see Roy Morris, Jr., *Lighting Out for the Territory: How Samuel Clemens Headed West and Became Mark Twain* (New York: Simon and Schuster, 2010).

9. *San Francisco Alta California,* December 15, 1866.

10. MTP, Notebook 32:20; Mark Twain, "Concerning the Jews," in *Collected Tales, Speeches, & Essays, 1891–1910* (New York: Library of America, 1992), 355.

1. INNOCENTS ABROAD

1. *San Francisco Alta California*, March 27, 1867, quoted in Fred Kaplan, *The Singular Mark Twain: A Biography* (New York: Anchor, 2003), 173.

2. *San Francisco Alta California*, March 30, 1867.

3. Edward H. House, Mark Twain, and Charles C. Duncan, quoted in Justin Kaplan, *Mr. Clemens and Mark Twain* (New York: Simon and Schuster, 1966), 28.

4. Ron Powers, *Mark Twain: A Life* (New York: Free Press, 2006), 183.

5. MTL, 2:17; *New York Evening Post*, March 9, 1867.

6. MTL, 2:49–50; *Alta California*, June 23, 1867.

7. Ganzel, 16; *New York Daily Sun*, June 6, 1867; *San Francisco Alta California*, April 9, 1867.

8. N&J, 2:332; Ganzel, 28–29; MTL, 2:58.

9. Henry T. Tuckerman, "The Philosophy of Travel," *United States Magazine and Democratic Review* 14 (1844): 527, quoted in Melton, 17.

10. Henry James, "Americans Abroad," *Nation* 3 (October 1878): 209; Ralph Waldo Emerson, "Self-Reliance," in *Anthology of American Literature: Colonial through Romantic*, ed. George McMichael (New York: Macmillan 1980), 1061.

11. Richard S. Lowry, "Framing the Authentic: The Modern Tourist and *The Innocents Abroad*," *New Orleans Review* 18, no. 2 (1991): 23; Melton, 17.

12. Washington Irving, *The Sketch-Book of Geoffrey Crayon, Gent.* (New York: Putnam, 1860), 15.

13. Larzer Ziff, *Return Passages: Great American Travel Writing, 1780–1910* (New Haven, CT: Yale University Press, 2000), 121.

14. Frederick Marryat, "How to Write a Book of Travels," in *The Works of Captain Marryat*, vol. 1 (New York: Peter Fenelon Collier, 1900), 529.

15. Jeffrey Steinbrink, "Why the Innocents Went Abroad: Mark Twain and American Tourism in the Late Nineteenth Century," *American Literary Realism* 16 (1983): 279.

16. IA, v, 19; Wilbur Fisk, *Travels in Europe* (New York: Harpers, 1841); Mark Twain, *Adventures of Huckleberry Finn*, ed. Sculley Bradley, Richmond Croom Beatty, E. Hudson Long, and Thomas Colley (New York: W. W. Norton, 1977), 2.

17. Albert Bigelow Paine, ed., *Mark Twain's Letters* (New York: Harper and Brothers, 1917), 127.

18. N&J, 1:57; Ganzel, 21.

19. Kaplan, *Mr. Clemens and Mark Twain*, 43; Samuel C. Webster, ed., *Mark Twain, Business Man* (Boston: Little, Brown, 1946), 97.

20. Mark Twain, quoted in Jerome Loving, *Mark Twain: The Adventures of Samuel Clemens* (Berkeley: University of California Press, 2010), 139–140; Ganzel, 50.

21. Ganzel, 41–42; Emily Severance, *Journal Letters of Emily A. Severance*, ed. Julia S. Millikan (Cleveland: Gates Press, 1938), 25.

22. Ganzel, 51; Severance, *Journal Letters*, 7.

23. IA, 26–27.

24. Ganzel, 35; IA, 39.

25. IA, 43.

26. IA, 49–51; Ganzel, 65.

27. Ganzel, 77; IA, 63–65.

28. W. Pembroke Fetridge, *Harper's Hand-Book for Travellers in Europe and the East* (New York; Harper and Brothers, 1865), 551; IA, 78.

29. MTL, 2:68.

30. IA, 78–84.

31. Ibid., 92–93; Ganzel, 96.

32. IA, 94, 113, 150.

33. Ibid., 126; *San Francisco Daily Alta*, September 5, 1867.

34. IA, 132–133.

35. Ibid., 136.

36. Daniel Morley McKeithan, ed., *Traveling with the Innocents Abroad* (Norman: University of Oklahoma Press, 1958), 42; IA, 164–165.

37. Ibid., 190–192; *San Francisco Alta California*, September 22, 1867.

38. IA, 199; *New York Daily Herald*, August 22, 1867.

39. IA, 217–218.

40. Ibid., 238, 249, 294–295.

41. Ibid., 262, 267, 279–283.

42. Ganzel, 164.

43. Ibid., 165: IA, 308–312.

44. IA, 312; Severance, *Journal Letters*, 24.

45. IA, 324–325.

46. Ibid., 331–335.

47. Ibid., 337; *San Francisco Alta California*, September 26, 1867.

48. Ganzel, 173–175; IA, 340.

49. Ben Jonson, "To the Memory of My Beloved Master William Shakespeare," in *The Norton Anthology of English Literature*, ed. M. H. Abrams (New York: W. W. Norton, 1974), 1229; IA, 354.

50. IA, 342–343, 347.

51. *New York Sun*, September 18, 1867; Ganzel, 179–180; Severance, *Journal Letters*, 118–119; *San Francisco Alta California*, October 29, 1867.

52. Ganzel, 185; IA, 361–362.

53. *San Francisco Alta California*, October 23, 1867; IA, 363–364, 368; *New York Sun*, September 23, 1867.

54. Ganzel, 185–186.

55. IA, 384–385.

56. *San Francisco Alta California*, November 3, 1867.

57. Ibid., November 6, 1867.

58. IA, 393–397; *Cleveland Herald*, October 8, 1867.

59. IA, 403–406.

60. Ibid., 410, 419–420.

61. Ibid., 430.

62. Ibid., 431.

63. Ibid., 432.

64. Ibid., 436, 439–440.

65. Ibid., 443, 451.

66. Ibid., 460, 463; *San Francisco Alta California*, January 19, 1868.

67. IA, 465; *San Francisco Alta California*, January 19, 1868.

68. IA, 498–499.

69. Ibid., 537.

70. Ibid., 530, 532; *San Francisco Alta California*, February 16, 1868; *Cleveland Herald*, November 22, 1867.

71. IA, 476; Ganzel, 241; N&J, 1:96.

72. McKeithan, *Traveling with the Innocents Abroad*, 465.

73. IA, 558–560.

74. *San Francisco Alta California*, March 19, 1868; IA, 570; Severance, *Journal Letters*, 177.

75. *San Francisco Alta California*, April 5, 1868; IA, 567; *Cleveland Herald*, December 5, 1867.

76. IA, 601–602; Harold T. McCarthy, "Mark Twain's Pilgrim's Progress: *The Innocents Abroad*," *Arizona Quarterly* 26 (1970): 250–252.

77. *San Francisco Alta California*, April 12, 1868; N&J, 1:468.

78. IA, 609, 613–614.

79. Ibid., 621–622, 626–627.

80. Ibid., 628–629.

81. *Cleveland Herald*, November 25, 1867; IA, 636.

82. IA, 640–642.

2. TRAMPS ABROAD

1. MTL, 2:120, 160.

2. Mark Twain, *Adventures of Huckleberry Finn*, ed. Sculley Bradley, Richmond Croom Beatty, E. Hudson Long, and Thomas Colley (New York: W. W. Norton, 1977), 83.

3. Howard G. Baetzhold, *Mark Twain and John Bull: The British Connection* (Bloomington: Indiana University Press, 1970), 264.

4. "The American Vandal Abroad," in *Mark Twain's Speeches*, ed. Albert Bigelow Paine (New York: Harper and Brothers, 1923), 21, 30; *Cleveland Herald*, November 18, 1868.

5. Bret Harte, quoted in Leslie Fiedler, "An American Abroad," *Partisan Review* 33 (1966): 78; Bruce Michelson, "Mark Twain the Tourist: The Form of *The Innocents Abroad*," *American Literature* 49 (1977), 396.

6. MTL, 4:52.

7. Mark Twain, *Roughing It* (Berkeley: University of California Press, 1993), 67–68.

8. Steven Marcus, *The Other Victorians: A Study of Sexuality and Pornography in Mid-Nineteenth Century England* (New York: Basic Books, 1964), 67–73.

9. Olivia Langdon Clemens, quoted in Ron Powers, *Mark Twain: A Life* (New York: Free Press, 2006), 319; MTL, 5:151–152.

10. Mark Twain, quoted in Robert M. Rodney, *Mark Twain Overseas* (Washington, D.C.: Three Continents Press, 1974), 74.

11. Roy Morris Jr., *Ambrose Bierce: Alone in Bad Company* (New York: Crown, 1995), 4.

12. Carey McWilliams, *Ambrose Bierce: A Biography* (New York: A. and C. Boni, 1929), 98–100; *San Francisco News Letter*, July 30, 1870.

13. Ibid., 100.

14. MTL, 5:200, 196, 183–184.

15. *London Times*, November 7, 1872; MTMF, 168; Arthur L. Scott, "Mark Twain Looks at Europe," *South Atlantic Quarterly* 52 (1953), 403.

16. *London Spectator*, September 21, 1872; M. E. Grenander, "Ambrose Bierce, John Camden Hotten, *The Fiend's Delight*, and *Nuggets and Dust*," *Huntington Library Quarterly* 28 (August 1965): 365.

17. MTL, 5:388. Justin Kaplan, *Mr. Clemens and Mark Twain* (New York: Simon and Schuster, 1966), 171.

18. Albert Bigelow Paine, *Mark Twain: A Biography* (New York: Harper and Brothers, 1912), 489; MTL, 5:439.

19. Powers, *Mark Twain*, 338; Charles Warren Stoddard, *Exits and Entrances, A Book of Essays and Sketches* (Boston: Lothrop, 1903), 73–74.

20. Mark Twain, quoted in Rodney, 86–87; MTL, 5:497, 508, 3.

21. MTL 6:158.

22. Mark Twain, *Life on the Mississippi* (New York: Penguin Putnam, 2001), 166, 118, 48.

23. Powers, *Mark Twain*, 251.

24. Dee Brown, *The Year of the Century: 1876* (New York: Scribner's, 1966), 247–249; John D. Bergamini, *The Hundredth Year: The United States in 1876* (New York: Putnam, 1976), 277. For the 1876 election, see Roy Morris Jr., *Fraud of the Century: Rutherford B. Hayes, Samuel Tilden, and the Stolen Election of 1876* (New York: Simon and Schuster, 2003).

25. William Dean Howells, *My Mark Twain: Reminiscences and Criticism* (Baton Rouge: Louisiana State University Press, 1967), 51.

26. Mark Twain, "The Whittier Birthday Speech," in *Selected Shorter Writings of Mark Twain*, ed. Walter Blair (Boston: Houghton Mifflin, 1962), 151–154.

27. Howells, *My Mark Twain*, 52; George Arms and Christoph K. Lohmann, eds., *Selected Letters* [W. D. Howells] (Boston: Twayne, 1979), 182; Mark Twain, "The Story of a Speech," in *Speeches* (New York: Oxford University Press, 1996), 11–12; *Boston Daily Globe*, December 18, 1877.

28. Frederick Anderson, William M. Gibson, and Henry Nash Smith, eds., *Selected Mark Twain-Howells Letters 1872–1910* (Cambridge: Harvard University Press, 1967), 105; MTP, Mark Twain to Jane Clemens, February 17, 1878.

29. MTHL, 1:227, 237; N&J, 2:75, 80; MTP, Mark Twain to William Dean Howells, May 4, 1878.

30. TA, 83–84, 87.

31. Ibid., 200–201; N&J, 2:123.

32. N&J, 2:113n; TA, 221.

33. Mark Twain, quoted in Hamlin Hill, ed., *Mark Twain's Letters to His Publishers* (Berkeley: University of California Press, 1967), 109–110. MTHL, 1:250.

34. TA, 102, 103, 207, 215.

35. Ibid., 126, 129.

36. Ibid., 203, 154–155.

37. Ibid., 245.

38. Ibid., 285.

39. Ibid., 286, 292, 302–303.

40. Ibid., 397–398.

41. Ibid., 418.

42. Ibid., 438, 446, 449.

43. Ibid., 505.

44. Ibid., 515, 519–521.

45. MTL, 1:338–339; N&J, 2:182, 227–228.

46. MTL, 1:248–249, 348–350.

47. MTMF, 228–229; Hill, *Mark Twain's Letters to His Publishers*, 111; N&J, 2:309.

48. N&J, 271–272, 308; MTMF, 229–230; Hill, *Mark Twain's Letters to His Publishers;* MTP, Mark Twain to Joseph Twichell, June 10, 1879.

49. Mark Twain, quoted in Baetzhold, *Mark Twain and John Bull*, 42; N&J, 2: 293, 318.

50. N&J, 2:333. MTHL, 534. Paine, *Mark Twain*, 648. Geoffrey West, *Charles Darwin: A Portrait* (New Haven: Yale University Press, 1938), 298–299.

51. *New York Sun*, September 3, 1879; *New York Times*, September 3, 1879.

52. William Dean Howells, "A Tramp Abroad," *Atlantic Monthly*, May 1880, 111; Frederick Anderson, ed., *Mark Twain: The Critical Heritage* (New York: Barnes and Noble, 1977), 76–77; Powers, *Mark Twain*, 422; Horst H. Kruse, "A Tramp Abroad," in *The*

Mark Twain Encyclopedia, ed. J. R. Lemaster and James D. Wilson (New York: Garland, 1993), 743.

53. Scott, "Mark Twain Looks at Europe," 404; Melton, 78–79.

3. INNOCENTS ADRIFT

1. Mark Twain, *Life on the Mississippi* (New York: Penguin Putnam, 2001), 298; Powers, *Mark Twain*, 494.

2. Mark Twain, *The Prince and the Pauper* (New York: Library of America, 1994), 4, 206.

3. MTHL, 2:645.

4. MTN, 72–73.

5. Justin Kaplan, *Mr. Clemens and Mark Twain* (New York; Simon and Schuster, 1966), 281–288; William Dean Howells, *My Mark Twain: Reminiscences and Criticism* (Baton Rouge: Louisiana State University Press, 1967), 80.

6. Albert Bigelow Paine, *Mark Twain: A Biography* (New York: Harper and Brothers, 1912), 831.

7. Susy Clemens, *Papa: An Intimate Biography of Mark Twain*, ed. Charles Neider (Garden City: Doubleday, 1985), 83–84; MTHL, 2:663.

8. Auto, 278.

9. Kaplan, *Mr. Clemens and Mark Twain*, 291.

10. MTP, Mark Twain to Orion Clemens, July 1, 1889; MTP, Mark Twain to Pamela Clemens Moffett, June 7, 1897.

11. MTP, Mark Twain to Orion Clemens, February 25, 1891; MTP, Mark Twain to J. P. Jones, February 13, 1891; Kaplan, *Mr. Clemens and Mark Twain*, 304.

12. LLMT, 258.

13. N&J, 3:621–623; MFMT, 87.

14. MTHL, 2:643–644.

15. Ibid., 645; MTMF, 267–268.

16. Mark Twain, "Aix, the Paradise of Rheumatics," in *Europe and Elsewhere* (New York: Harper and Brothers, 1923), 102–104.

17. Mark Twain, "At the Shrine of St. Wagner," in *What Is Man? And Other Philosophical Writings*, ed. Paul Baender (Berkeley: University of California Press, 1973), 4, 11; Kaplan, *Mr. Clemens and Mark Twain*, 312; MTP, Olivia Clemens to Grace King, August 23, 1891.

18. MTP, Notebook 31, 2–4.

19. Ibid., 5.

20. Mark Twain, "Down the Rhone," in *The Complete Essays of Mark Twain*, ed. Charles Neider (New York: Da Capo Press, 1991), 595.

21. Ibid., 602–603, 616.

22. Susy Clemens, *Papa*, 15.

23. Olivia Susan Clemens to Louise Brownell, March 5, September 3, November 8, 1893, quoted in Jerome Loving, *Mark Twain: The Adventures of Samuel L. Clemens* (Berkeley: University of California Press, 2010), 332, 336.

24. MFMT, 91–93.

25. Mark Twain, "The German Chicago," *Complete Essays*, 88–89.

26. Rodney, 139; MTP, Mark Twain to Clara Clemens, January 21, 1893.

27. Harriet Elinor Smith, ed., *Autobiography of Mark Twain*, vol. 1 (Berkeley: University of California Press, 2010), 456.

28. Robert Underwood Johnson, *Remembered Yesterdays* (Boston: Little, Brown, 1923), 321.

29. MTMF, 269; Grace King, *Memories of a Southern Woman of Letters* (New York: Macmillan, 1932), 179.

30. MTP, Olivia Langdon Clemens to Clara Clemens, December 11, 1892; MTP, Olivia Susan Clemens to Clara Clemens, November 11, 1892.

31. Mark Twain, *Tom Sawyer Abroad / Tom Sawyer, Detective*, ed. John C. Gerber, and Terry Firkins (Berkeley: University of California Press, 1980), 189–190.

32. Hamlin Hill, ed., *Mark Twain's Letters to His Publishers* (Berkeley: University of California Press, 1967), 359.

33. MTMF, 269; MFMT, 126–127.

34. Hill, *Mark Twain's Letters*, 343–344.

35. For the Panic of 1893, see H. W. Brands, *The Reckless Decade: America in the 1890s* (Chicago: University of Chicago Press, 1995); and Mark Wahlgren Summers, *The Gilded Age: Or, The Hazard of New Functions* (Upper Saddle River, NJ: Prentice-Hall, 1997); Hill, *Mark Twain's Letters*, 350–351.

36. MTN, 232.

37. Powers, *Mark Twain*, 544–545.

38. Kaplan, *Mr. Clemens and Mark Twain*, 321.

39. LLMT, 270.

40. Ibid., 293; MTP, Olivia Susan Clemens to Clara Clemens, October 1893.

41. LLMT, 99.

42. Olivia Langdon Clemens to Susan Crane, April 22, 1894, quoted in Paine, *Mark Twain*, 986–987; LLMT, 308–309.

43. Mark Twain, "Fenimore Cooper's Literary Offenses," in *Collected Tales, Sketches, Speeches, & Essays 1891–1910* (New York: Library of America, 1992), 180–192.

44. Susy Clemens, *Papa*, 23–28.

45. Mark Twain to Susy Clemens, February 7, 1896, quoted in Powers, *Mark Twain*, 570, 614.

46. MTP, Olivia Langdon Clemens to Alice Day, July 1, 1894; MTP, Mark Twain to Olivia Langdon Clemens, July 26, 1894; MTP, Notebook 32:19–20; *Chicago Evening Post*, December 21, 1871.

47. N&J, 2:308–309, 316; Mark Twain, "The French and the Comanches," in *Letters from the Earth*, ed. Bernard DeVoto (New York: Harper and Row, 1962), 146–151.

48. MTHHR, 108, 126; Paine, *Mark Twain*, 996.

49. LLMT, 312.

4. STOWAWAYS WILL BE PROSECUTED

1. *San Francisco Examiner*, August 17, 1895; MTHHR, 121.

2. MTHHR, 138.

3. MFMT, 136; MTP, Olivia Langdon Clemens to Franklin Whitmore, June 18, 1895.

4. MTP, Mark Twain to Orion Clemens, May 26, 1895.

5. MTL, 2:663.

6. MTHHR, 167.

7. Ibid., 171; *Cleveland Plain Dealer*, July 16, 1895.

8. MTN, 244.

9. *Winnipeg Daily Tribune*, July 27, 1895.

10. *Duluth Statesman*, July 23, 1895; MFMT, 139.

11. Rodney, 46; MTHHR, 177; J. B. Pond, *Eccentricities of Genius: Memories of Famous Men and Women of the Platform and Stage* (New York: G. W. Dillingham, 1900), 219; Ruth A. Burner, "Mark Twain in the Northwest," *Pacific Northwest Quarterly* 42 (1951), 194.

12. MTP, Mark Twain to Samuel Moffett, August 14, 1895.

13. Pond, *Eccentricities of Genius*, 211, 220.

14. Alan Gribben and Nick Karanovich, eds., *Overland with Mark Twain: James B. Pond's Photographs and Journals of the North American Lecture Tour of 1895* (Elmira, NY: Center for Mark Twain Studies at Quarry Farm, Elmira College, 1992), 11; Pond, *Eccentricities of Genius*, 217.

15. *New York Times*, August 17, 1895.

16. MTP, Mark Twain to Samuel Moffett, August 14, 1895.

17. Pond, *Eccentricities of Genius*, 224, 221.

18. FE, 25–26.

19. Ibid., 27–28.

20. Ibid., 48, 57; MTP, Notebook 35:38, 250.

21. FE, 65–66.

22. Ibid., 81–86.

23. *Sydney Morning Herald*, September 16, 1895; Herbert Low, *Sydney Worker*, April 2, 1908, 11.

24. Mark Twain, "What Paul Bourget Thinks of Us," in *The Complete Essays of Mark Twain* (New York: Da Capo Press, 1991), 167.

25. Max O'Rell, "Mark Twain and Paul Bourget," *North American Review* (March 1895): 307; *Sydney Evening News*, September 16, 1895.

26. *Melbourne Argus,* September 17, 1895; Auto, 136; *Melbourne Argus,* September 20, 1895; *Sydney Sunday Times,* September 22, 1895.

27. *Sydney Daily Telegraph,* September 17, 1895; *Sydney Australian Star,* September 17, 1895.

28. *London Sketch,* November 27, 1895, 245.

29. *Melbourne Herald,* September 26, 1895.

30. Coleman O. Parsons, "Mark Twain in Australia," *Antioch Review* 21, no. 4 (1961): 456; *South Australian Register,* October 14, 1895; MTP, Mark Twain to H. Walter Barnett, October 3, 1895.

31. *Adelaide Advertiser,* October 14, 1895; FE, 207.

32. FE, 211–213.

33. *Melbourne Mercury,* November 4, 1895; *Otago Daily News,* November 6, 1895.

34. Olivia Langdon Clemens, quoted in E. Daniel Potts and Annette Potts, "The Mark Twain Family in Australia," *Overland* 70 (1978): 47; FE, 262–265, 284.

35. FE, 163.

36. Ibid., 287, 297.

37. Robert Cooper, *Around the World with Mark Twain* (New York: Arcade, 2000), 139; FE, 287–288.

38. FE, 319.

39. Ibid., 321–322.

40. Ibid., 301–303; MFMT, 151.

41. MTL, 2:630; MTP, Olivia Langdon Clemens to Susy Clemens, December 5, 1895; Olivia Langdon Clemens to Susan Crane, quoted in Potts and Potts, "The Mark Twain Family in Australia," 137–138.

42. *Sydney Morning Herald,* December 21, 1895.

43. FE, 351–352.

44. Harsharan Singh Ahluwalia, "Mark Twain's Lecture Tour of India," *Mark Twain Journal* 34, no. 1 (1996): 43; FE, 345, 347–348.

45. Albert Bigelow Paine, *Mark Twain: A Biography* (New York: Harper and Brothers, 1912), 1014; MFMT, 154.

46. FE, 403.

47. Ibid., 390.

48. Ibid., 426.

49. For divergent views on the Thuggee cult, see Mike Dash, *Thug: The True Story of India's Murderous Cult* (London: Granta Books, 2005); Kevin Rushby, *Children of Kali: Through India in Search of Bandits, the Thug Cult, and the British Raj* (New York: Walker, 2003); Martine van Woerkins, *The Strangled Traveler: Colonial Imaginings and the Thugs of India* (Chicago: University of Chicago Press, 2002); Kim Wagner, *Thuggee: Banditry and the British in Early Nineteenth-Century India* (London: Palgrave Macmillan, 2007).

50. FE, 428–435.

51. MTN, 275–276; FE, 464.

52. FE, 480, 497–499.

53. Ibid., 520–523.

54. Ibid., 529.

55. Ibid., 530, 543.

56. Ibid., 532, 543.

57. MTN, 278; FE, 556, 570–571.

58. *Lahore Civil and Military Gazette*, March 20, 1896; MTHHR, 212.

59. MFMT, 161; Auto, 258.

60. FE, 622–625.

61. Ibid., 630, 654–685; *Johannesburg Times*, May 18, 1896.

62. MTN, 295; FE, 688.

63. FE, 708–710; MTL, 2:694–695.

64. MFMT, 170; FE, 712; Mildred Howells, ed., *Life in Letters of William Dean Howells*, 2 vols. (Garden City: Doubleday, Doran, 1918), 2:71.

5. THIS EVERLASTING EXILE

1. Auto, 351.

2. MTN, 315, 319; Auto, 351.

3. MFMT, 171; LLMT, 322.

4. MTHL, 2:662–663; MTHHR, 235.

5. Clara Clemens, quoted in Jerome Loving, *Mark Twain: The Adventures of Samuel L. Clemens* (Berkeley: University of California Press, 2010), 371; MFMT, 179–181; Alfred, Lord Tennyson, *In Memoriam,* in *The Oxford Anthology of English Literature,* ed. Frank Kermode, John Hollander, Harold Bloom, Martin Price, J. B. Trapp, and Lionel Trilling, vol. 2 (New York: Oxford University Press, 1973), 1228; MTP, Olivia Langdon Clemens to Mary Mason Fairbanks, December 28, 1896.

6. MFMT, 180–181.

7. MTP, Mark Twain to Wayne MacVeagh, August 22, 1897.

8. FE, 212.

9. Mary Louise Pratt, *Imperial Eyes: Travel Writing and Transculturation* (New York: Routledge, 1992), 4; Melton, 139.

10. Michael Shelden, *Mark Twain: The Man in White: The Grand Adventure of His Final Years* (New York: Random House, 2010), xv–xx.

11. MTHHR, 309–310; Rodney, 207; MTHL, 2:690.

12. Mark Twain, "Queen Victoria's Jubilee," *The Complete Essays of Mark Twain,* ed. Charles Neider (New York: Da Capo Press, 1991), 192, 196–199.

13. *New York Herald,* June 13, 1897.

14. MTP, Mark Twain to Joseph Twichell, July 31, 1897; MTN, 315.

15. Mark Twain, "Villagers of 1840–3," in *Huck Finn and Tom Sawyer Among the Indians and Other Unfinished Stories,* ed. Dahlia Armon, Paul Baender, Walter Blair, William M. Gibson, and Franklin P. Rogers (Berkeley: University of California Press, 1989), 98.

16. Mark Twain, "Hellfire Hotchkiss," in Armon, *Huck Finn and Tom Sawyer Among the Indians and Other Unfinished Stories,* 121.

17. MFMT, 203–204.

18. Mark Twain,"Stirring Times in Austria," in *Complete Essays,* 228–229, 231, 235.

19. Mark Twain, "Concerning the Jews," in *Complete Essays*, 236–237, 242–243, 248.

20. Mark Twain, "The Memorable Assassination," in *Collected Essays*, 537.

21. MTL, 2:672; Albert Bigelow Paine, *Mark Twain: A Biography* (New York: Harper and Brothers, 1912), 1079.

22. MFMT, 193.

23. MTL, 5:487–488; William M. Gibson, ed., *No. 44, Mark Twain's Mysterious Stranger Manuscripts* (Berkeley: University of California Press, 1982), 49–51; William Shakespeare, *King Lear*, in *William Shakespeare: The Complete Works*, ed. Alfred Harbage (New York: Viking Press, 1969), 1090.

24. Mark Twain, "The Great Dark," in *Collected Tales, Sketches, Speeches, & Essays 1891–1910* (New York: Library of America, 1992), 297.

25. Ibid., 319.

26. MTP, Mark Twain to Mollie Clemens, December 11, 1887.

27. MTHHR, 325; MTHL, 2:684.

28. MTL, 2:663.

29. MTP, Mark Twain, "Jean's Illness."

30. MTHHR, 400.

31. MTP, Mark Twain, "Diary of a Kellgren Cure," August 11, 1899.

32. Mark Twain, quoted in Thomas Packenham, *The Boer War* (New York: Random House, 1979), 257; MTHHR, 419; MTL, 2:693–694.

33. MTN, 43; MTL, 2:697; MTHHR, 434.

34. MTHHR, 414, 424, 448; MFMT, 216.

35. Paine, *Mark Twain*, 1110; *New York Sun*, October 16, 1900.

36. *New York Herald*, October 16, 1900.

37. Ibid.; *Hartford Courant*, October 26, 1900; Paine, *Mark Twain*, 1112.

38. MTL, 2:704–705.

39. Mark Twain, "Introducing Winston S. Churchill," in *Collected Tales*, 455.

40. *London World*, October 6, 1900.

41. Bernard DeVoto, ed., *Mark Twain in Eruption* (New York: Harper and Brothers, 1940), 201; *St. Louis Post-Dispatch*, May 30, 1902.

42. LLMT, 344.

43. Mark Twain, "Villa di Quarto," in *Autobiography of Mark Twain*, ed. Harriet Elinor Smith, vol. 1 (Berkeley: University of California Press, 2010), 241.

44. Auto, 190.

45. MTP, Mark Twain to Joseph Twichell, June 8, 1904; MTP, Mark Twain to John MacAlister, November 9, 1904.

46. Ron Powers, *Mark Twain: A Life* (New York: Free Press, 2006), 618. For Isabel Lyon, see Karen Lystra, *Dangerous Intimacy: The Untold Story of Mark Twain's Final Years* (Berkeley: University of California Press, 2004).

47. MTP, Clara Clemens to Mark Twain, November 7, 1904; MTP, Mark Twain to Susan Crane, January 25, 1905; MTP, Mark Twain to Mrs. Andrew Carnegie, n.d., 1905.

48. MTP, Mark Twain to Clara Clemens, February 21, 22, and 23, 1906; DeVoto, *Mark Twain in Eruption*, 49.

49. Justin Kaplan, *Mr. Clemens and Mark Twain* (New York: Simon and Schuster, 1966), 374.

50. Mark Twain, "Seventieth Birthday Speech," in *Collected Tales*, 713–718.

51. MTHL, 2:853.

52. John Cooley, ed., *Mark Twain's Aquarium: The Samuel Clemens—Angelfish Correspondence, 1905–1910* (Athens: University of Georgia Press, 1991), 49, 94.

53. Marion Schuyler Allen, quoted in Shelden, *Mark Twain: Man in White*, 218.

54. Lystra, *Dangerous Intimacy*, 131–133.

55. *London Daily Express*, June 19, 1907.

56. *Harper's Weekly*, July 20, 1907; Rodney, 262–263.

57. Thomas Pinney, ed., *The Letters of Rudyard Kipling*, vol. 3 (Iowa City: University of Iowa Press, 1996), 242; *New York Times*, June 27, 1907.

58. Clara Clemens, *My Husband Gabrilowitsch* (New York: Harper, 1938), 50–51.

59. Mark Twain, "The Death of Jean," *Harper's Monthly*, January 1911, 210–218; Lystra, *Dangerous Intimacy*, 249.

60. MTP, Mark Twain to Clara Clemens, February 21, 1910.

61. Paine, *Mark Twain*, 1562–1563.

62. Ibid., 1570–1573.

63. Powers, *Mark Twain*, 627.

AFTERWORD

1. Ernest Hemingway, *Green Hills of Africa* (New York: Charles Scribner's Sons, 1935), 22; George Bernard Shaw, quoted in Justin Kaplan, *Mr. Clemens and Mark Twain* (New York: Simon and Schuster, 1966), 382.

2. Richard Bridgman, *Traveling in Mark Twain* (Berkeley: University of California Press, 1987), 4.

3. MTP, Mark Twain to William Dean Howells, February 15, 1887.

4. Harold H. Hellwig, *Mark Twain's Travel Literature: The Odyssey of a Mind* (Jefferson, NC: McFarland, 2008), 15; Bernard DeVoto, ed., *Mark Twain in Eruption* (New York: Harper and Brothers, 1940), 304–305.

5. Melton, 4.

6. Ibid., 155–157; MTL, 2:49–50.

7. *Hartford Courant*, September 20, 1877.

INDEX

Jaffa, failed religious commune at, 58–59
Jail(s): in Tangier, 28–29; Twain speaks in New York, 148; Twain visits Tasmanian, 167; Twain visits South African, 185. *See also* Arrest, of Twain in New York City
Jaipur, India, 182–183
James, Henry, 3, 16, 100–101, 235
James, Henry, Sr., 16
James, William E., 37–38, 55, 125, 216
James I, King, 168
Jameson, Leander Starr, 184
Jameson Raid, 184–185
Jay Cooke and Company, 79
Jefferson, Joseph, 113
Jerusalem, 54–57
Jews, 202–204
"Jim Baker's Blue Jay Yarn," 146
Joan of Arc, 130–131
John A. Gray Company, 9
Johnson, Robert Underwood, 126
Jonas Smith, 239–240
Jones, John P., 114–115
Judas Iscariot, 33, 58

Kanawha, 218–219
Kellgren, Jonas Henrik, 211, 212, 213
King, Grace, 126
King Lear, operatic performance of, 89
"King Leopold's Soliloquy," 216
Kipling, Rudyard, 133, 231
Klimt, Gustav, 202

Kookaburra, 164–165
Kruger, Paul, 185
Kumar, Prince, 175
Kurzwell, Maximilian, 202

Lahore, India, 183
Lake Lucerne, 199–200
Lampton, James, 128
Langdon, Charles Jervis "Charley," 21, 27, 49–50, 190, 223
Langdon, Jervis, 69
Langdon, Olivia Louise ("Livy"): Twain sees, for first time, 49–50; courtship and marriage of, 68–69, 74–75; depression of, 72; accompanies Twain to England, 77–80; gives birth to Clara Clemens, 81; sails to Europe, 87; in Italy, 98; on Henry James, 101; family life of, 112; leaves Hartford house, 116; tours health facilities in Europe, 118; love of, for classical music, 118–119; reaction of, to Clara's social life, 123; in Berlin, 124; as Twain's primary creditor, 135; on bankruptcy of Webster & Company, 136; on Clara's solo travels, 138; and loan repayments, 140; leaves Europe following financial difficulties, 145; accompanies Twain on lecture tour, 146; in Melbourne, 165; on Twain trying to make kookaburra laugh, 165; on